Debates in Economic History

Edited by Peter Mathias

The Growth of English Overseas Trade in the Seventeenth and Eighteenth Centuries

The Growth of English Overseas Trade in the Seventeenth and Eighteenth Centuries

edited with an introduction by
W. E. MINCHINTON

METHUEN & CO LTD
11 NEW FETTER LANE LONDON EC4

First published 1969 by Methuen & Co Ltd
Introduction © 1969 by W. E. Minchinton
Printed in Great Britain by
Richard Clay (The Chaucer Press), Ltd,
Bungay, Suffolk

Distributed in the U.S.A.
by Barnes & Noble Inc.

Contents

Preface

The chronological conventions of textbooks, and examination syllabuses, commonly see the economic history of 'modern' Britain beginning in 1700 or 1750. This book underlines how foreshortened a perspective is given to the role of commercial developments in the general process of economic change by such a chronology. Indeed it can be argued that, when considering the propensities for economic growth and industrialization in the eighteenth century, the economic evolution of western Europe during the two previous centuries provides the crucial historical sequence which sets apart the most advanced regions of this area from virtually all other societies known to history.

Professor Minchinton's widely-ranging introduction shows how deeply structured into the whole fabric of the economy were these developments in foreign trade – involving changing levels of purchasing, new patterns of consumption, changing structures of industrial production, new regional growth, expanding political and naval commitments overseas – with the sword (in result if not always in intention) so often in the service of the counting house. Changes in foreign trade (as agricultural change in the same period) show just how responsive main sectors of the British economy had become, long before the industrial revolution, to commercial pressures and opportunities. Equally, the multifarious institutions, policies, practices and attitudes fostering the expansion of trade reveal how commercially sophisticated was the 'pre-industrial' economy in England, and how widespread were these commercial links with subsequent phases of economic growth. Even if historians are only now, for the first time, seeking to quantify the importance of foreign markets in comparison with home demand during the eighteenth century (to which topic a later book in this series is devoted), this volume emphasizes how formative an influence foreign trade had already become; while, from the vantage point of the twentieth century, we can see exactly how powerfully Britain's international economic commitments shaped the industrial structure of Victorian England. The interdependencies between exports, imports and changes in the level of internal demand are many and intricate, but it should still be acknowledged that the processes of economic change in Britain have been more intimately moulded by foreign trade than has been the case with any other major industrial economy, excepting only, perhaps, Japan. As Sir George Savile, Marquis of Halifax, remarked in the 1680s – and he was voicing a sentiment already long traditional – 'we are to consider that we are a very little spot in the map of the world and make a great figure only by trade'.

7 May 1969   PETER MATHIAS

Acknowledgements

The editor and publishers wish to thank the following for permission to reproduce the articles listed below:

Professor W. A. Cole for 'Trends in eighteenth-century smuggling' (*Economic History Review*, 2nd series, X (1958), 395–410); Professor Ralph Davis for 'English foreign trade, 1660–1700' (*Economic History Review*, 2nd series, VI (1954), 150–66) and 'English foreign trade, 1700–1774' (*Economic History Review*, 2nd series, XV (1962), 285–303); Professor F. J. Fisher for 'London's export trade in the early seventeenth century' (*Economic History Review*, 2nd series, III (1950), 151–61); Dr H. E. S. Fisher for 'Anglo-Portuguese trade, 1700–1770' (*Economic History Review*, 2nd series, XVI (1963), 219–33) and Professor A. H. John for 'Aspects of English economic growth in the first half of the eighteenth century' (*Economica*, new series, No. 28 (1961), 176–90).

They would also like to thank the Oxford University Press for permission to reproduce tables I–IV from Elizabeth Schumpeter, *English overseas trade statistics, 1697–1808* and Macmillan & Co Ltd for permission to reprint tables V and VI from Ralph Davis, *The rise of the English shipping industry in the seventeenth and eighteenth centuries*.

Editor's Introduction

The main subject of this volume has not been one of violent contemporary controversy, rather it is one where the broad course of commercial history, the changing pattern of foreign trade, has been more clearly delineated in writing which has occurred too recently to have been embodied in textbooks. It is concerned with the trading activities of England in the early modern period on the eve of the industrial revolution, a period of nearly two centuries when foreign commerce played a major part in the transformation of English economic life. This collection of essays considers three issues: the level and character of English overseas trade between 1600 and the 1770s, including a more detailed account of the trade with Portugal; a discussion of the statistical sources on which such accounts have to be based; and, thirdly, an examination of the connection between the course of English overseas trade and the process of industrialization.

THE NATURE OF TRADE

As a result of the Discoveries at the end of the fifteenth century, the old European trading system based on the Mediterranean, with the Italian merchants in the van, and on the Baltic, under the leadership of the cities of the Hanseatic League, began to break down and the seaboard of western Europe became the main focus of economic activity. First Spain and Portugal in the sixteenth century and then the Netherlands, France and England in the seventeenth and eighteenth centuries were able to exploit their favourable geographical position by using the developments in ship construction, in cartographic skills and in navigational techniques which had recently become available. The decline of the predominantly land-based European empires was completed by the severe economic crisis of the early seventeenth century and they were superseded by sea-based hegemonies. Europe entered a more avowedly expansionist phase which was based on an exploitation of the sea-routes of the world and on the development of trade. Overseas commerce was the bond which linked Europe and the wider world because Spain and Portugal, England, France and the Netherlands were able, in different ways, to make fuller use of the wide range of commodities which became available through an extended geographical division of labour.

Apart from a small quantity of Eastern products such as spices and silk, the bulk of the trade of medieval Europe had been in the products of the European world. The volume of trade was accordingly limited by the restricted climatic and product range of these countries and by the small differences in technology. With the Discoveries the divergence in factor endowments of territories within the wider trading area was increased, creating new opportunities for trade based on comparative advantage. This growing geographical sphere of European activity overseas was important in a number of ways for England: it supplied a larger market for the sale of English manufactures; it provided supplies of raw materials such as dyestuffs and wool which were used by existing industries or provided, with sugar and cotton, the basis for new ones and it was the source of a wider range of foodstuffs – tea and coffee – and manufactured goods such as silks and calicoes; it helped to augment the standard of living and provided the basis for increased domestic demand; it encouraged service industries based on a substantial re-export trade. Such developments inevitably had repercussions on the organization, finance and conduct of trade, on the size and character of the English merchant fleet and on the attitude of governments and private individuals towards trade and related economic matters.

The year 1600 is an appropriate date to begin such a volume as this for it is contemporary with two important events in the history of English trade – the eviction of the Hanse in 1598 and the formation of the English East India Company in 1601, which were symptomatic of the changing character of English trade at the end of the sixteenth century. The first event was of importance because it marked the end of the period of tutelage when a substantial part of English overseas trade had been in the hands of foreign merchants. The Venetians who had once controlled English cloth exports left London in 1533 and Southampton in 1587 and the Hanse, the last group of foreign merchants with extra-territorial rights in England, were deprived of their privileges in 1552 and finally evicted in 1598. In a symbolic way this latter event was a sign that England was moving from the periphery towards the centre of a new trading system.

The new trading system was to be based on the exploitation of extra-European trade. In developing this trade, as other countries also recognized, there were considerable problems of organization and finance to which they all tended in the first phase of development to find a similar solution – the establishment of joint-stock trading companies. Earlier attempts to found such companies had been made in England but the East India Company was the most important and the most successful. Whenever substantial sums of capital were involved, when there was a high risk element, when there were factories or bases to be supported, when the prospect of immediate profits was absent, and when political representation was necessary, the trading company had an important contribution to make.

Yet the contribution of the trading company should not be exaggerated. Because their protests were more vocal and their records, albeit fragmentary, were more easily available in the public archives, the achievements of the trading companies have sometimes received disproportionate attention. A key figure in the expansion of English overseas trade was the individual English merchant. Because of the scarcity of commercial papers, studies of merchant houses are extremely sparse and until we know more about their trading operations we shall not be able to appreciate them fully. Nevertheless it is already clear that the main agents in the growth of the Atlantic trading area were the English merchant or the small trading partnership rather than the chartered trading companies.

Like the other pre-industrial countries of Europe, England was able to win an increasing trade for herself through the energies and enterprise of her merchants and seamen. This process also involved considerable activities on the part of her politicians and armed forces. In the first phase of the challenge to the Iberian powers, harrying the Spanish in the New World and the Portuguese in the Far East, it was the Dutch who set the pace by establishing new colonies and settlements and profiting from the commerce with them. For more than a century, English and French forays were more tentative until, in the seventeenth century, first from envy not only of the Spanish and Portuguese but also of the Dutch and later from rivalry with the Dutch, the English and the French learned how to exploit overseas territories to their own economic advantage.

The political dynamic for such a policy was clear. In an age of mercantilism, there seemed to be a connection between political control and economic access. Although some manufactured goods were forthcoming, the essence of colonial policy was that the ownership of colonies provided European countries with a closed source of raw materials and a closed market for the sale of the manufactured goods which they produced. To attempt to secure such a situation seemed for the European colonial powers a legitimate and appropriate policy, in an age of heightened political nationalism, for a particular stage of economic development when the resources, and particularly the capital, available to foster the growth of colonies were comparatively limited. No more need be said here on this topic since mercantilism has been considered by this author in another place[1] and by Professor Coleman in a companion volume in this series.[2]

Before proceeding further, there is need to stress that this volume is concerned with *English* trade. Although the Act of Union by which Scotland became part of the United Kingdom was passed in 1707, these discussions exclude Scotland which for purposes of trade remained a separate country. Separate statistics of imports and exports were returned and the trade of Scotland is separately analysable. Thus a discussion of an important trade – the Glasgow tobacco trade – is excluded from our terms of reference. It should also be stated that in most cases when 'English' is used in this volume it is the adjective used to denote the political area which we now talk about as England and Wales. The adjective is used for shorthand purposes because no convenient alternative exists. In the sixteenth, seventeenth and early eighteenth centuries the trade that was carried on from England and Wales both with Europe and the wider world was in fact conducted predominantly by English merchants, using English crews and vessels, financed by English capital and carrying English products, using 'English' in the narrower sense to denote 'England' rather than the wider territorial area,

[1] Walter E. Minchinton, *Mercantilism: system or expediency?* (Lexington, Mass.: D. C. Heath, 1969).
[2] D. C. Coleman, *Revisions in mercantilism* (Methuen, 1969).

England and Wales. Not until the industrial revolution, when the coal and iron resources of south Wales and the copper of north Wales came to be exploited, did Wales make a significant contribution to English overseas trade.

The articles printed here are concerned with a particular phase of economic experience which came to an end, as far as England was concerned, sometime in the later eighteenth century. With the onset of the industrial revolution both the character of English overseas trade and the nature of England's relationship with the wider world altered. From roughly the last quarter of the eighteenth century, England was, for a period, the workshop of the world. Then the expanding sale of English cotton goods, ironware and coal in return for an inflow of raw materials and foodstuffs which dominated her trading pattern for a century or more make the expansion of overseas trade in the industrial age another story.

THE COURSE OF TRADE

About the general course of trade in the period between 1600 and 1770 there has been little debate. Recent contributions have extended our knowledge and given a firmer statistical basis to our understanding although the evidence on which judgements have to be based for the earlier years is still rather limited. Earlier historians based their accounts of trade under the Stuarts and Georges on the writings of Anderson, Davenant, Macpherson, Missenden, Sheffield and others or drew on the publications of the Historical Manuscripts Commission as they were issued. The available figures of trade were patchy and lacking in comparability; the conclusions which were drawn from them were therefore impressionistic. Colouring the accounts of these historians was the Whig bias of progressive development which led them to suggest that from the sixteenth century, if not earlier, the onward progress of English overseas trade was ever expanding and unchecked. More recent accounts have corrected this simplistic view.

In the later middle ages England, on the periphery of the European trading system, was a less developed country which supplied the more advanced centres of Europe with raw materials, notably wool, tin and leather, with growing amounts of unfinished cloth, the product of England's major industry, and, intermittently in times of surplus, with agricultural products. From the fifteenth until the eighteenth century, English exports were dominated by the cloth industry. Moving into the countryside and developing the use of water-power, the English cloth industry was able to lower costs and produce a cheaper product. Although the demand for cloth, so it is argued, was relatively inelastic so that sales to Europe were not greatly increased in the later fifteenth and early sixteenth centuries by price reductions alone, England's market share was increased by developments in the producing areas in Europe which greatly reduced the competition encountered by English cloth. Under the influence of unique trading conditions, exports of English woollen textiles grew. Information is only available for the export of shortcloth which expanded more than twofold in the first half of the sixteenth century from about 50,000 cloths a year to about 120,000 cloths a year, while wool exports were shrinking. At the English end this trade was funnelled through London, thereby seriously reducing the activity of the other south- and east-coast ports; at the other end the trade was concentrated on Antwerp which, after the Portuguese transfer of the spice staple there in 1504, became the commercial and financial capital of Europe until shaken by the religious wars of the 1540s. The Antwerp market for cloth collapsed in the 1550s and the decline of this entrepôt, hastened by the Spanish and French repudiation of debts in 1557 and the sack of Antwerp by Spanish troops in 1576, was completed by the Dutch blockade in 1585.

The loss of the Antwerp market forced the Merchant Adventurers to set up their staple at Middelburg, Stade, Emden and other places in order to continue their sales to the central European market. It also provoked a search for new markets outside the traditional areas of English trade. This search had several repercussions: it forced the English cloth industry to diversify its activities, led English merchants and seamen to explore more distant trade routes and stimulated the growth of the English shipping industry. These developments, in turn, necessitated new forms of business organization and resulted in a wider range of imports. To cater for new markets, English woollen manufacturers, who had previously concentrated on the production of unfinished cloth, were led not only to attempt to reduce costs but also to develop dyeing and finishing processes so that the proportion of finished cloth exports began to increase. More important, they were encouraged to expand, with the aid of immigrant skilled workers, the manufacture of lighter bays, says, fustians, etc., called collectively the new draperies. The exploration of more distant trade routes had two aspects: the maritime enterprises carried out by partnerships of London merchants and west-country seamen (which were part trading ventures and part privateering expeditions) and a search for other European markets. Balancing the famous voyages of Hawkins, Frobisher, Drake and others was the quest for new markets in the Mediterranean which was facilitated by the grain crisis there. From the 1560s the English competed with Dutch and Hanseatic ships in transporting Baltic grain to the needy cities of Italy and the Ottoman empire. So successful were the English merchants, whose trading concessions from the Sultan in 1581 led to the foundation of the Levant Company, that the Venetians became concerned from the later 1570s about the growing activity of English shipping. Obviously more than a mere foothold in the Mediterranean had been won.

All these enterprises increased the demand on the shipping industry. In the middle of the sixteenth century, though England had an effective navy, her merchant fleet was insignificant by European standards.[1] In the following century the effective expansion of the English mercantile marine came as a combined result of the coastal coal trade, the Newfoundland and Greenland fisheries and the expansion of the Mediterranean and African trades. To meet these needs larger and better armed ships were built.

The requirement for more capital had its effect on business organization. From the 1550s the joint-stock company form was employed for trading enterprises. The Muscovy Company was founded in 1555, the Spanish Company in 1577 and the Senegal Adventurers in 1588. Finally, the ships voyaging in more distant seas brought back a wider range of commodities. But the extent of these changes must not be exaggerated; they were merely portents of the widening scope of English commerce. In 1600 as in 1500, the major English export continued to be cloth and by far the greater part of English overseas sales were concentrated

[1] Ralph Davis, *The rise of the English shipping industry in the seventeenth and eighteenth centuries* (Macmillan, 1962), p. 2.

on the seaboard of north-western Europe, though there was some redistribution of trade to France and the Baltic after the collapse of Antwerp.

The periodization of the century and three-quarters after 1600 is not without problems. The period 1660–1775 can be divided into three phases: a quarter of a century of rapid growth during the reign of Charles II from 1660 to 1686–8; a period of slow growth until the 1740s; and then, from about 1750 until the War of American Independence, another phase of rapid commercial expansion. But, largely because of statistical limitations, the relationship of the period 1600 to 1660 to the following years has not been fully explored.

The seventeenth century opened bright with promise. Peace in Ireland and a truce in the Netherlands after a long and exhausting war with Spain in 1604 seemed to presage more stable conditions. In rivalry with other European powers, the foundations of wider trading connections were laid. Like the French who founded an East India Company in 1598 and the Dutch who established one in 1603, the English East India Company set up trading stations in India and the East Indies and promoted ventures to China. Driven from the spice islands by the massacre of Amboyna in 1623 by the Dutch, who came in the following years to dominate the trades with the Baltic and with Spanish America as well, the East India Company were nevertheless able after this check to develop trade with the East, which grew more rapidly than trade with America.

Along the seaboard of mainland North America settlements were established by the French, the Dutch and the Swedes as well as the English. A string of English settlements was started there by the Virginia Company at Jamestown in 1607, by the Pilgrims at Plymouth in 1620–1 and by the Massachusetts Bay Company in 1629. In the next decade Maryland, Providence and New Haven were colonized. The Dutch, French, English and Swedes all established trading posts or colonies in the West Indies as well before 1640 but because of the enormous pioneering difficulties involved, none of these enterprises yielded anything but a slow return. Although there was some growth in the imports of sugar and tobacco, the English possessions in America did not make a sizeable contribution to English trade before the mid-century.

The main expansion of English overseas trade in the early seventeenth century took place nearer home. Though the Mediterranean and Irish seas were menaced by pirates – in 1609 there were said to be a thousand pirates at large off the Irish coast – English merchants were able to extend their trade with European countries. With the Merchant Adventurers settled at Hamburg from 1611, London's exports of traditional woollens reached a final peak in 1614 but the hopes of a continued expansion in the sales of the heavier woollen textiles went unrealized. Further, when Alderman Cockayne's project, floated in 1613 to promote the export of dyed and finished cloth and so end English dependence on foreign finishers, collapsed in 1616, it led to heavy unemployment in the clothing areas. While the outbreak of the Thirty Years War and the collapse of the cloth markets in eastern Europe underlined the depression in the old draperies, exports of the new draperies to southern Europe and the Mediterranean grew. While contemporaries concentrating on short-run phenomena, vociferously proclaimed the decay of trade on the eve of the Civil War, an analysis of the figures available suggests that in the period between 1600 and 1640, English exports increased by about 75 per cent (an annual rate of approximately 1·5 per cent)[1]. This comparatively slow rate reflects the still

---

[1] According to Professor Fisher's figures given below (pp. 68–9) exports of the new draperies and hosiery amounted to £454,914, almost equal to the value of the exports of shortcloths. If the value of the shortcloth exports accordingly is assumed to be £500,000, total London exports in 1640 amounted to £609,722 (the official value of commodities other than shortcloths, but including re-exports) + £500,000 or approximately £1·1 million. Professor Fisher goes on to say that London's trade was some two-thirds or three-quarters of the nation's trade. On this arithmetic the trade of the outports in 1640 would therefore range between £370,000 and £550,000 and the total trade of England in 1640 between £1·47 million and £1·65 million. (These figures may however be too low as Professor Ralph Davis suggests that English exports alone amounted to £2·5–3 million in 1640 (*A commercial revolution: English overseas trade in the seventeenth and eighteenth centuries* (Historical Association, 1967), p. 9) while re-exports amounted to a few score thousand in addition. Applying the same kind of arithmetic to Professor Fisher's figures for 1601 and assuming constant prices, we get the following result. If the value of the 87,000 shortcloths exported in 1640 was (as suggested above) £500,000, then the value of 100,000 shortcloths exported in 1601 was approximately £600,000, giving a total London export trade of £720,000. Taking the same proportions as above – between two-thirds and three-quarters – the trade of the outports ranged between £240,000 and £360,000. Thus in 1601 English exports totalled between £960,000 and £1·08 million. This arithmetic therefore suggests that English exports rose from between £0·96–1·08 million in 1601 to at least £1·6–1·8 million in 1640.

limited purchasing power in Europe and the fact that time was needed before the investment of capital and labour effectively expanded production and demand outside Europe. Taking into account also the facts of political dislocation in Europe and the reorientation of the cloth industry at home, this increase in trade was a considerable achievement.

Though the outbreak of the Civil War increased uncertainty, trade soon recovered in 1642. This improvement quickened after 1646 only to be halted by unfavourable reaction abroad to the execution of Charles I. In the 1650s merchants enjoyed considerable prosperity, largely from increased dealings in re-exports, but trade was to some extent affected by the first Anglo-Dutch War of 1652–4 and by the outbreak of war with Spain later in the decade. While the Civil War may have interrupted domestic production it had less effect on overseas trade and the period 1640–60 is overall a period of growth. English exports expanded from £2·5–3 million (using the higher estimates) in 1640 to £3·2 million in the early 1660s and re-exports grew from under £100,000 to about £900,000. The increase of total exports from £2·5–3 million to £4·1 million, an increase of between 37 and 64 per cent (or an annual average of from 1·3 to 2·1 per cent), is thus largely attributable to the growth of re-exports.

Yet it was not so much the short-run changes in this decade which were of importance but their long-run consequences. The growth in trade led to an expansion of the English merchant shipping fleet. Total tonnage grew from 101,000 tons in 1609–15 and 115,000 tons in 1629 to 162–200,000 tons in 1660.[1] This increase in the number of ships and the growth in wealth and expertise of the English merchant class enabled the Dutch dominance of the carrying trade, which was also threatened by the French, to be challenged. The navigation acts of 1650 and 1651 confined English trade with English colonies to English ships and thus laid the foundation of a protected trading system, such as the Spanish and French tried to establish. It was based on the geographical division of labour including the exchange of English manufactures for tropical and semi-tropical products,

[1] The 1609–15 and the lower 1660 figures are taken from Lawrence A. Harper, *The English navigation laws* (New York: Columbia University Press, 1939), p. 339 and the 1629 and the higher 1660 figures come from Davis, *Shipping industry*, p. 15. For figures of the tonnage of English owned shipping 1572–1775 see table 6, p. 62 below.

organized by English merchants and carried out by English ships. While trade with Spain languished, the alliance with Portugal in 1654 provided English merchants with the opportunity of developing connections with Portuguese territories in Brazil, Africa and Asia. Finally, the victory over the Spaniards in 1655 added Jamaica, soon to be a major sugar producer, to the English West Indian possessions.

Some nineteenth-century historians, like Ranke and Gardiner, linked the commercial expansion of the seventeenth century with the name of Cromwell, but this view finds little support today. Rather it is argued that the Restoration was the economic exit from medievalism and the period from 1660 to 1688 a period of commercial expansion. Consideration of this period is not easy because of the paucity of statistical information but some statements can be made about these years. Immediately after the Restoration the navigation system was virtually completed by the Act of 1660 which introduced the 'enumeration' of certain commodities, such as tobacco, sugar, ginger, cotton, indigo and other dyewoods, and laid down that these goods could only be shipped to a European market through an English entrepôt, the Act of Frauds of 1662 and the Staple Act of the following year which required European goods to be sent to the colonies through an English port and in English ships. While the Dutch continued to dominate the European short-sea routes, these Acts gave English manufacturers a cost advantage and stimulated the expansion of the English mercantile marine.

Across the Atlantic the Restoration inaugurated a new wave of expansion and settlement and within twenty-five years there was a continuous line of English colonies along the American seaboard from Maine to Spanish Florida. Victory over the Dutch after two further wars not only brought New York into English hands but also did much to break the hold of the Dutch on the oceanic trades. In the West Indies, where the French with fourteen islands by the 1660s were the main rivals, the Leeward Islands in 1672 were separated from Barbados which became a royal colony in the following year. In the East the foundations of trade with China and of English territorial power in India were more securely laid and the ports of Bombay and Tangiers became English possessions as the result of Charles II's marriage to Catherine of Braganza in 1661.

To develop the more distant trades was still the task of the joint-stock company. Despite frequent attacks, the East India Company, which had received a new charter in 1672, expanded its activities in the later seventeenth century; the African and the slave trades came into the hands of the Royal African Company in 1672 and the much smaller Hudson's Bay Company was founded in 1670. At the same time the corporate control of the European trades by the regulated companies was relinquished to private traders. In 1673 the monopoly of the Eastland Company was ended and the trade with Norway, Sweden and Denmark was thrown open while the Levant and Russia companies also declined. Concerned with a product – broadcloth – whose market was shrinking, the activities of the Merchant Adventurers who had moved their staple to Dordrecht in 1655, also waned and their monopoly rights were abolished in 1689.

After 1660 the expansion of trade was checked in the middle of the decade by the second Anglo-Dutch War (1664–7), plague and the Great Fire of London and again in 1672 by the stop of the Exchequer. With the ending of the third war with Holland in 1674 trade revived and apart from the threat of war which led to the prohibition of trade with France in 1678, overseas trade prospered between the mid-1670s and the mid-1680s, to reach a new peak in 1686–8. Estimates suggest that English exports rose from £4·1 million in the early 1660s to £6·5 million in the mid-1680s. In promoting this growth both supply and demand factors operated. The expansion of the production of colonial products in the plantations sharply reduced their price, increasing the quantity demanded and bringing them within the reach of a wider range of people within Europe. The growth of trade also stimulated the expansion from an estimated 180–200,000 tons in 1660 to 340,000 tons in 1686[1] of the English merchant fleet, which was by that date responsible for the greater part of the English carrying trade.[2]

In the late 1680s the expansion of English overseas trade came to a halt and the growth of the English mercantile marine slowed down for about half a century. For this a number of factors were responsible. First of all, there were market changes. The new

[1] See table 6, p. 62.

[2] In 1686 of 466,000 tons of shipping entering English ports, 399,000 was English and of 361,000 tons clearing English ports, 331,000 was English. See below, table 5, p. 61.

draperies encountered competition from East Indian cottons and silks which, though helping to extend the European market for textiles, shifted the demand away from English cloth. Then the re-export trades encountered fiercer competition in European markets. After the Act of Union, Glasgow came to dominate the re-export trade in tobacco while the French encouragement of sugar production in Hispaniola, acquired from Spain in 1697, severely reduced the sales of English sugar in Europe, particularly after 1713. Then the growth of policies of national self-sufficiency in Europe tended to hamper commerce. Anti-French measures had been imposed under the Commonwealth and rivalry with France led to their extension after 1689. In the fifteen years after the accession of William III to the English throne, 'the English tariff structure was transformed from a generally low-level, fiscal system into a moderately high-level system, which, though still fiscal in its purposes, had become in practice protective'.[1] The system of industrial protection was consolidated by Walpole's customs reform of 1722. At the same time sales of English manufactured goods and agricultural products abroad were assisted by the removal of export duties in 1699 and 1722. In their turn, France, the German states and other European countries endeavoured to give their own industries protection.

Meanwhile merchants sought greater freedom to carry on their business and the tide continued to run against the trading companies. The monopoly of the Royal African Company was breached in 1698 and the Newfoundland and Russian trades were thrown open in the following year. A renewed assault on the companies came in the 1740s. While the East India Company, the Hudson's Bay Company and the Russia Company were able to ward off these attacks, the Royal African Company, which had been virtually ineffective for several decades, was transformed in 1750 and the monopoly of the Levant Company was ended in 1753.

Then, war disrupted trade. War, together with the accompanying financial strains and the failure of the banking schemes, brought depression during the war of the League of Augsberg in the 1690s and the war of Spanish Succession (1702–13) also

[1] R. Davis, 'The rise of protection in England, 1689–1786', *Economic History Review*, 2nd series, XIX (1966), 307.

caused trade to fall to a low level between 1704 and 1708. But for English merchants, these wars were not fought in vain. The conclusion of the Methuen treaty with Portugal in 1703 provided a stimulus to trade and helped in time to make London a major market in bullion and with the treaty of Utrecht, England enlarged her American holdings at the expense of France who gave up her claims to the Hudson's Bay region, to Newfoundland, to St Christopher and ceded Acadia. These gains opened the way to westward expansion, improved the position of the New England fishermen and, more important, brought peace to the North American continent for a period of time. The growing population of the American colonies took into cultivation more land which expanded exports of tobacco, rice and indigo to England and wheat, beef, pork, livestock and lumber to the West Indies. From Spain England won Gibraltar and the *Asiento* which gave English and colonial slave traders a thirty-year legal monopoly of the supply of slaves to the Spanish American colonies. This opened the way to other trade until after renewal it was relinquished in 1750.

Recovery from the war of Spanish Succession was checked by the internal troubles of 1715, by the English dispute with the Baltic powers in 1717–19 and by the brief war with Spain in 1718. Renewed hostilities with Spain in 1727–8 and the threat of war in 1734 also had their effect on trade but more serious were the consequences of the War of Jenkin's Ear in 1739. War made trade difficult for most of the following decade and particularly in the period 1744–8. Bad harvests also adversely affected trade in the 1690s and in the 1720s while the last visitation of the plague in Europe in 1721[1] following on the collapse of the South Sea Bubble also caused a sharp contraction of trade. In consequence of all these factors, the periods of active trade were limited and short between the late 1680s and 1748, the best years being 1699–1701 when, aided by the removal of export duties on woollens and grain, trade recovered to the level of 1686–8, 1711

[1] Though the disease did not spread beyond Provence and Languedoc and was over by August 1721, the catastrophe caused grave anxiety throughout Europe and in England produced an unexpected boom in the textile trades, as people stopped buying French manufactures and transferred their demand to English goods. K. F. Helleiner, 'The vital revolution reconsidered' reprinted in D. V. Glass and D. E. C. Eversley (eds.), *Population in history* (Arnold, 1965), p. 81.

when woollen exports reached a new peak, 1714 when there was
a substantial stockbuilding boom, the mid-1720s following Walpole's abolition of the customs duties on English manufactures
and some imports, and the years 1735–8, a period of active trade
when exports of manufactured goods to the colonies began to
expand. Exports were also high in 1743 because of government
shipments, French purchases of woollens for their armies and
the building up of stocks by foreign merchants in anticipation
of a further extension of the war.[1]

As a result of these various factors – market changes, protec-
tionism and war – English overseas trade grew more slowly between the later 1680s and the late 1740s than in the previous
twenty-five years – at the rate of only 1 per cent a year.[2] The
course of imports, exports and re-exports is set out in the following table:

ENGLISH IMPORTS, EXPORTS AND RE-EXPORTS, 1700–1749[3]
(annual averages)

£ million	1700–9	1710–19	1720–9	1730–9	1740–9
Imports	4·7	5·5	6·8	7·5	7·3
Exports	4·5	4·8	4·9	5·8	6·5
Re-exports	1·7	2·1	2·8	3·2	3·6
Exports and re-exports	6·1	6·9	7·7	9·0	10·1

Source: E. B. Schumpeter, *English overseas trade statistics, 1697–1808* (Oxford
University Press, 1960), pp. 15–16, tables II–IV.

Imports stagnated in the 1700s, grew in the 1710s and 1720s and
then were more stable in the 1730s and 1740s; re-exports grew
more slowly until the 1730s and then levelled off while exports
remained fairly constant until the 1730s. The upward movement

[1] For a more detailed discussion of the movements of trade in these years see
T. S. Ashton, *Economic fluctuations in England, 1700–1800* (Oxford University
Press, 1959), pp. 53–62, 138–61.
[2] This figure of the compound rate per cent per annum in volume (decade
averages) of domestic exports plus retained imports is taken from Phyllis Deane
and W. A. Cole, *British economic growth, 1688–1959: trends and structure* (Cambridge
University Press, 1962), p. 29, table 8.
[3] For the problem of eighteenth-century trade statistics see Professor Davis's
comments below (p. 100). The figures of value in this table may be taken as
giving a reasonable indication of the trend since this was not a period of inflation
and the general trend of prices was downward from 1700 to the 1730s, then
stable until about 1760 after which date it began to move slowly upwards. The
annual figures are given below in tables 1–4 (pp. 58–60).

of exports between 1735 and 1738 was checked by the outbreak of war, not to be resumed until the late 1740s.

The ending of the war in 1748 was followed by a post-war boom which set in motion a further wave of expansion which lasted for nearly a quarter of a century, as this table shows:

ENGLISH IMPORTS, EXPORTS AND RE-EXPORTS, 1740–1775
(annual averages)

£ million	1740–9	1750–9	1760–9	1770–5
Imports	7·3	8·4	10·8	12·8
Exports	6·5	8·7	10·0	10·0
Re-exports	3·6	3·5	4·4	5·6
Exports and re-exports	10·1	12·2	14·4	15·6

Source: Schumpeter, *Overseas trade statistics*, pp. 15–16, tables II–IV.

In the period between 1750 and 1775 the average annual rate of growth was 1·9 per cent per annum, a high rate for a pre-industrial country[1] but the same factors did not operate throughout the period. The impetus for growth in the 1750s came from an expansion of exports of English manufactured goods (notably to the American colonies) while the dynamic in the 1760s and early 1770s was due to a swelling volume of re-exports made possible by the continued expansion of imports.

When war ended in 1748 markets re-opened abroad and exports, stimulated by a general boom in commerce in Western Europe,[2] expanded steadily in the 1750s with slight checks in 1754–5 and in 1759 until the sales of English exports reached a new peak in 1760 before war affected overseas sales in 1761–2. By the treaty of Paris which brought the Seven Years War to an end England gained Canada, Cape Breton Island and all of the region east of the Mississippi. The annexation of Tobago, Domi-

[1] Deane and Cole, *British economic growth*, p. 29.

[2] French trade also boomed in these years, as the following figures show:

ANNUAL AVERAGES OF FRENCH IMPORTS AND EXPORTS
(million livres)

1733–5	1736–9	1740–6	1749–56	1756–63
277·5	361·0	430·1	616·7	323·5

E. Levasseur, *Histoire du commerce de la France* (Paris: Librarie Nouvelle de Droit et de Jurisprudence, 1911), I, 512 cited in A. H. John, 'Agricultural productivity and economic growth in England, 1700–1760' in E. L. Jones (ed.), *Agriculture and economic growth, 1650–1815* (Methuen, 1967), p. 181.

nica, Grenada and St Vincent in the West Indies was followed by the Free Port Act of 1766 by which England endeavoured to capture trade with the Spanish American empire. The French colonies in India (except Pondicherry and Chandernagore) and Senegal and Goree in West Africa were also acquired and Florida was taken from Spain. Thus French power in India and America was broken, Spain was subdued and the British navy ruled the waves. These years too saw a notable expansion of the English merchant fleet.[1] It must have seemed as if Raleigh's dictum that 'whosoever commands the sea, commands the trade; whosoever commands the trade of the world commands the riches of the world: and consequently the world itself' had come true. But appearances were illusory for within two decades England was to lose most of her American mainland possessions.

After the Seven Years War had come to an end, trade was extremely active in 1764 and 1765 as merchants built up stocks again and entrances and clearances of shipping reached a new peak.[2] Thereafter the sales of English manufactures were affected by the persistence of unsettled conditions in the American colonies and by the effects of the non-importation agreements, as the following figures of shipments to New England, New York, Pennsylvania, Maryland, Virginia, the Carolinas and Georgia show:

EXPORTS TO THE AMERICAN COLONIES, 1764–1769

	1764	*1765*	*1766*	*1767*	*1768*	*1769*
£ *million*	2·49	1·94	1·80	1·90	2·16	1·34

Source: Ashton, *Economic fluctuations*, p. 154.

The influence of the colonial struggle on English exports in the 1760s should not be exaggerated in comparison with the more serious decline in shipments to Germany – from £2·4 million in 1764 to £1·3 million in 1769 – the result of the stagnation of incomes rather than of foreign competition, and the shrinkage of trade with Portugal from 1762 and with Spain at the end of the decade.[3] As a result of these factors the level of exports dropped in 1769 to its lowest point for more than a decade. A revival of trade in America contributed to a substantial expansion of exports in 1771 and 1772, years when English ports were more

[1] See table 6, p. 62 below.   [2] See table 5, p. 61 below.
[3] See below, pp. 147, 158–62.

active than ever before,[1] but this boom was then checked by the British credit crisis, by the worsening situation in America and by more difficult trading conditions in Europe. By the middle of 1774 recovery had begun as trade expanded to the East Indies and with Spain as well as the American colonies.

The outbreak of the war of American Independence ushered in a period of more unsettled trading conditions in which exports did not again exceed the peak total of 1771 until peace had been restored in 1784. Re-exports recovered even more slowly and did not reach the peak figure of 1773 until 1794. But in 1775 our discussion of the course of English overseas trade must end. When the expansion of trade was resumed in the 1780s it took place on a new basis, on the basis of the new English manufactures. The age of the commercial revolution was over.

COUNTRIES AND COMMODITIES

Throughout the period covered by this volume, English export trade was predominantly with Europe and was dominated by the traffic in woollen cloth. But the two important new and linked developments were the growth of extra-European trade and the widening range, particularly in the eighteenth century, of English manufactured goods which were sent overseas. At the same time the character of English imports changed as trade outside Europe grew. An increasing volume of tropical and semi-tropical foodstuffs and raw materials found their way to these shores. Some of these commodities were consumed in England but a substantial and growing quantity went to supply the re-export trade. English ports, and especially London, became entrepôts as well as terminals. The backing of English finance and the expertise of English merchants allowed England to move towards a leading position in world trade in the century after 1660.

In 1600 England's exports were based on the exploitation of her natural resources: the products of mining such as tin, of agriculture (butter, cheese, grain in times of surplus and indirectly leather) and of her industries (notably iron and cloth, made from home-produced wool). Cloth was by far the most important, accounting for 80–90 per cent of the total exports. When sales

[1] See table 5, p. 61 below.

of broadcloths to the traditional war-torn northern European markets declined in the early seventeenth century, exports of lighter fabrics to Spain and the Mediterranean grew. It is probable, however, that the shift from northern to Mediterranean markets was more marked in London than elsewhere because of that port's larger interests in southern markets and it is also possible that Professor Fisher's figures exaggerate the growth of trade in the new fabrics to some extent. The decline in London's export of undressed shortcloths was dramatic between 1606 and 1640 while the value of the new draperies was increasing sharply to reach £454,914 in the latter year.

	1604	*1614*	*1620*	*1632*	*1640*
No. of cloths (rounded to 100)	90700	87800	48000	45700	30300
Percentage of London's exports	72·0	68·7	56·3	46·1	34·8

Source: B. E. Supple, *Commercial crisis and change in England 1600–1640* (Cambridge University Press, 1959), p. 137.

This change in the market for woollen textiles had two repercussions. As mentioned earlier, it reduced the importance of the Merchant Adventurers who had previously controlled most of the cloth export trade, though they continued to be of some account as far as northern Europe was concerned. The relative geographical importance and manufacturing significance of the woollen industry was also affected. By the mid-seventeenth century the manufacture of old draperies in Suffolk, Wiltshire, Somerset and Oxfordshire was in decline while the new draperies were taken up with varying degrees of enthusiasm in East Anglia, Yorkshire and the West Country. In some cases, new and old manufactures existed side by side: in others, some areas declined while others prospered.

Opinions differ about the origins of this shift in the pattern of the export trade in woollen cloth. In the article printed here, Professor Fisher sees the growth in the trade in the 'new draperies' as the response of English industrial enterprise to the changed political and commercial situation in Europe. The ending of the war with Spain, he argues, opened up prospects there and in the Mediterranean while the outbreak of the Thirty Years War closed them in the north. But Dr Bowden has urged that the change was technological rather than commercial and resulted from the changing character of the English wool supply. The new enclosures, an expanding source of raw material, produced coarser wool with a longer staple, which was less suited to the needs of woollens and more to those of the newer fabrics.[1] Professor Charles Wilson has added a further dimension in arguing that the relative success of the English cloth industry in the Mediterranean was based, in addition, on the decline and virtual disappearance of Italy as a leading producer in the course of the seventeenth century. The Mediterranean market was won by the English cloth industry because it produced a more marketable type of cloth than its main rival, the Netherlands cloth industry centred on Leiden. At the same time the English cloth industry made little impact on the markets of northern Europe because the product of the Low Countries made of Spanish or Turkish wool was more acceptable there than the English product. Throughout the seventeenth century Anglo-Dutch competition remained a major force in the division of markets.[2] And there is a further general point: the ability of English manufacturers and merchants to sell overseas depended not only on raw material supply conditions and on the level of technique and costs at home but also on conditions in the competing industries in Europe and on the less predictable vagaries of fashion. 'It cannot be argued', Professor Supple has written, 'that the export of English cloth, after decades of growth, had reached a ceiling beyond which it could not rise, that sales, having saturated a static market, could no longer expand. Rather, what happened was that competition developed which English textiles were unable to meet, so that they had to accept a smaller absolute share of total demand.'[3]

Even in the early seventeenth century, the cloth trade was not the whole of the story of English overseas trade. The fish trade to Spain and the Mediterranean expanded and exports of other English manufactures, of mineral products and of agricultural produce also grew. The most rapidly expanding trade was not in the native manufactures of England but in the re-export of commodities brought from overseas as a consequence of the

[1] P. Bowden, 'The wool supply and the woollen industry', *Economic History Review*, 2nd series, IX (1956), 44–58.

[2] Charles Wilson, 'Cloth production and international competition in the seventeenth century', *Economic History Review*, 2nd series, XIII (1960), 209–21.

[3] B. E. Supple, *Commercial crisis and change in England 1600–42* (Cambridge University Press, 1959), p. 138.

widening area of English overseas trade. Of these East Indian products – calicoes, saltpetre, indigo, silks and spices – tobacco from America and Mediterranean cotton, dyestuffs and raw silk were the most important. Nevertheless this trade was but a beginning, and even by 1640 re-exports only accounted for 6 per cent of total English exports.

While imports consisted of a wider range of commodities than exports, there were four main categories of commodities brought in: textile materials, groceries, timber and wine and then a host of miscellaneous commodities including metal goods. In the sixteenth century linen and metalware brought from Germany via the Netherlands and French wines had predominated. With the widening orbit of trade after 1600, these were joined by a growing quantity of Baltic iron, flax, hemp and timber in addition to silk, dyestuffs, fruits and drugs from the Mediterranean. Finally, there were the colonial imports of which initially the most important was tobacco. Almost all this trade came through London and the London port books provide evidence for the growth of this trade. In 1620, when this commodity was eighth in the list of all imports, London tobacco imports were rated at £55,143; by 1633 it had risen to fifth position and by 1640, when £230,840 worth was brought in, tobacco had become the most important single import.[1] Declared tobacco imports rose in quantity from 173,372 lbs in 1620 to 1·25 million lbs in 1640[2] and to 9 million lbs in the 1660s. This was the earliest American staple to emerge: the others developed later – sugar in the 1650s and furs in the 1670s. Some of the imports, such as Spanish wool for the new draperies, silk and cotton, provided raw materials for English industry but more consisted of luxury articles which were in growing demand by the more affluent aristocracy and middle class.

The increased range of commodities in which England traded between 1600 and 1660 reflected the widening geographical range of commerce. While most of English trade still went on the short North Sea or English Channel routes where Dutch

[1] Neville Williams, 'The London port books', *Transactions of the London and Middlesex Archaeological Society*, XVIII (1955), 15.
[2] A. M. Millard, 'Analyses of port books recording merchandises imported into the Port of London by English and alien and denizen merchants for certain years between 1588 and 1640' (unpublished), table 3.

shipping predominated,[1] a growing number of English ships ranged further afield – and demanded naval protection from piracy in the process – along the coasts of Spain and Portugal and into the Mediterranean, to Leghorn and Naples, to Venice and the Greek islands and to Turkey and Egypt. More English vessels also sailed for Norway or penetrated into the Baltic.[2] The East India trade grew particularly between 1618 and the early 1630s and English vessels ranged the Atlantic, taking part in the Newfoundland fisheries (which alone employed over 300 vessels a year in the 1630s), and in the much smaller African trade. Although growing slowly until 1642, the trade with the American mainland colonies and the West Indian islands had become a substantial business by 1660. The Iceland fishery, said to employ nearly a quarter of all English seamen in 1615, contracted in the middle years of the century while the Spitzbergen whaling industry, which had encountered severe Dutch competition in the 1630s, was almost extinct by 1660.[3]

In the century or so after 1660 an important feature of English imports was the growth of trade in non-European products. No figures are available for the whole period but the following table, which groups imports by category rather than by place of origin, indicates the trend in the eighteenth century.

Of particular importance amongst the textiles were linen yarn and linen imported from Germany and the Baltic countries. Raw silk imports grew from 357,966 lbs in 1700 to a peak of 697,529 lbs in 1769 while, paralleling the growth of the English cotton industry, raw cotton imports grew after the mid-century to reach 6·7 million lbs in 1775.[4] Hemp, flax and wool were also to

[1] In 1601 714 ships entered London; of these 40 (2,656 tons) were German, 207 (15,601 tons) English and 360 (9,328 tons) Dutch. L. R. Miller, 'New evidence on the shipping and imports of London, 1601–1602', *Quarterly Journal of Economics*, XLI (1926), 740.

[2] These trades, where the Dutch had the lead, were affected adversely by the wars in the 1650s. Down to 1651 the Dutch had been out-trading England in the Baltic; then, between 1654 and 1656, only two Dutch ships a year went from England to the Sound until in 1657–8, thanks to the Spanish war, Dutch and Lübeck ships began to recover ground. Christopher Hill, *Reformation to industrial revolution* (Weidenfeld & Nicolson, 1967), pp. 125–6.

[3] Davis, *Shipping industry*, pp. 8–16.

[4] But still a small amount compared with imports later in the century: an average of 31·4 million lbs were imported in the years 1795–99. B. R. Mitchell and Phyllis Deane, *Abstract of British historical statistics* (Cambridge University Press, 1962), p. 178.

be found among the textile materials imported. Sales of East Indian products grew in the seventeenth century as they became cheaper: 240,000 pieces of calico were imported in 1600 and 861,000 pieces a century later. This trade was checked by the Acts of 1700 and 1721, which prohibited the importation of printed calicoes and cottons for domestic consumption, though their import for re-export was allowed.

PERCENTAGE OF ENGLISH IMPORTS, 1700–1772 (by value)[1]

	1700	1750	1772
Textile materials*	30·8	30·6	28·7
Groceries†	16·9	27·6	35·8
Timber	4·0	4·2	2·2
Wine	10·8	4·7	2·8
Other	37·5	32·9	30·5

*Linens, calicoes, silk (raw and thrown), flax and hemp, cotton wool.
†Tea, coffee, rice, sugar, pepper, etc.
Source: Ashton, Introduction to Schumpeter, *Overseas trade statistics*, p. 11.

The course of trade in the most important colonial imports is set out in the following table, which gives annual averages of legal imports by volume:

	1700–4	1720–4	1750–4	1770–1
Coffee (cwts)	5,764	13,648	8,810	40,192
Sugar (million cwts)	0·38	0·64	0·91	1·56
Tea (million lbs)	0·07	1·03	3·55	9·95
Tobacco (million lbs)	32·4	31·2	55·2	48·7

Source: Schumpeter, *Overseas trade statistics*, pp. 52–5, table XVI.

While imports mounted, coffee remained the drink of the well-to-do and most of the coffee which came in was re-exported. The major stimulus to the consumption of sugar came on the supply

[1] These are the years for which Professor Ashton provided figures. The following table has been drawn up from the more limited range of statistics printed in E. B. Schumpeter, *Overseas trade statistics, 1687–1808* (Oxford University Press, 1960) pp. 48–51, table XV. It confirms the picture given in the text.

	1700–4	1720–4	1750–4	1770–1
Textile materials*	22·1	19·7	17·4	17·9
Groceries†	11·2	16·9	20·8	27·8
Timber	2·1	2·3	2·0	2·0
Wine	8·5	8·7	4·6	3·2

* Flax, hemp, silk, wool and yarns.
† Coffee, brown sugar and tea.

B

side from the fall in price as output expanded and on the demand side from the spread of tea and coffee drinking which grew as the price, particularly of tea, fell. As Professor Cole describes below, the official figures of tea imports were considerably affected by smuggling but demand grew as tea became cheaper.[1] In the 1700s it cost £1 a lb; in 1750 it cost 5s. Although affected by smuggling, tobacco imports also increased early in the century but after the Scottish trade began its most imposing growth about 1740, the English trade ceased to grow. Even so apart from a single year it always remained larger than the Scottish trade. The peak English import figure was 65·2 million lbs in 1763; the peak Scottish figure was 47·0 million in 1771, at which time Glasgow attained its greatest relative importance in the trade.[2] Other significant imports were rice, which was an important newcomer to the list of colonial imports, grain, timber and port. From 1765 overseas supplies of grain began to come in as the English surplus came to an end. Together with some Swedish iron, timber was imported from the Baltic and North America, mainly for houses and ship-building. Finally, while the consumption of port expanded because of England's special relationship with Portugal, imports of wine did not increase. The majority of imports therefore continued to be tropical and sub-tropical foodstuffs, drink and tobacco and raw materials, whose volume expanded to meet the demand created by the rising level of incomes in England and the expansion of the textile and ship-building industries.

On the export side two aspects are notable in the century after 1660: the declining contribution of the woollen textile industry to English manufactured exports and the continued contribution of re-exports to the export account. Though the value of woollen cloth exported grew with the opening up of markets in the Americas and in the slave trade, the overseas market was affected

[1] See below, pp. 127–31.
[2] Scottish tobacco imports amounted to 1·5 million lbs a year immediately after the Union, 6 million lbs in 1722, 8 million lbs in 1741, 21 million lbs in 1752 and 32 million lbs in 1760. As late as 1738 the Scottish trade was only 10 per cent of the British total; in 1744 it was 20 per cent; in 1758 it was 30 per cent and in 1765 40 per cent. The 51·8 per cent of 1769 was the only occasion on which Scottish imports exceeded English imports. In the years 1771–5 it slipped back to about 45 per cent. Jacob M. Price, 'The rise of Glasgow in the Chesapeake trade, 1707–1775' in Peter L. Payne (ed.), *Studies in Scottish business history* (Cass, 1967), p. 300.

thproductAshtonton, ...

as European demand for woollen cloth was checked by the expansion of protected domestic industries. The relative import-

PERCENTAGE OF ENGLISH EXPORTS, 1700-1772 (by value)[1]

	1700	1750	1772
Woollens	57·3	45·9	42·2
Grain	3·7	19·6	8·0
Fish	2·6	1·0	0·7
Lead	2·5	1·6	1·7
Iron	1·6	4·4	8·0
Linens	—	2·1	7·3
Cotton fabrics	0·5	—	2·3
Others	31·8	25·4	29·8

Source: Ashton, Introduction to Schumpeter, *Overseas trade statistics*, p. 12.

ance of cloth exports, which in the early seventeenth century accounted for about 80–90 per cent of total English exports, continued to decline, a trend accelerated by the continued shift of demand to the cheaper fabrics. Among the other exports the pace was set by iron, whose exports, particularly to the American colonies, rose sharply after the mid-century. Even before the coming of the major industrial inventions, overseas sales of coal, cotton goods, linen and refined sugar grew, aided by the removal of export duties or prohibitions on manufactures. Corn exports expanded in the first half of the eighteenth century and sharply declined from the mid-1760s,[2] while fishing entered a more prolonged decline. As employment grew in manufacturing industry, the labour force in in-shore fishing (always a residual employment) decreased and the amount of fish caught fell.[3]

[1] These are the years for which Professor Ashton provided figures. The following table has been drawn up from the more limited range of statistics printed in Schumpeter, *Overseas trade statistics*, pp. 19–22, 29–30, 35–6, tables VII, X and XII. It confirms the picture given in the text.

	1700–4	1720–4	1750–4	1770–1
Woollens	72·6	73·5	57·7	54·3
Fish	2·1	2·9	1·5	0·8
Lead	2·8	2·1	1·8	1·7
Iron	1·7	2·4	4·7	7·9
Linens	0·2	0·5	2·4	6·3
Cotton fabrics	0·4	0·4	0·8	2·4

[2] See table 7, p. 63.

[3] The Newfoundland and Greenland fisheries, whose product did not normally enter into the English trading account, enjoyed great prosperity between 1729 and 1763. See R. G. Lounsbury, *The British fishery at Newfoundland, 1634–1763* (Cambridge, Mass.: Harvard University Press, 1934), p. 311. Professor Harper suggests that the tonnage of shipping employed in these fisheries rose from 20,330 tons in 1660 to 38,585 tons in 1773 (*Navigation laws*, p. 339).

In the period 1660–1775 re-exports remained of considerable importance in the trading account. In the 1660s re-exports accounted for just over 30 per cent of total exports: in the 1770s they accounted for over 37 per cent. In both periods they were dominated by East Indian and colonial products. Re-exports of sugar and tobacco grew in the later seventeenth century and by the turn of the century one-third of English imports of sugar and two-thirds of English imports of tobacco were being sent abroad. Both these commodities suffered from competition in the first half of the eighteenth century, sugar from the French West Indian islands and tobacco – where leaf found a better market than treated – from the concentration of re-exports on Glasgow, but new re-exports such as rice and coffee helped maintain total re-exports. In 1772 grocery re-exports (tea, coffee, rice, sugar, pepper, etc.) worth £2·1 million accounted for 37·4 per cent of total re-exports; piece goods (calicoes, etc) worth £1·1 million for 19·7 per cent; tobacco (£0·9 million) for 16·5 per cent, linens (£346,000) for 6·1 per cent and dyestuffs (£191,000) for 3·4 per cent.[1]

Generally exports and re-exports moved in the same direction but sometimes, as in 1728–9, 1762–3, 1768 and 1773 when English exports were depressed, partial compensation was provided by a rise in re-exports. When European purchases of tropical produce declined because of war or other adverse circumstances, goods piled up in warehouses in London and the other ports. When demand recovered, it was possible to put them onto the market quickly: hence re-exports sometimes rose in advance of domestic exports for which the facilities for storage were small.[2]

The changing commodity composition of English overseas trade was reflected in its changing geographical pattern but, as the following table shows, a substantial trade continued to be carried on with continental Europe and with Ireland. As late as the early 1770s almost half of domestic exports and more than four-fifths of re-exports were sent to Europe which was the source of almost half of English imports. Two main tendencies may be noted in England's trading relations with Europe. The first was England's changed position within the European agricultural market. The dislocation of Baltic supplies of grain after

[1] Ashton, Introduction to Schumpeter, *Overseas trade statistics*, p. 13.
[2] Ashton, *Fluctuations*, p. 54.

1700 provided a large market for English agriculture. Total exports of grain rose from 2·8 million quarters in the decade 1700-9 to over 6 million in the 1740s and 1750s and maintained this level during the early 1760s.[1] As Professor John has pointed out,

THE GEOGRAPHICAL DISTRIBUTION OF ENGLISH TRADE (by value)

	Percentages of totals for England and Wales		
	1700–1	*1750–1*	*1772–3*
Total imports from:			
Europe	66	55	45
North America	6	11	12
West Indies	14	19	25
East Indies and Africa	14	15	18
Re-exports to:			
Europe	85	79	82
North America	5	11	9
West Indies	6	4	3
East Indies and Africa	4	5	6
Domestic exports to:			
Europe	85	77	49
North America	6	11	25
West Indies	5	5	12
East Indies and Africa	4	7	14

Source: Phyllis Deane, *The first industrial revolution* (Cambridge University Press, 1965), p. 56.

this development had a number of consequences. It 'meant more work at home and, by providing a bulk outward cargo, the more efficient use of English shipping. Above all, it gave an extra command over foreign currency at a time when European markets for British manufactures were sluggish. According to the Procureur-Général of the Breton Parliament, for example, France alone spent 10·5 million livres for British grain in 1748–50. Money earned in this way could be used by means of the European money market to offset debts incurred with other countries'.[2] Between 1763 and 1776, by contrast, increased imports of grain, wool, tallow and dairy produce helped to sustain English exports to Europe.

[1] Figures derived from J. Marshall, *A digest of all the accounts* (London, 1833), II, 88. Figures for net exports of wheat (including flour) are given in table 7, p. 63.
[2] John, 'Agricultural productivity' in Jones, (ed.), *Agriculture and economic growth*, p. 180. The figures for France are taken from G. S. Keith, *Tracts on the corn laws of Great Britain* (London, 1792), p. 220.

The second change in trade with Europe was a geographical shift away from the Netherlands. In the early seventeenth century, the Netherlands had been both the main market for English exports and the main source of supply of imports. In the eighteenth century while both English exports and imports grew in total, English trade with Holland stagnated. As a result the Dutch share of imports into England fell from 14·6 per cent to 3·6 per cent between 1696–7 and 1772–3 and her share of English exports fell from 41·5 per cent to 12·7 per cent in the same year.[1]

England imported comparatively little from Germany and, affected by war, exports thence developed only slowly between 1700 and 1760 to rise steeply in 1761–5 and to decline thereafter. Protectionist policies inhibited trade between England and France which remained small while commercial relations with the Scandinavian countries expanded only after 1760. Imports from the Baltic increased – particularly naval stores for the English merchant marine and iron – but English merchants were unable to persuade those nations to take any substantial quantity of English manufactured goods. In southern Europe trade was affected by the recurrent wars with Spain and, while exports to the Mediterranean rose in the course of the century, imports were depressed between 1735 and 1760. Two brighter spots were Portugal and Ireland. As Dr Fisher demonstrates below, trade with Portugal expanded until the early 1760s both as a result of the growth of the Portuguese home market and indirectly because of the expansion of Brazilian demand for European manufactures.

Trade with Ireland was circumscribed by legislation. In 1667 the import of Irish sheep and cattle into England had been forbidden and this was followed by a prohibition on the import of Irish butter and cheese in 1681 and on the export of Irish wool or cloth except to England in 1698. Some changes were made in the eighteenth century. Exempted from duty in England from 1696, Irish linens also benefited from the bounties on re-export from 1743. Irish beef, pork and cattle were re-admitted

---

[1] The actual figures were:
1696–7 total English imports £ 3·5 million, from Holland £0·5 million
1772–3   „   „   „   £11·4 million, „   „   £0·4 million
1696–7 total English exports £ 3·5 million, to Holland £1·5 million
1772–3   „   „   „   £14·8 million, „   „   £1·9 million
Charles Wilson, *England's apprenticeship, 1603–1763* (Longmans, 1965), p. 272.

to the English market after 1758–9 and the duty on tallow was removed. By these changes Irish products gained an easier access to the English market than to the European markets where they faced high tariff barriers. As a result trade between England and Ireland expanded rapidly after the mid-century and Ireland's share of total English imports increased from 3·9 per cent in 1700 to 9·9 per cent in 1771. But these figures conceal an important shift from wool to linen. In 1698 wool and yarn formed 46 per cent of total Irish exports to England and linen cloth and yarn 23·3 per cent while in 1768 the former accounted for 11·2 per cent and the latter 66·9 per cent. By 1768 imports of Irish beef, butter and pork had reached appreciable quantities and amounted to 9·5 per cent of the total. Irish imports from England also grew in these years. And the proportion of English exports destined for Ireland rose from 4·2 per cent in 1700 to 14·9 per cent in 1771. There were again significant changes in commodity composition.

IMPORTS FROM ENGLAND (GREAT BRITAIN) AS A PROPORTION OF TOTAL IMPORTS FROM ENGLAND (GREAT BRITAIN)*

	Coal	Woollens	Sugar	Hops	Tea	Tobacco	Silk manufactures	Raw silk	Others
1698	9·1	1·7	2·3	5·2	—	26·0	4·7	4·1	46·9
1768	7·9	11·4	15·2	3·2	4·5	2·3	4·4	5·2	45·8

*Based on Irish valuations of imports from England, 1698: from Great Britain, 1768.
Source: L. M. Cullen, *Anglo-Irish trade, 1660–1800* (Manchester University Press, 1968), p. 52.

Because of the alteration in base the comparisons in this table should not be pressed too far but they provide some indication of the shift in composition of English exports to Ireland, notably the increase in woollen exports and the decline in tobacco exports, where the fall in tobacco prices exaggerates the change. Coal imports rose from 46,519 tons in 1700 to 197,136 tons in 1770. The overall change in trade is shown in the following table:

£ million	English exports to Ireland	English imports from Ireland
1700	0·43	0·37
1770	1·88	2·40

Source: Cullen, *Anglo-Irish trade*, p. 45.

From the mid-eighteenth century trade with Ireland was of growing importance for the English economy.[1]

The main development in English trade in the eighteenth century was the expansion of trade with America: the growth of imports of tobacco, sugar, rice, indigo, furs, dyewoods, grain and lumber and of exports of English manufactures, notably iron and woollens. Exports to the American mainland colonies rose from an annual average of £259,000 in the years 1701–5 to a peak of £1·8 million in the period 1766–70 while exports in official values to the British West Indies increased from £305,000 to £1·4 million in the same years. Similarly imports from the American mainland colonies expanded from an annual average of £264,000 in 1701–5 to a peak of £1·45 million in 1771–5 and imports from the British West Indies increased from an annual average of £609,000 in 1701–5 to £3.11 million in 1771–5. Trade with the American colonies also increased relatively in importance. In 1701–5 the American market took nearly 10 per cent of English imports while in 1766–70 it took nearly 25 per cent. Similarly the colonial share of English imports rose from 15 per cent in 1700 to 40 per cent in 1760.[2] The growth of the American and West Indian trades had important consequences for the English shipping industry. The moderate expansion of these trades in the 1720s and 1730s did much to prevent an actual decline in the total size of the industry while their rapid expansion after the mid-century was both the major cause of the increase in size of the English merchant marine – since by the end of our period nearly half of all English shipping was engaged in the Atlantic trades[3] – and also a stimulus to the import of naval stores from the Baltic.

Finally there were the Africa and Asian trades. Direct trade with Africa was small though the expansion of the slave trade after 1750 brought a marked growth of exports to expedite that trade. Imports from the East Indies rose from about half a million pounds in 1701–5 to a peak of £1·85 million in 1766–70 and exports to that area increased from a mere hundred thousand

---

[1] This paragraph is based on L. M. Cullen, *Anglo-Irish trade, 1660–1800* (Manchester University Press, 1968).

[2] The figures in this paragraph come from Schumpeter, *Overseas trade statistics*.

[3] Davis, *Shipping industry*, p. 42.

pounds to £1·1 million in the same years. Attempts to reduce
the bullion drain to the Far East and to increase the shipments
of woollens and other manufactures finally began to have some
effect in the 1760s and 1770s.

All the discussions of trade centred on England inevitably
understate the involvement of English merchants in overseas
commerce for they also came to be concerned in vessels and
cargoes which did not come to England. Early sixteenth-
century English trade was mainly bilateral between London and
Antwerp or between some other English port and a nearby
European port but eighteenth-century trade was more roundabout and by the middle of this century a much more complex
pattern had evolved. The Atlantic was criss-crossed by a series
of multilateral trading patterns such as England–West Africa–
West Indies or American plantation colonies and back, or
England–Newfoundland–Mediterranean and back,[1] or England–
South Carolina–Hamburg–Stockholm and back. Given the conditions of the time, moreover, the expansion of plantation agriculture in America or the West Indies would have proved slower
and much more difficult without negro labour. Trade goods or
guns manufactured in Birmingham, Indian cottons, rum and
spirits found a market in West Africa in exchange for slaves who
were transported across the Atlantic. Even here there was
change, for in the course of the eighteenth century imported
products formed a decreasing proportion of the trade goods as
more home manufactures became available. Recent research has
been tending to reduce the volume of the Atlantic slave trade
but all the same a considerable number of negroes were carried
across the Atlantic.[2] With slave labour the profits of a sugar
plantation were 'generally much greater than those of any other
cultivation that is known either in Europe or America'.[3] Finally,
English merchants profitably engaged in trade between the
Iberian peninsula and Spanish and Portuguese overseas
possessions, particularly in America.

Between 1600 and the 1770s English overseas commerce

[1] With some exaggeration, H. A. Innis wrote: Cod from Newfoundland was
the lever by which England wrested her share of the riches of the New World
from Spain. *The cod fisheries* (Toronto University Press, 1940), p. 53.
[2] See Philip D. Curtin, 'Epidemiology and the slave trade', *Political Science
Quarterly*, LXXXIII (1968), 191, note 1.
[3] *Wealth of nations* (Cannan ed., Methuen, 1904), 1, 365.

widened its horizons considerably and diversified the commodities in which it traded. Nevertheless, while there was a relative decline of the old markets for both purchases and sales and the development of new sources of supply and outlets for English products in more distant parts of the world, the extent of the changes should not be exaggerated. English trade throughout this period continued to be almost entirely an exchange of manufactured goods for primary products. Further, although because of their requirements for finance and the demands they placed on the shipping industry, attention has often been focused on the growing oceanic trades, it must be emphasized that though of declining importance, Europe was still the main customer for English exports and the main supplier of English imports.

THE ENGLISH PORTS

The growing volume, changing geographical pattern and shifting commodity composition of English overseas trade in the period between 1600 and 1770 inevitably affected the relative importance of English ports. In the course of the sixteenth century the concentration of the trade in broadcloth on the London–Antwerp axis had adversely affected the trade of many provincial ports and this decline in the share of the outports of cloth exports appears to have continued in the first half of the seventeenth century. According to calculations made by Dr Stephens the outports were responsible for about 26 per cent of the trade in the old draperies and about 23 per cent in the new in 1612: nearly thirty years later they accounted for 32 per cent of the depleted export of old draperies and only 17 per cent of the increased export of the new draperies. These changes were not equally felt by all ports. Whereas in the earlier years of James I's reign many of the south-western ports – Southampton, Lyme Regis, Exeter, Dartmouth and to a lesser extent Plymouth, Bristol and Barnstaple – had some stake in the cloth trade, by the later 1630s only Exeter and Lyme Regis were really significant in this branch of commerce. The most important development on the east coast was the shift of the trade of the major cloth port, Hull, from the Baltic to the Netherlands by forcing its way, together with Newcastle, into a market which London had previously virtually monopolized. But cloth was not the only trade in which the outports participated: herrings at Yarmouth, pilchards at Plymouth, coal at Newcastle, the Newfoundland fisheries at Southampton, Plymouth and other western ports, lead at Plymouth, Southampton, Hull and Newcastle, tin at Plymouth and coal, general goods and re-exports from Chester to Ireland were among the more important. With its interests in the Newfoundland fisheries, in the lead trade, in the trade with Ireland and in the wine trade, Bristol had become by 1640 the 'greatest town for shipping except London'.[1]

Statistics are not readily available for the trade of individual ports in the seventeenth century but the following table of customs revenue for selected years in the century gives some indication of the changes in the relative importance of the main English ports:

CUSTOMS REVENUE AT THE CHIEF ENGLISH PORTS (£s)

Port	1614	1617	1672	1676	1687*
London	105,131	121,887	502,312	569,531	586,905
Hull	7,664	5,904	22,527	20,213	18,649
Exeter	4,096	4,427	15,727	17,038	20,761
Bristol	3,599	3,568	56,922	65,908	46,820
Newcastle	3,781	2,957	8,889	9,419	10,583
Plymouth	2,316	3,462	14,102	16,564	19,139
Lyme Regis	3,010	2,938	6,518	4,438	5,269
Southampton	2,350	3,220	9,803	6,632	4,310
Dartmouth	2,294	3,516	2,217	1,263	745

*This year's figures cannot be compared with those of previous years because of the inclusion of new duties levied from 1685.
Source: W. B. Stephens, *Seventeenth-century Exeter* (University of Exeter, 1958), pp. 8, 162.

Two points above all are evident: first, the revenue figures indicate a notable expansion of English imports in the later seventeenth century: second, those ports which expanded fastest were the western ports which benefited from the 'Americanization' of English overseas trade. The most marked development was the growth of Bristol after 1660 which found an expanding role as a major participant in the Atlantic trade by engaging in the tobacco and sugar trades and in the Newfoundland fisheries and by interloping in the African slave trade. By

[1] This paragraph has drawn on W. B. Stephens, 'The cloth trade of the provincial ports, 1600–1640' (unpublished). I am most indebted to Dr Stephens for allowing me to see his work.

1686–7 shipping in these trades amounted to between one-third and one-quarter of the total. While in 1700 49·5 per cent of the vessels entering Bristol were from the American colonies and the West Indies, 20·5 per cent were from Spain and Portugal and 11 per cent from Ireland.[1] Like Bristol, Plymouth also gained from the expansion of trade with the New World. Other strands also contributed to the growth of outport trade. With the boom in the serge trade to the Netherlands and an increasing stake in the Newfoundland fisheries, Exeter became one of the most vigorous ports in the kingdom.[2] Elsewhere in the south-west there was change. The trade of the north Devon ports began to grow but Dartmouth decayed rapidly after the Civil War and Lyme Regis suffered from its dependence on the trade with France. On the east coast, Hull (which rivalled Exeter in the cloth trade) and Newcastle exported woollens, mainly to the Baltic for flax, hemp, iron, pitch, tar and timber. Overtopping all, as the figures show, was London which throughout most of the seventeenth century was increasing its share of the total volume of trade. It handled between two-thirds and three-quarters of the nation's trade and remained without serious challenge.

The outports continued to grow in the eighteenth century. Of those engaged in the oceanic trades, Bristol, with its large stakes in the sugar and tobacco trades, was the most important until it was overtaken by the mid-century by Liverpool which increased rapidly in importance after 1730. In the same years Whitehaven, a coal-exporting port, became the major English provincial tobacco entrepôt and the growth of the Baltic trades made Hull and Newcastle, whose coal exports also grew, busier ports. Yarmouth benefited from the boom in corn exports between 1700 and 1750 and then declined. At the same time other ports, notably Lyme Regis and Dartmouth, lost ground

[1] See W. E. Minchinton, *The trade of Bristol in the eighteenth century* (Bristol Record Society, xx, 1957), p. 5.

[2] Professor Davis's statements about Exeter below (p. 90) are somewhat misleading. Exeter's direct foreign trade in serges was not the product of the previous decade or so (i.e. the 1690s): substantial quantities of perpetuanas were exported from Exeter between 1676 and 1686: 1676, 1·31 million lbs; 1680, 1·79 million lbs; 1683, 1·66 million lbs; 1686, 1·72 million lbs. W. B. Stephens, *Seventeenth-century Exeter: a study of industrial and commercial development, 1625–1688* (University of Exeter, 1958), p. 105. 'By the 1680s', writes Dr Stephens, 'Exeter was recognized as the serge-exporting port *par excellence* among the outports'. Stephens, *Exeter*, p. 110.

as did Exeter, after reaching a peak of prosperity in 1715–20.
The great growth of the trade of the major provincial ports
in the third quarter of the century is strikingly demonstrated
by figures of the tonnage of English and foreign shipping clearing outwards from the five principal English ports for the years
1750 and 1770:

(*tons*)	London	Whitehaven	Liverpool	Newcastle	Bristol
1750	179,860	100,778	42,662	45,336	27,636
1770	212,876	189,445	76,578	54,264	24,839

Source: *Political Magazine and Parliamentary, Naval, Military and Literary Journal*,
IV (1783), 202.

While Whitehaven and Liverpool grew quickly, Newcastle and
London grew more slowly and Bristol stagnated. The forces
which had led to the growth of the trade of the outports slightly
eroded London's dominance.[1]

LONDON'S PERCENTAGE SHARE OF ENGLISH OVERSEAS TRADE, 1700–1770

	1700	*1710*	*1720*	*1730*	*1740*	*1750*	*1760*	*1770*
Imports	80	72	81	80	73	71	72	73
Exports*	69	71	66	69	65	62	73	63
Re-exports	86	80	85	83	75	70	75	69

*Of English produce and manufactures
Source: T. S. Ashton, Introduction to Schumpeter, *Overseas trade statistics*, p. 9.

For London's larger share of imports and re-exports than of
exports there were several reasons: its monopoly of the East
India trade, the existence in the metropolis of extensive facilities
for warehousing and the requirement in some legislation, as for
example, the Iron Act of 1750, that London should be the sole
port of import. More generally London's dominance derived
from its position as a major market for imported foodstuffs and
raw materials, as a major distribution centre both coastwise and
by water and land carriage within England and as a convenient
entrepôt, favoured by the enumeration clauses of the Navigation
Acts, for the European trades. These factors were reinforced by
the growth in wealth and expertise of the London merchants
and by the proliferation of financial and other services available
in the metropolis. In the later eighteenth century, because of its

[1] See also Professor John's comment, p. 181.

credit facilities and financial resources, London was on the verge of ousting Amsterdam from its position of dominance.

ENGLISH FOREIGN TRADE AND ECONOMIC DEVELOPMENT

Economic growth, or the reasons why some nations become wealthier than others and why some economies undergo improvement, is not a recent concern. Interest can be seen in the writings of seventeenth-century Englishmen who sought reasons for Dutch economic pre-eminence and these issues also exercised men's minds in the eighteenth century. Was not Adam Smith's own contribution 'An inquiry into the nature and causes of the wealth of nations'?

The acceptance of Keynesian economics and the political necessity of dealing with the issue of economic development since 1945 has focused the attention of economists and many economic historians anew on the problems of economic growth. For British economic historians this interest was given a greater momentum by the publication first of Rostow's *Stages of economic growth*[1] and then of Deane and Cole's *British economic growth, 1688–1959* and the subsequent debate, in which a variety of explanations of the quickening pace of industrialization in England in the eighteenth century have been offered.[2] The purpose of the ensuing discussion is not to examine the whole question of economic development in England. It is rather a more limited one – to consider how the changes in English overseas trade between 1600 and 1775, already outlined above and discussed in the articles printed below, contributed to the evolution of the English economy at this time.

Certainly many contemporaries in the seventeenth and eighteenth centuries were in little doubt that an increase in trade provided the route to expanding national wealth and numerous pamphlets and polemics embroidered on this theme. As Daniel Defoe wrote:

[1] W. W. Rostow, *The stages of economic growth* (Cambridge University Press, 1960).

[2] For a more detailed discussion of the alternative theories see R. M. Hartwell, 'The causes of the industrial revolution: an essay in methodology' in R. M. Hartwell (ed.), *The causes of the industrial revolution in England* (Methuen, 1967), pp. 53–79.

Upon the whole, to sum it up in a few words trade is the wealth of the world; trade makes the difference as to rich and poor, between one nation and another; trade nourishes industry, industry begets trade; trade dispenses the natural wealth of the world, and trade raises new species of wealth, which nature knew nothing of; trade has two daughters, whose fruitful progeny in arts may be said to employ mankind; namely manufactures and navigation.

Or in Postlethwayt's view: commerce is that alone by which our nation supports its head.

British experience in the nineteenth century when overseas trade appeared to be the engine of growth contributed to the judgement of an earlier generation of historians, which included Bowden, Cunningham, Mantoux and Redford, that foreign trade played a crucial role in early English economic development.[1] And these notions still strike responsive chords. Professor Charles Wilson has argued that the period between 1660 and 1760 was 'a time when commercial enterprise, often closely allied with state power and aided by legislation and military or naval force, was changing the face of the old agrarian customary economy. . . . The dynamic of the time was commercial'.[2] More recently Dr Hobsbawm has stated that 'the industrial revolution was generated in these decades – after the 1740s, when this massive but slow growth in the domestic economies combined with the rapid – after 1750 extremely rapid – expansion of the international economy; and it occurred in the country which seized its international opportunities to corner a major share of the overseas markets'.[3]

Though it was not the main concern of most of the authors of the articles printed in this volume to discuss the influence of overseas trade on English economic development as a central issue, they all deal with this question incidentally. Both

[1] See in particular Witt Bowden, *Industrial society in England towards the end of the eighteenth century* (New York: Macmillan, 1925), pp. 65, 68; W. Cunningham, *The growth of English industry and commerce in modern times* (Cambridge University Press, 4th ed. 1907), II, 610; Paul Mantoux, *The industrial revolution in the eighteenth century* (Cape, 1928), p.94 and Arthur Redford, *The economic history of England, 1760–1860* (Longmans, 2nd ed. 1960), pp. 3–4.

[2] *England's apprenticeship*, p. x.

[3] E. J. Hobsbawm, *Industry and empire: an economic history of Britain since 1750* (Weidenfeld & Nicolson, 1968), p. 38.

Professor F. J. Fisher and Dr H. E. S. Fisher might echo the more recent statement of Professor Davis – which goes further than the conclusion of his first paper in this collection[1] – that 'we may well attach to the period running from the English Restoration to American Independence the title of "The Commercial Revolution"'.[2]

The following discussion will consider some of the ways in which foreign trade affected English economic life between 1600 and 1775. It is a commonplace of discussions of market growth to cite Adam Smith's view that the division of labour is limited by the extent of the market. Increasing demands for products can result from a growth of population or from rising real incomes. In its turn population growth may be a consequence of an increase in population within a given market area or may be a consequence of an increase in the geographical limits of the market area. In either case the factor of rising real income would apply. Total demand for the products of English industry in the period under review was composed of the sum of home and foreign demand so that the relative importance of each type of market needs to be considered. Following the contemporary example of David Macpherson, who in 1760 asserted that 'the home trade is with good reason believed to be a vast deal greater in value than the whole of the foreign trade, the people of Great Britain being the best customers to the manufacturers and traders of Great Britain',[3] historians have in the past devoted some attention to the importance of the home market but more attention has recently been paid to this aspect of eighteenth-century economic life.[4] In the article printed below,[5] Professor

[1] See below, p. 95.

[2] *Commercial revolution*, p. 3; a term used earlier by Bolingbroke, see J. Plumb, *The growth of political stability in England* (Macmillan, 1967), p. 3.

[3] *Annals of commerce* (London, 1805), III, 340. In a footnote Macpherson cites an estimate by an unknown author that home consumption was thirty-two times as much as exports to foreign countries. But as Deane and Cole point out (*British economic growth*, p. 42, note 1) this is clearly an over-estimate and probably refers to the estimates of consumption and exports of *grain* in the early part of the century which were made by Charles Smith in his *Three tracts on the corn trade and corn laws* (1766).

[4] See R. B. Westerfield, *Middlemen in English business* (New Haven, Conn.: Yale University Press, 1915: Newton Abbot: David & Charles, 1969) and T. S. Ashton, *An economic history of England: the 18th century* (Methuen, 1955), pp. 63–90.

[5] Pp. 165–83. See also his 'Agricultural productivity' in Jones (ed.), *Agriculture and economic growth*, p. 177.

John has set out the case for asserting that in the first half of the eighteenth century the increase in agricultural output increased consumer incomes and so stimulated home sales of woollens, metal goods and pottery. Though some of the income released by cheaper bread may have been spent on meat, tea, sugar and gin, there was, it is suggested, a net expansion of demand for English industrial products before 1750.

This view that the domestic market was less influential after 1750 has recently been challenged by Dr Eversley. His proposition of the continuance of home demand as an important factor in maintaining aggregate demand is based on a very tentative attempt to assess the size of the domestic market from a consideration of estimates of national income.[1] Taking the two estimates of Gregory King of 1688 and Arthur Young of 1770, he suggests that while exports rose from £5 million in 1688 to £9·5 million in 1770, domestic consumption increased from £10·5 million to £34 million in the same period. Thus he argues home demand was both larger and grew faster than overseas demand. Further he holds that during the thirty years from 1750 to 1780 purchasing power was maintained by the expansion of a middle-class market, by 'the existence of a free, mobile, prudent section of the population which was able to assert some choice in the pattern of its expenditure sufficiently often to provide the stimulus which . . . neither foreign markets nor luxury consumers could have given.'[2] More research is necessary before

[1] The detailed account is as follows:

THE COMPOSITION OF THE NATIONAL INCOME, 1688 AND 1770

	Gregory King, 1688	*Arthur Young, 1770*
Gross national product	£50 million	£128 million
Of which manufactures, distribution and transport	£15·5 million	£43 million
Of which exports	£5 million	£9·5 million
Home market	£10·5 million	£34 million
Population	5·5 million	7 million
Home consumption per household	£9 10s.	£25
Exports per head	£1	£1 7s.

Source: D. E. C. Eversley, 'The home market and economic growth in England, 1750–1780' in E. L. Jones and G. E. Mingay (eds.), *Land, labour and population in the industrial revolution* (Arnold, 1967), p. 227. This table is derived from figures in Deane and Cole, *British economic growth.*

[2] See Eversley, 'Home market' in Jones and Mingay (eds.), *Land, labour and population*, p. 259.

the relative importance of the home and overseas markets can be fully assessed.

Though home sales were substantial and growing, the activities of English merchants, shipowners and seamen also significantly extended the market for English manufactures by adding the wider world to a greater interest in European trade. By the early eighteenth century when 85 per cent of English domestic exports consisted of manufactured goods, overseas sales probably accounted for up to one-third of total English industrial production.[1] In the early seventeenth century the Mediterranean was the growing area, while in the eighteenth century the impact of the American colonies, whose population grew quickly from under half a million in 1715 to over 2·5 millions in 1775, was particularly important for English manufacturers. Not only was the market there growing quickly but outside agriculture the level of incomes tended to be higher than in England.[2] Thus, in the aggregate, foreign trade provided a substantial market for English manufactures and the stimulus for growing production came from the combined pressures of the home and export markets. Nevertheless, it may not always have been the case that the growth of the industries producing exports kept pace with the expansion of trade. It has been suggested that the surge in exports after 1748 – of which increased grain shipments formed a part – was met in part by transfer of output from the home to the foreign market.[3]

Foreign demand was important for a wide range of English industries but three – woollens, metal goods and agriculture – call for special consideration. Though of declining relative importance, woollen textiles, the major English manufacturing industry, was also the major exporting industry. Based on the meagre information available the following table suggests how important exports were for the industry.

These contemporary estimates suggest that there was a marked expansion of output in the English woollen textile industry between 1700 and 1775. For this the growing overseas market for

---

[1] Deane and Cole, *British economic growth*, pp. 41–2.

[2] 'The wages of labour, however, are much higher in North America than in any part of England.' Smith, *Wealth of nations*, I, 71.

[3] See John, 'Agricultural productivity' in Jones (ed.), *Agriculture and economic growth*, pp. 186–9.

woollen cloth provided a stimulus,[1] augmented after 1750 by increased home demand as population began to increase. Exports not only affected the size of the English industry but also influenced the type of product produced and hence the nature of the labour force. Foreign demand provided an incentive for the development of the manufacture of lighter kinds of fabrics which in turn affected employment because the new draperies which replaced broadcloths as the more saleable cloths overseas were more labour-intensive. In the short-run, moreover, the level of foreign sales considerably influenced the profitability of the industry. When, for one reason or another, export markets declined, unemployment in the English clothing areas resulted. As incomes were reduced, the demand for other goods fell and depression became more widespread through the economy.

PRODUCTION AND EXPORTS OF WOOLLEN TEXTILES, 1688–1772

£ million	1688	1700	1741	1772
Production	5	5	7·9	10·2
Exports	2	3	3·5	4·7

Source: Phyllis Deane, 'The output of the British woolen industry in the eighteenth century', *Journal of Economic History*, XVII (1957), 207–23.

For other textiles, foreign markets were also of some significance. With the expansion of the slave trade and plantation agriculture, which required a specialized product, the demand for printed cottons and linens abroad grew. There was a steep rise after the mid-century: exports of checked cottons were half as much again and those of checked linen about two and a half times as much in 1770 as they had been in 1756.[2]

The second main group of industries involved in overseas trade in this period were the metal industries for whose products demand grew abroad, and particularly in the American colonies, in the course of the eighteenth century. Nails, pots and pans, axes and ploughshares, kitchen and dairy utensils, buttons and buckles, anchors and other ship's ware were among the articles sent overseas. Professor John has shown that in the first half of the eighteenth century, home demand for iron was much greater

[1] For example, it is said 'the recovery of the 1730s was largely due to increased sales of woollen cloth'. John, 'Agricultural productivity' in Jones (ed.), *Agriculture and economic growth*, p. 180.

[2] A. P. Wadsworth and J. de L. Mann, *The cotton trade and industrial Lancashire, 1660–1780* (Manchester University Press, 1931), pp. 145–69.

than export demand.[1] But his figures also imply that export demand was growing faster than home demand and that the proportion of total English iron supplies exported rose from 8 per cent in 1715–19 to 16 per cent in 1748–52. This trend continued in the following quarter of a century and exports accounted for something of the order of 20 per cent of total English iron production in 1770. The weight of all iron exports rose from 8,710 tons at the mid-century to a peak of 21,000 tons.[2] Exports of other metal ware such as brass and copper goods also increased significantly.[3] Moreover overseas sales may well have been much more important than these figures suggest for specific trades in certain areas at particular times. And this growth of overseas markets for metal goods may have had further consequences. 'The expansion of the American market for iron- and brass-ware', it has been suggested, 'was on so great a scale that it must have contributed very significantly to the eighteenth-century development of those industries in England, and so to the process of rationalization, of division of labour, of search for new machines and new methods which helped so much towards the Industrial Revolution.'[4]

In addition to its effect on the woollen industry, the character of English overseas trade also influenced the location of other manufacturing in England, encouraging the establishment and expansion of industries at the ports. Though Bristol is commonly thought of as a port, according to one contemporary, even at the end of the eighteenth century, it was not more a commercial than

[1] See below, p. 175. The figures are as follows:

tons	1715–19	1734–8	1748–52
Home supplies of iron	28,768	41,465	48,452
Iron exports	2,385	4,294	8,710

[2] Total imports of iron amounted to an average of 50,000 tons in the years 1767–71. No figures are available for total production but it is estimated that 30,000 tons of iron were made in England in 1760 and 68,000 tons in 1788. If production in 1770 is assumed to be of the order of 45–55,000 tons, then total iron available in England was 95–105,000 tons and imports were approximately one-half of this amount. These figures are drawn from Schumpeter, *Overseas trade statistics* and Deane and Cole, *British economic growth*.

[3] Exports of wrought brass increased from 1,742 tons in 1700 to 33,211 tons in 1775 and of wrought copper from 1,636 tons to 32,314 tons in the same period. Schumpeter, *Overseas trade statistics*, p. 63, tables XIX and XXI.

[4] Davis, *Commercial revolution*, p. 20.

a manufacturing town. Sugar refining, with some twenty works in operation in the middle of the century, glass-making both for home sales and for exports, tobacco processing, soap-making and a range of metal manufactures were carried on. A chocolate industry was set up there in 1731. Similar manufactures were developed at other ports. Moreover such trades had linkage effects with the rest of the economy as in the case of the coal industry. While duties and high transport costs kept down the direct export of coal, the industry received a stimulus from the demand for coal for outlets such as soap, sugar, glass and metal goods. Thus the expansion of exports might involve not only directly but also indirectly an expansion of industry.[1]

Thirdly there was the importance of exports for agriculture. The fortunes of English farming at this time can only be understood in the context of European agriculture. During the seventeenth century, England was only intermittently an exporter of agricultural produce. But, as the result of changes in the European market for grain and particularly the dislocation of Baltic supplies[2] and of the improvement visible in English agriculture, England was generally a net exporter of grain during the first sixty years of the eighteenth century. In the peak year, 1750, over one million quarters of grain were exported, accounting for, it is estimated, about 20 per cent of exports by value and 7 per cent of total agricultural production.[3] Although grain exports therefore formed only a small proportion of the total produced it is nevertheless held – with perhaps an element of circularity – that one of the major reasons for the continued growth of agricultural productivity in parts of southern England in the first half of the eighteenth century was the existence of an overseas market for grain.[4]

[1] The growth of exports may also have affected the structure and organization of English industry by facilitating the division of labour. See Davis, *Commercial revolution*, p. 20.

[2] Danzig wheat exports declined from 1·1 million quarters in 1680–9 to 0.6 million quarters in 1700–9 and 0·5 million quarters in 1710–19. Marshall, *Digest of all the accounts*, II, 88, 99 cited in A. H. John, 'The course of agricultural change, 1660–1760' in L. S. Pressnell, (ed.) *Studies in the industrial revolution* (Athlone Press, 1960), p. 131.

[3] Deane and Cole, *British economic growth*, p. 65, table 17.

[4] See below, p. 170: Professor John then goes on to discuss the indirect effects of this trade. As a bulk export, grain contributed to the more efficient use of shipping by providing a back cargo since commonly vessels coming to England were more heavily laden than those clearing from this country.

Foreign trade also provided a source of raw materials which enabled some existing industries to cut their costs, expand production or improve their products and certain new industries to be founded. All the textile industries employed imported dyestuffs such as logwood, braziletto and indigo and all the established textile industries came to use imported fibres – wool, silk, flax and hemp. Used both for houses and ship-building, timber (together with tar, pitch and naval stores) was brought mainly from the Baltic but there were also imports from colonial America. Bar iron also came mainly from the Baltic but again, after 1750, there were growing quantities brought in from the American colonies. Then there were the new industries based on imported raw materials. A tobacco processing industry was set up in the ports and a substantial sugar refining industry was established. Finally, of growing importance was the cotton industry which was entirely dependent on imported supplies from the Levant and the West Indies. Thus foreign trade helped to create new industries and to sustain existing ones.

But not all overseas trade had industrial consequences for the English economy. Imported manufactured goods, luxury articles and some groceries were consumed at home without further processing while a wide range of re-exports – which amounted to between one-third and one-quarter of total English exports – were sent abroad again without further treatment in England. The development of the English entrepôt involved a large investment in commerce which was not accompanied by industrial investment.[1] Yet it was not without significance for the English economy. Because trade was carried out over greater distances over longer periods of time, using bigger ships which, in certain trades, had to carry guns, the capital requirements of merchants engaged in foreign trade grew faster than the expansion of trade itself. Capital no longer turned over quickly but was tied up for a longer time – as Adam Smith commented critically – and the element of uncertainty tended to be increased.

[1] For the case of the 'enclave' development where the expansion induced by the growth of foreign trade affects only a small part of the country and leaves the rest largely untouched, see K. Berrill, 'International trade and the rate of economic growth', *Economic History Review*, 2nd series, XII (1960), 355. Professor Campbell argues that the commercial prosperity of Glasgow was largely isolated from the industrial and agricultural areas of the rest of Scotland in the eighteenth century. R. H. Campbell, *Scotland since 1707* (Oxford: Blackwell, 1964), p. 46.

Assuming the control of English trade also meant assuming financial responsibility for its conduct. Moreover, since the expanding sector of English trade was outside Europe, growth depended on purchasing power being provided by the English merchant. Both stocks and long terms of credit were financed by the English exporter. Most markedly was this so in the case of trade with the American colonies. As Adam Smith commented:

> The greater part both of the exportation and coasting trade of America is carried on by the capitals of merchants who reside in Great Britain. Even the stores and warehouses from which goods are retailed in some provinces, particularly in Virginia and Maryland, belong many of them to merchants who reside in the mother country, and afford one of the few instances of the retail trade of a society being carried on by the capitals of those who are not resident members of it.[1]

The financial links stretched from the English merchant to the frontier of settlement in the American backcountry. But there was some change. There seems to have been a tendency during the eighteenth century for some of the financing of trade to shift a stage further back from the English merchant to the English manufacturer, particularly the woollen manufacturer.

The profits from all branches of commerce contributed greatly to the country's financial strength and facilitated the development of financial institutions, especially in London.[2] The expansion of trade in the later seventeenth century led to the growth of the London marine insurance market and 'forms part of that remarkable period of financial activity culminating in the South Sea Bubble, which gave rise to the Bank of England, the Funded Debt and an embryonic Stock Exchange'.[3] In the eighteenth century marine insurance developed in the major English outports such as Bristol, Exeter, Hull, Liverpool and Newcastle. Foreign trade also provided a stimulus to the development of other commercial institutions such as Lloyds as a source of maritime intelligence and banks up and down the country and to the emergence of specialists such as shipbrokers, exchange bullion dealers, warehousemen and ship-chandlers. More generally the

---

[1] *Wealth of nations*, I, 346. [2] See below, pp. 76, 164, 169.
[3] A. H. John, 'The London Assurance Company and the marine insurance market of the eighteenth century', *Economica*, new series, xxv (1958), 126.

growth of merchant firms assisted the spread of business techniques which were of importance in domestic as well as in foreign trade. The inflow of bullion affected the availability of credit and helped to lower the rate of interest thus affecting the finance of concerns in every line of business. And the income effect of foreign trade was also of significance. Both through its influence on industrial and on commercial employment, overseas trade contributed to total employment and hence helped to raise the level of aggregate demand throughout the community.

In a much more diffuse way the conduct of foreign trade may have helped to facilitate economic growth. The business skills the merchants acquired were not specific but could be applied elsewhere. With their business sense and knowledge of the market, merchants not only helped to create an appropriate institutional structure and provided capital but they also contributed a greater awareness of commercial and technical possibilities. The needs of trade were among the forces which led to a reform of education – more appropriate curricula in the old grammar schools, the foundation of dissenting academies and the establishment of private schools.[1] So there emerged an educational system from which others could benefit too. Further, by apprenticeship the merchant provided an instruction in skills such as book-keeping which were not specific to their own businesses. The merchant also more generally fostered the creation and acceptance of a business ethic and assisted in the creation of an intellectual climate which was favourable to enterprise. 'A merchant is commonly a bold, a country gentleman, a timid undertaker.'[2] And not least the merchants were able to secure sustained government concern in the problems of trade, to obtain legislation to promote their activities and the use of military and naval force to protect their interests.[3]

Merchants commonly used some of their profits to extend their scale of operations but since the benefits of size were limited,

[1] W. E. Minchinton, 'The merchants in England in the eighteenth century', *Explorations in Entrepreneurial History*, x (1957), 65.

[2] W. Petty, *Economic writings* (Hull's edition, Cambridge University Press, 1899), I, 261.

[3] Yet there were limits: in a choice between the interests of commerce and those of industry, the domestic producer commonly prevailed. The merchant could mobilize only London and a few ports in his interest, the manufacturer, the political interests of large stretches of the country and of government. See Hobsbawm, *Industry and empire*, p. 17.

they tended also to diversify their activities. Foreign trade accordingly provided a surplus to finance industrial expansion, banking and agricultural improvement. Merchant capital went into a wide range of concerns. Taking Bristol as an example, it is clear that mercantile capital flowed into a number of enterprises both in that city and its hinterland. In Bristol itself merchants invested in iron, glass, pottery, soap, sugar, brass and copper, and other metal-working industries while Bristol capital is also to be found in the south Wales iron, tinplate and brass and copper industries.[1] Similarly Liverpool capital went into industrial businesses and merchant capital found its way into manufacturing enterprises in other ports. But, significant though it was in particular areas, trade was but a limited source of industrial finance and Dr Eric Williams's claim that 'the profits obtained [from the West African and West Indian trades] provided one of the main streams of accumulation of capital in England which financed the Industrial Revolution'[2] is clearly an exaggeration.

Merchant capital also found its way into banking. Again to cite Bristol as an example, merchants figure predominantly among the shareholders of the first banks founded in Bristol from the establishment of Bristol Old Bank in 1750.[3] And a similar situation obtained elsewhere. Of the fourteen banks of any importance listed for Liverpool, ten sprang from merchant houses while half of the early Newcastle banks had partners concerned with trade.[4]

Foreign trade also undoubtedly contributed to the wealth of the English middle class. Some of the profits made possible greater conspicuous expenditure, a higher standard of living and better and more impressive town houses. Leisure and consumption were financed out of the proceeds of trade. Agriculture also benefited from the transfusion of trading capital as rich

---

[1] See W. E. Minchinton, 'Bristol–metropolis of the west in the eighteenth century', *Transactions of the Royal Historical Society*, 5th series, IV (1954), 69–89.

[2] *Capitalism and slavery* (Chapel Hill, NC: University of North Carolina Press, 1944), p. 52. See also Richard Pares, *Merchants and planters* (Cambridge: *Economic History Review*, Supplement 4 (1960)), pp. 38–50. Pares suggests that profits made by English merchants from the sugar trade were ploughed back into the West Indian plantations.

[3] C. H. Cave, *A history of banking in Bristol from 1750 to 1899* (Bristol, 1899).

[4] L. S. Pressnell, *Country banking in the industrial revolution* (Oxford University Press, 1956), p. 51.

merchants bought country seats.[1] But these were often purchases for status more than for exploitation and so tended to be
off-setting drains on capital accumulation, reducing rather than
adding to the resources available for profitable investment. And
movement into land became much less frequent after 1730 than
it had been in the previous two hundred years.[2] As a result there
began to develop in London and other provincial towns a
society of families of considerable wealth who were permanently
committed to an urban way of life. Such a change reflected a
more self-confident attitude on the part of 'the mercantile part
of the nation'.

Mercantile activities therefore had a considerable influence on
urban development in England. Within the ports there were
four main changes. First, the demands of foreign trade provided
a stimulus to port improvement. Though the major investment
was to come from the end of the eighteenth century, some development took place earlier. The first wet dock was constructed
at Rotherhithe in 1711 and other steps were taken to improve
the accommodation for vessels in the port of London. In Bristol
the wharves were extended, a wet dock was built at Sea Mills in
1712 and a second at Hotwells in 1765 and extra cranes were
provided.[3] In Liverpool too there was substantial improvement
and wet docks were opened there in 1715, 1753 and 1771. Other
ports – notably Whitehaven, Sunderland, Grimsby and Yarmouth – built improved quays, piers and other installations in
the eighteenth century.[4] The growing size and number of vessels
made such improvement imperative if trade was to be successfully
and expeditiously carried out. Then there was the expansion of
the commercial sectors of the ports, the establishment of ware-

[1] *Agriculture and economic growth*, p. 6. Dr Jones further suggests that 'capital
originally generated by foreign trade was often filtered . . . out again [from agri-
culture] through the early industrial activities of landowners', but elsewhere he
quotes Defoe: an estate is but a pond but trade is a spring. 'Industrial capital and
landed investment: the Arkwrights in Herefordshire, 1809–43', in Jones and
Mingay (eds.), *Land, Labour and population*, p. 48.

[2] H. J. Habakkuk, 'The English land market in the eighteenth century' in J. S.
Bromley and E. H. Kossman (eds.), *Britain and the Netherlands* (Chatto, 1960), p.
155.

[3] A. F. Williams, 'Bristol port plans and improvement schemes of the eighteenth century', *Transactions of the Bristol and Gloucestershire Archaeological Society*,
LXXXI (1962), 138–88.

[4] D. Swann, 'The pace and progress of port investment in England, 1660–
1830', *Yorkshire Bulletin of Economic and Social Research*, XII (1960), 32–44.

houses, exchanges, coffee houses, insurance offices and all the ancillary activities of trade. Thirdly, as already described, it resulted in the growth of industrial activity in the ports. And fourthly it led to a substantial increase in the wealth and population of these towns.

Of all English ports, London is clearly a special case. It was not only far and away the largest English port but it had other roles as capital, administrative centre, metropolis and focus of conspicuous consumption as well. Nevertheless London's prime economic foundation was its trade with its merchant community augmented anew by aliens, Danes, Germans, Huguenots and Jews. About 1700 it has been estimated that a quarter of London's population of 575,000 – about one-tenth of the entire population of England and Wales – depended directly on employment in port trades and allowing for the multiplier effect of this employment, it is clear that 'the greatness of London depended, before anything else, on the activity of the port of London'.[1] Further, 'it was the fact that the growth of her trading wealth enabled London herself to grow, to develop as a centre of consumption, and to dominate English society, which formed her greatest contribution to the total process of change in the country as a whole'.[2]

Though it expanded less rapidly than some of its inhabitants expected, it was foreign trade which made Bristol for a period in the eighteenth century, the second city in the land. Hull and Exeter also owed their expansion to overseas trade but, as Mantoux has written, 'the most striking instance is the story of the town and port of Liverpool . . . [which] had begun earlier and was progressing faster than that of local industry. It seems to be bound up with the general trade of the country and to run parallel with it in the most marked and most constant manner' and he concludes, 'the growth of Lancashire, of all English counties the one most deserving to be called the cradle of the factory system, depended first of all on the development of Liverpool and of her trade'.[3] As the eighteenth century wore on, the industrial towns of Birmingham, Leeds, Manchester, Nottingham and Sheffield

---

[1] Davis, *Shipping industry*, p. 390.
[2] See E. A. Wrigley, 'A simple model of London's importance in changing English society and economy, 1650–1750', *Past and Present*, 37 (1967), 63.
[3] Mantoux, *Industrial revolution*, pp. 107, 110, 111.

grew more quickly than the ports but their manufactures were not entirely dependent on the home market and overseas demand also played a part in stimulating their growth.[1]

Finally, there was the contribution overseas trade made to consumption. Foreign trade was not just a means of obtaining cheaper commodities, it was also a means to increase the range of goods available. As Malthus pointed out:

> The great mass of our imports consists of articles as to which there can be no kind of question about their comparative cheapness, as raised abroad or at home. If we could not import from foreign countries our silk, cotton and indigo, our tea, sugar, coffee and tobacco, our port, sherry, claret and champagne, our almonds, raisins, oranges and lemons, our various spices and our various drugs, with many other articles peculiar to foreign climates, it is quite certain we should not have them at all.[2]

Some of them, like the Chinese goods, influenced the level of taste, some of them, like silk, ministered to a rising standard of living and some of them led to a transformation of social habits. While coffee failed to find a mass market, tea moved from a luxury drink in the seventeenth century to a more popular drink by the middle of the eighteenth. Without the possibility of enhancing their standard of living by the consumption of imported goods, it is arguable that the energy devoted by the middle class to building up their businesses might have been that much less. To quote Malthus again:

> And the trader or merchant, who would continue in his business in order to be able to drink and give his guests claret or champagne, might think the addition of homely commodities by no means worth the trouble of so much constant attention.

In addition to its other effects trade could therefore generate expansion by broadening the boundaries of choice of consumers within the trading area.

Thus foreign trade made an important contribution to English economic development between 1600 and 1775. As indicated

[1] Macpherson, *Annals*.

[2] T. R. Malthus, *Principles of political economy* (1820 ed.), p. 461. I owe this and the following quotation to J. F. Wright, 'British economic growth, 1688–1959', *Economic History Review*, 2nd series, XVIII (1965), 402–3.

[3] Malthus, *Principles of political economy*, p. 405.

above, it significantly extended the market for English manufactures. A substantial proportion of the produce of English
industries was sent overseas and the importance of foreign demand was greater than these totals themselves suggest because
the growth of foreign trade brought about shifts in the disposi-
tion of factors of production at the margin which were crucial
to the whole industrial process.[1] Then foreign trade supplied
needed raw materials to increase or diversify production in existing industries and to enable new manufactures to be established.
Its capital requirements grew faster than the expansion of trade
itself because of the growth of extra-European trade, the more
roundabout trades and the re-export trade. Not all the profits of
trade were ploughed back into commerce or dissipated in consumption so that foreign trade assisted more generally the process of capital accumulation in the seventeenth and eighteenth
centuries. It also provided a basis for the development of London's financial activities and for the expansion of the commercial
sector of the economy. To some extent too overseas trade was
a source of entrepreneurial ability. Both directly and indirectly
it increased the purchasing power of a significant section of the
English population. The less tangible influences of foreign trade
on business procedures, on the regard for economic activities
and in the widening of man's economic horizons should also not
be disregarded.

   Though foreign trade absorbed no more than a limited proportion of total output – about 10–12 per cent of the national product
– the demand for English goods overseas – and the English demand for foreign products – was an expanding one. Moreover
foreign trade was important for particular industries in certain
areas at different times – the Mediterranean demand for woollen
textiles in the early seventeenth century, the European demand
for grain in the early eighteenth century and the American colonial demand for iron and textiles in the middle of the century.
Overall foreign demand was of particular importance for the

---

[1] The importance of overseas trade for early seventeenth-century England
'cannot be measured solely by the amount of capital involved ... Directly im-
pacting on the prosperity of England's largest industry [woollen cloth manufac-
ture], sharply altering the demand for goods and the supply of capital and cash
to an economy whose instability and sensitivity it is easy to underestimate, overseas economic relationships deserve a large chapter in any story of England's
economic development'. Supple, *Commercial crisis*, p. 14.

English economy in the twenty-five years after the Restoration and in the period of trade expansion from the 1740s until the 1760s when the diversification of English exports exerted a wider multiplier effect through the English economy. By its effect on the supply of the factors of production, on the demand for English manufactures, on the location and finance of industry, on urban development among others and by its income effects, foreign trade made a vital and necessary contribution to that mix of factors which started England along the road of faster economic growth in the eighteenth century. Moreover, in the period between 1600 and 1775 foreign trade played a more important role in stimulating economic development than at any other period in the history of this country.

A NOTE ON THE STATISTICS

For some time historians have recognized that if they want to say anything useful about the course of trade, they must use figures, they must quantify. But, if not so long ago a British prime minister could say that, as far as the statistics relating to the British economy in the late 1950s were concerned, the British government was in the position of trying to make decisions with last year's railway timetable as the only guide, the plight of the historian is much worse. More than half a century ago Archdeacon Cunningham did what he could with figures gathered from a variety of sources.[1] But more recently, with a greater statistical awareness, the tests imposed on such figures as are now available have become more rigorous and historians are not now satisfied with a rather random selection of figures drawn from disparate sources.

Although there were medieval attempts to estimate the quantity of imports and exports, they have severe shortcomings[2] and the real beginnings of commercial statistics date from the late sixteenth and early seventeenth centuries. Tudor and Stuart statesmen had a twofold concern with the trade statistics for income and trade balance purposes. The revenue from the cus-

[1] Cunningham, *The growth of English industry*, II, 931. See below, p. 92, note 1.
[2] See E. M. Carus-Wilson and Olive Coleman, *England's export trade, 1275–1547* (Oxford: Clarendon Press, 1963) and G. N. Clark, *Guide to English commercial statistics, 1696–1782* (Royal Historical Society, 1938).

toms provided the main source of national finance and they needed information about imports and exports to provide the basis for policy about the balance of trade.

The major problem to be faced in dealing with English over-seas trade between 1600 and 1775 is that there are no continuous series available. Consequently it is not easily possible to get a picture of the changing volume, commodity composition and geographical distribution of trade over the whole period. Then there are problems related to the nature of the statistics avail-able. For what purpose were they compiled? Finally, there is the question of their accuracy. How far do they reflect the actual situation? Is their usefulness vitiated by attempts to avoid cus-toms regulations and to evade the payment of duties by smug-gling?

For the seventeenth century there are not, as far as is known, any continuous series of customs or commercial statistics. From 1601 the annual customs accounts ceased to be enrolled in the office of the King's Remembrancer and a new series of centrally compiled accounts of imports and exports does not start until near the end of the century. The historian is therefore faced with the problem of trying to compile a run of meaningful statistics from diverse and discontinuous sources.[1] In recent years work has been done on two sets of records not used in the articles below – the port books[2] and the pretermitted customs returns[3] – to provide more statistical information for the early Stuart period. And now that data-processing equipment is more readily available further work should be possible, particularly on the port books which exist not in a continuous series but in broken runs for many ports (though unhappily not for London) until the late eighteenth century.[4]

[1] See below, p. 92.

[2] A growing number of historians are indebted to Mrs A. Millard for her analyses of port books recording merchandises imported into the port of London, 1588–1640. See also Sven–Erik Åström, *From cloth to iron, the Anglo-Baltic trade in the late seventeenth century, Part II, The customs accounts as sources for the study of trade* (Helsingfors: Societas Scientarum Fennica, 1965).

[3] These returns (PRO E 351/779–94) exist for the years 1618–40 and have been used by Dr Stephens for his study of the cloth trade of the provincial ports, 1600–40. See W. B. Stephens, 'The pretermitted customs duties at Exeter, Dart-mouth and Barnstaple, 1620–1639', *Devon and Cornwall Notes and Queries*, xxxi (1968), 84–5.

[4] See PRO, *Descriptive list of Exchequer, Queen's Remembrancer Port Books (E 190), Part I, 1565–1700* (HMSO, 1960).

From the Restoration a growing interest in the quantification of information relating to trade, which was a product of the concern with political arithmetic, led to the compilation of a series of returns.[1] Nevertheless, statistical material continues to be sparse and no trade statistics, apart from the port books, appear to have survived for the 1670s and 1680s. Experiments in the 1690s transformed the situation and led to the commencement in 1696 of the first continuous series of trade returns, the *Ledgers of Imports and Exports* (PRO Customs 3), compiled by the Inspector-General, which run from Michaelmas 1696 to 1780.[2] As a number of historians have pointed out,[3] the interpretation of these Ledgers is not devoid of problems since the figures of total imports and exports were obtained by multiplying the quantity of each commodity by an official price, and adding together the values so obtained. As, with few exceptions, no adjustments were made in the official prices used to take account of changes in market prices, the aggregate figures reflect changes in the quantity and not in the value of trade.[4] In consequence these figures cast no light on such matters as the balance of payments but can be used to document discussions of other trading matters, including short-term fluctuations. Information contained in the Ledgers has now been made available by Mrs Schumpeter in her volume of *English overseas trade statistics*.[5] In

[1] See below, p. 84–6.

[2] It is believed that the Ledgers originally continued to 1791 but that the volumes from 1781 to 1791 were destroyed in the London Custom House fire in 1814. Clark, *Guide*, p. 31.

[3] See Ashton's introduction to Schumpeter, *Overseas trade statistics*, pp. 1–9; Deane and Cole, *British economic growth*, pp. 42–3, 315–22; Phyllis Deane, *The first industrial revolution* (Cambridge University Press, 1965), pp. 60–2.

[4] Henry Martin commented in 1718 that 'If the thing intended by these valuations was to discover at one view the increase or decrease of the quantitys of goods, imported or exported, it must be acknowledged that the keeping allways to the same price of the same species of goods serves best for this purpose, since the increase or decrease of the quantitys must show at once in some measure this last increase or decrease: whereas if it had been possible to have brought into the total values the numberless variations of prices of all sorts of goods, this had not been sufficient to show the increase or decrease of the quantitys imported or exported, since it often happens that a less quantity of goods in one year is of more value than a greater of the same goods in another.' 'Observations upon the account of exports and imports for 17 years' in Clark, *Guide*, p. 63.

[5] In her volume Mrs Schumpeter tried to overcome the problem of changes in the official valuations by revaluing imports and exports at a standard set of official values throughout the century. This method, however, does not produce statistics which provide an entirely satisfactory measure of the change in the

addition to the Ledgers there are many returns which were drawn
up for special purposes in the eighteenth century which cast
light on particular areas of trade or trade in particular commodities.[1] They are joined in 1772 by the second major series, the
Reports of the Navigation, Commerce and Revenues of Great Britain
(PRO Customs 17). Thus, despite the limitations which they
have, from 1696 we do possess a series of commercial statistics
which enable us to speak with greater confidence statistically
about the course, commodity composition and geographical
distribution of English trade in the eighteenth century.

The second range of problems concerns the accuracy of the
returns available. Every attempt was made by most eighteenth-
century officials to make their returns as accurate as possible but
they did not achieve perfection. Here the major, but not the
only, problem was that of smuggling. All the authorities who
have attempted to assess the importance of smuggling now agree
that, by and large, the level of smuggling varied directly with
the level of duties and the complexity of administration.
Generally speaking, though not invariably, when customs
duties were high it was profitable to smuggle: when duties were
low or non-existent there was no profit to be gained from
smuggling. Thus in the first half of the sixteenth century, which
has been called one of the great free trade periods of English
history, there was little motive to smuggle. The origins of large-
scale smuggling are to be discerned in the later sixteenth century
with the increase of duties and regulations. From then until his
disappearance with the advent of free trade in the nineteenth
century, the smuggler engaged in his nefarious activities. A well-
organized activity, smuggling was carried on by persons of
rank[2] as well as by skilled and resolute men of humble station.

---

volume of trade since it is based on the assumption that changes in the price level
were more important than changes in the price relatives and that the structure of
prices did not alter greatly during the period.

[1] See Clark, *Guide*. For a collection of statistics relating to a single port, see
Minchinton, *The trade of Bristol*.

[2] Including Sir Robert Walpole: see J. H. Plumb, *Sir Robert Walpole, the makings
of a statesman* (Cresset Press, 1956), pp. 121–2. Adam Smith sympathized with
the smuggler who, 'though no doubt highly blameable for violating the laws of
his country, is frequently incapable of violating those of natural justice and would
have been, in every respect, an excellent citizen, had not the laws of his country
made that a crime which nature never meant to be so'. *Wealth of nations*, II, 381.

Basing his conclusions on a detailed investigation of tea-running, Professor Cole provides a case study for a single commodity.[1] Smuggled tea, he suggests, probably represented three-quarters of the total imported in the 1730s and early 1740s before the reduction of the tea duty in 1745 but the amount entering illegally declined sharply from that date until the new increase in tea duties during the American revolution gave rise to an increase in smuggling. For illicit trade in general, Cole suggests that smuggling followed the same course during the greater part of the eighteenth century, increasing in most cases until about 1745 and then falling off until the late 1760s or 1770s. The import trade was affected by smuggling much more seriously than the export trade. Among imports, wines and spirits, pepper, tobacco and silk as well as tea were the major items smuggled: among exports, in spite of its bulk, raw wool was exported illegally in quantity. Depending on technological developments and changing consumer demand as well as on the level of duties, other commodities appeared in and disappeared from the smugglers' trade.[2]

As there were variations over time and between commodities, so might there be between ports. One example will make the point. Fabricius, the factor of a Norwegian landowner, who was sent to England in 1759–60 to report on means of increasing exports to England from his employer's large saw-mills and ironworks, noted that smuggling timber into London was difficult as the customs officers were too knowledgeable. It was better to try it in the smaller ports, he suggested.[3]

Since the smuggler aimed to leave as few traces as possible of his activity, it is impossible to do more than guess at the proportion of English foreign trade involved but one conservative estimate made in 1733, which has commanded some support from later historians, is that the share of English smugglers in

---

For a criticism of the customs laws as class legislation, which artificially kept up prices to the detriment especially of poorer consumers, see Hill, *Reformation to industrial revolution*, pp. 194–5.

[1] See below, pp. 121–43.

[2] See F. G. James, 'Irish smuggling in the eighteenth century', *Irish Historical Studies*, XII (1961), 301–4.

[3] H. S. Kent, 'The Anglo-Norwegian timber trade in the eighteenth century', *Economic History Review*, 2nd series, VIII (1955), 66.

English commerce with France and Holland was equal to about a third of the legitimate traffic.[1]

Smuggling apart, there were other reasons why the customs returns do not reflect a true picture of the volume of trade. First, an undetermined but possibly substantial amount of illicit trade was carried on under the eyes of the customs officials, some of it with their connivance and some of it without their knowledge. Then, particularly when an import duty was imposed or raised, there were under-entries of dutiable goods to avoid duty. Especially after the removal of export duties in 1700 and 1721 there were over-entries of dutiable goods which were later to be re-exported in order that a larger amount of draw-back could be claimed. Further, as a trick to deceive other exporters who might thereby be induced to believe that a particular market was in danger of being glutted, some merchants declared greater quantities than were actually exported. Because of collusive frauds in which merchants and customs officials were involved, it is likely that the official returns of imports understate the actual volume of goods which passed through the customs. They may well also overstate the actual volume of exports. It is clear therefore that the volume of trade revealed by the customs records in the seventeenth and eighteenth centuries cannot be taken as representing the full amount of English overseas trade.

The purpose of the foregoing discussion has been to point out some of the difficulties involved in handling what statistical material is available for the discussion of trade in the seventeenth and early eighteenth centuries. It is in the nature of a warning, however, and not a prohibition.

[1] Clark, *Guide*, p. 34.

STATISTICAL TABLES

Table 1 EXPORTS (INCLUDING RE-EXPORTS) OF COMMODITIES AND
SPECIE FROM ENGLAND AND WALES (£000)

	Commodities	Specie		Commodities	Specie
1700	6,469	834	1738	10,196	2,094
1701	6,869	751	1739	8,844	652
1702	4,797	439	1740	8,198	672
1703	6,170	474	1741	9,571	1,900
1704	6,187	365	1742	9,574	2,010
1705	5,309	193	1743	11,310	3,313
1706	6,251	261	1744	9,191	2,239
1707	6,440	327	1745	9,072	1,426
1708	6,564	405	1746	10,767	594
1709	5,913	714	1747	9,775	1,667
1710	6,295	396	1748	11,141	1,210
1711	5,963	484	1749	12,679	1,421
1712	6,869	600	1750	12,700	2,433
1713	6,892	461	1751	12,419	1,548
1714	8,004	354	1752	11,695	1,526
1715	6,922	457	1753	12,244	2,021
1716	7,050	564	1754	11,788	1,609
1717	7,997	1,151	1755	11,065	1,117
1718	6,361	1,894	1756	11,721	797
1719	6,835	875	1757	12,339	1,100
1720	6,911	1,026	1758	12,618	2,417
1721	7,201	1,480	1759	13,948	749
1722	8,265	1,386	1760	14,695	884
1723	7,396	2,094	1761	14,973	1,493
1724	7,601	1,543	1762	13,750	589
1725	8,482	2,871	1763	14,667	1,673
1726	7,693	1,714	1764	16,261	310
1727	7,275	2,278	1765	14,573	997
1728	8,707	2,924	1766	14,082	869
1729	8,240	3,236	1767	13,867	439
1730	8,549	3,425	1768	15,120	948
1731	7,862	3,305	1769	13,438	996
1732	8,871	2,916	1770	14,268	641
1733	8,838	2,939	1771	17,123	585
1734	8,229	2,701	1772	16,159	1,012
1735	9,329	4,215	1773	14,763	279
1736	9,702	1,914	1774	15,916	319
1737	10,082	1,761	1775	15,202	621

Source: Schumpeter, *Overseas trade statistics*, p. 15, Table I.

Table 2 EXPORTS OF ENGLISH PRODUCE AND MANUFACTURES (£000)

1700	4,337	1719	4,514	1738	6,982	1757	8,574
1701	4,641	1720	4,611	1739	5,572	1758	8,763
1702	3,621	1721	4,512	1740	5,111	1759	10,079
1703	4,521	1722	5,293	1741	5,995	1760	10,981
1704	4,262	1723	4,725	1742	6,095	1761	10,804
1705		1724	5,107	1743	6,868	1762	9,400
1706	4,768	1725	5,667	1744	5,411	1763	9,522
1707	4,795	1726	5,001	1745	5,739	1764	11,536
1708	5,069	1727	4,605	1746	7,201	1765	10,122
1709	4,406	1728	4,910	1747	6,744	1766	9,900
1710	4,729	1729	4,940	1748	7,317	1767	9,492
1711	4,088	1730	5,326	1749	9,081	1768	9,695
1712		1731	5,081	1750	9,474	1769	8,984
1713	4,490	1732	5,675	1751	8,775	1770	9,503
1714	5,564	1733	5,823	1752	8,226	1771	11,219
1715	5,015	1734	5,403	1753	8,732	1772	10,503
1716	4,807	1735	5,927	1754	8,318	1773	8,876
1717	5,384	1736	6,118	1755	7,915	1774	10,049
1718	4,381	1737	6,668	1756	8,632	1775	9,729

Source: Schumpeter, *Overseas trade statistics,* p. 15, Table II.

Table 3 RE-EXPORTS FROM ENGLAND AND WALES (£000)

1700	2,132	1719	2,321	1738	3,214	1757	3,755
1701	2,229	1720	2,300	1739	3,272	1758	3,855
1702	1,177	1721	2,689	1740	3,086	1759	3,869
1703	1,649	1722	2,972	1741	3,575	1760	3,714
1704	1,925	1723	2,671	1742	3,480	1761	4,069
1705		1724	2,494	1743	4,442	1762	4,351
1706	1,485	1725	2,815	1744	3,780	1763	5,146
1707	1,645	1726	2,692	1745	3,333	1764	4,725
1708	1,495	1727	2,670	1746	3,566	1765	4,451
1709	1,507	1728	3,597	1747	3,031	1766	4,193
1710	1,566	1729	3,299	1748	3,824	1767	4,375
1711	1,875	1730	3,223	1749	3,598	1768	5,425
1712		1731	2,782	1750	3,225	1769	4,454
1713	2,066	1732	3,196	1751	3,644	1770	4,764
1714	2,440	1733	3,015	1752	3,469	1771	5,905
1715	1,908	1734	2,897	1753	3,511	1772	5,656
1716	2,243	1735	3,402	1754	3,470	1773	5,888
1717	2,613	1736	3,585	1755	3,150	1774	5,868
1718	1,980	1737	3,414	1756	3,089	1775	5,474

Source: Schumpeter, *Overseas trade statistics,* p. 16, Table III.

Table 4 IMPORTS INTO ENGLAND AND WALES (£000)

1700	5,970	1719	5,367	1738	7,439	1757	9,253
1701	5,870	1720	6,090	1739	7,829	1758	8,415
1702	4,159	1721	5,908	1740	6,704	1759	8,923
1703	4,527	1722	6,378	1741	7,936	1760	9,833
1704	5,383	1723	6,506	1742	6,867	1761	9,544
1705	4,032	1724	7,394	1743	7,802	1762	8,870
1706	4,114	1725	7,095	1744	6,363	1763	11,199
1707	4,274	1726	6,678	1745	7,847	1764	10,391
1708	4,699	1727	6,799	1746	6,206	1765	10,981
1709	4,511	1728	7,569	1747	7,117	1766	11,513
1710	4,011	1729	7,541	1748	8,136	1767	12,074
1711	4,686	1730	7,780	1749	7,918	1768	11,879
1712	4,455	1731	6,992	1750	7,772	1769	11,909
1713	5,811	1732	7,088	1751	7,943	1770	12,217
1714	5,929	1733	8,017	1752	7,889	1771	12,822
1715	5,641	1734	7,096	1753	8,625	1772	13,298
1716	5,800	1735	8,160	1754	8,093	1773	11,407
1717	6,347	1736	7,308	1755	8,773	1774	13,347
1718	6,669	1737	7,074	1756	7,962	1775	13,548

Source: Schumpeter, *Overseas trade statistics*, p. 16, Table IV.

Table 5 ENTRIES AND CLEARANCES (000 tons)

		Entries			Clearances	
	Total	English	Foreign	Total	English	Foreign
1686	466	399	67	361	331	30
1692–3	177	70	107	181	89	92
1693–4	201	95	106	143	74	69
1696				175	92	83
1697				245	144	101
1699–1701				338	294	44
1700–2				318	274	44
1709				290	244	46
1710				311	244	67
1711				324	266	58
1712				356	327	29
1713				438	412	26
1714				479	445	34
1715				426	406	20
1716	349			456	439	17
1717	347			429	414	15
1718	369	354	15	445	428	17
1723	393			420	393	27
1726–8	421			457	433	24
1730		422				
1737		404				
1744		269				
1751	480	421	59	694	648	46
1758	413	283	130	526	427	99
1765	693	568	125	758	690	68
1772	780	652	128	888	815	73

Sources:

1686: Port Books giving numbers of ships; average tonnage of ships in each trade taken from PRO CO 388–9 (1715–17).

1692–3, 1693–4: *HMC House of Lords MSS. 1695–7*, pp. 419–22.

1696, 1697, 1699–1701, 1700–2, 1709, 1723, 1726–8: G. Chalmers, *Estimate of the comparative state of Great Britain* (1782), *passim*.

1710–14: PRO CO 388–18.

1715–17: PRO CO 390–8.

1718: PRO CO 390–5.

1730, 1737, 1744: Outports, BM Add. MSS. 11256; London: PRO Adm. 68–195/197. 1751, 1758, 1765, 1772: BM Add. MSS. 11256.

Entries for 1716–18, 1723, 1726–8 obtained by deducting recorded clearances from the figures of total entries and clearances in *The wealth and commerce of Great Britain considered* (1728), p. 7.

Source: Davis, *Shipping industry*, p. 26.

Table 6 TONNAGE OF ENGLISH-OWNED SHIPPING (000 tons)

	Total	London	Outports
1572	50		
1582	67		
1629	115		
1686	340	150	190
1702	323	140	183
1716			215
1723			219
1730			235
1737			248
1751	421	119	302
1752	449	131	318
1753	468	132	336
1754	458	120	338
1755	473	131	342
1763	496	139	357
1764	523	135	388
1765	543	134	409
1766	562	133	429
1767	557	139	418
1768	549	123	426
1769	574	128	446
1770	594	150	444
1771	577	133	444
1772	584	133	451
1773	581	136	445
1774	588	133	455
1775	608	143	465

Source: Davis, *Shipping industry*, p. 27.

Table 7 NET EXPORTS OF WHEAT (INCLUDING FLOUR) : NET IMPORTS (—)

(000 quarters)

1700	49	1726	142	1752	429
1701	98	1727	30	1753	300
1702	90	1728	—71	1754	356
1703	107	1729	—21	1755	237
1704	90	1730	94	1756	103
1705	96	1731	130	1757	—130
1706	188	1732	202	1758	—11
1707	74	1733	427	1759	227
1708	83	1734	498	1760	394
1709	170	1735	153	1761	442
1710	14	1736	118	1762	296
1711	77	1737	462	1763	400
1712	145	1738	581	1764	397
1713	176	1739	280	1765	62
1714	175	1740	54	1766	154
1715	166	1741	45	1767	—493
1716	75	1742	293	1768	—342
1717	23	1743	371	1769	46
1718	72	1744	232	1770	75
1719	128	1745	325	1771	7
1720	83	1746	131	1772	—18
1721	82	1747	267	1773	—49
1722	179	1748	543	1774	—273
1723	158	1749	629	1775	—470
1724	246	1750	948		
1725	204	1751	661		

NB: These figures refer to Great Britain.

Source: J. Marshall, *A digest of all the accounts* (London, 1833), pp. 88–9 cited in Ashton, *Fluctuations*, p. 183.

1 *London's Export Trade in the Early Seventeenth Century*[1]

F. J. FISHER

[This article was first published in *The Economic History Review*, 2nd series, Vol. III (1950).]

To the student of English commercial development the seventeenth century must always present peculiar difficulties. Few aspects of commercial organization or policy can be fully understood unless seen against the background of the general commercial trends of their time. Long- and medium-term trends can seldom, if ever, be satisfactorily established without the aid of statistics. And the seventeenth century is the one period in modern English history for which no continuous series of customs or commercial statistics appears to have survived or, indeed, ever to have been made. The annual customs accounts ceased to be enrolled in the Office of the King's Remembrancer at the accession of James I. The Inspectors-General of Imports and Exports did not begin to compile their ledgers until 1696. For the intervening years, the historian is driven back to sources that are both discontinuous and difficult to correlate. There is a wealth of statistical memoranda prepared by contemporaries for specific and immediate purposes; but the methods by which those memoranda were prepared are so obscure, and the purposes for which they were prepared so diverse, that their comparison is more dangerous than profitable. There still remain a few of the original Port Books in which all imports and exports were required to be entered; but years of neglect have reduced a once complete series to a sample which, if sufficiently random to refute all charges of bias, is too small to permit the accurate measurement of general trends. From such materials no definitive table of trade figures can possibly be constructed. But it is the purpose of this paper to suggest that, at least as far as the first

[1] This article is based on a paper read on 15 April 1950 before the annual conference of the Economic History Society.

four decades of the century are concerned, the fragmentary statistics that have by chance survived can be combined in such a manner as to indicate certain trends for which there is considerable supporting evidence in literary sources; for which a plausible explanation can be offered; and which, therefore, may merit some consideration by those working in this particular field. The investigation has been confined to the export trade of London but, since throughout this period the capital handled some two-thirds or three-quarters of the nation's foreign trade, any conclusions that can be drawn from the London figures must obviously provide a major theme in the story of that trade as a whole.

By the beginning of the seventeenth century, shipments of wool, woolfells and leather were sufficiently small for them to be safely ignored in any calculation of broad general trends. For the purposes of taxation, all other exports were divided into two categories. The older forms of woollen textiles were measured in terms of a notional shortcloth and paid custom at the rate of 6s. 8d. per shortcloth; all other commodities paid subsidy at the rate of 5 per cent *ad valorem* calculated on the basis of their official value as set out in the Book of Rates. Thus the records yield two sets of figures each; as is convenient for an age of rising prices, showing changes in the volume rather than in the value of the exports to which they relate. Neither set, it is true, would satisfy any rigid tests of statistical orthodoxy. The notional shortcloth was a clumsy unit for the measurement of fabrics which differed, not only in their weight and dimensions, but also in their fineness and their degree of finish. The figures for subsidy-paying exports would obviously be affected by any changes in the official values assigned to those exports in the Book of Rates and, although there was no general or substantial revision of export valuations during this period, it is impossible to be certain that none were altered. Yet, unsatisfactory though they may be, such are the figures which the historian must use. And although their division into two series makes the calculation of overall totals extremely difficult, as contemporaries found when they tried to assess the balance of trade,[1] it is convenient in so far as it is from the differences in behaviour between the two

[1] For the calculations made by Cranfield and Wolstenholme, and the different conclusions to which they came, see Lansdowne MSS. vol. CLII, f. 175.

series that some of the more interesting aspects of London's commercial history in the early seventeenth century may be deduced.

As will be seen from Table 1, both branches of London's
export trade shared in the expansion that reached its peak in the
middle of the second decade of the century. But from then on
they moved in different directions. Exports of shortcloths sank
back to a level below that from which the expansion had started
and for a generation showed a sluggishness comparable to that

Table 1 STATISTICS OF LONDON EXPORTS, 1598–1640*
(excluding wool, woolfells and leather)

Year	No. of 'shortcloths' exported		Official value of other goods exported (£)	
	By natives	*By aliens*	*By natives*	*By aliens*
1598–1600 (av.)	97,737	5,295	119,415	
1601	100,380	3,643	120,860	
1602	113,512	5,072	133,688	
1603	89,619	2,366	136,695	
1604	112,785	5	—	
1606	126,022	—	—	—
1609	—	—	198,266	—
1612	—	5,199	275,140	81,072
1614	127,215	—	—	—
1616	88,172	—	—	—
1617	—	—	338,598	—
1618	102,332	—	—	—
1619	—	—	371,572	—
1620	85,517	—	—	—
1622	75,631	—	—	—
1626	*c.* 91,000	—	—	—
1627	*c.* 88,000	—	—	—
1628	*c.* 108,000	—	—	—
1631	84,334	—	—	—
1632	99,020	—	—	—
1633	80,844	—	—	—
1634	—	—	594,849	—
1636	—	1,256	—	65,745
1640	86,924	503	609,722	85,136

* The figures for the years 1598–1604 are taken from the Enrolled Customs
Accounts. Those for 1626–8 are estimates based on the Abstract of the Accounts
of the General Farm of the Customs to be found in the Shaftesbury Papers,
bundle ii, no. 17; they are more likely to be too high than too low. The rest have
been calculated from the Port Books. The figures for shortcloths are exclusive of
duty-free wrappers. According to a memorandum among the papers of Lionel
Cranfield, the total number of shortcloths exported from London was 142,466 in
1614 and 126,134 in 1615.

which had characterized them during the latter half of the sixteenth century.[1] Other exports continued to expand – whether
steadily or erratically we do not know – until in 1640 they were
some five times as great in volume as they had been during the
closing years of Elizabeth's reign.

As can be seen from Tables 2 and 3,[2] the two branches of
London's export trade differed in their geographical direction as

Table 2 DISTRIBUTION OF SHORTCLOTHS EXPORTED BY ENGLISH
MERCHANTS FROM LONDON

Percentage shipped to	1614	1616	1620	1622	1632	1640
Russian, Baltic and North Sea ports	76	76	78	80	77	73
Spanish, African and Medi-terranean ports	16	18	17	16	18	25

well as in their long-term trends. The major markets for shortcloths were in northern, central and eastern Europe. Of the years
examined for this purpose only 1640, when, under the pressure
of the Thirty Years War, the trans-alpine route into central and
eastern Europe was being used, shows the Spanish, African and
other Mediterranean ports taking as many as a quarter of the
total shortcloths exported. By contrast, it was to those southern
ports that the bulk of the other exports went. The expansion of

Table 3 DISTRIBUTION OF GOODS OTHER THAN SHORTCLOTHS EXPORTED
BY ENGLISH MERCHANTS FROM LONDON

Percentage shipped to	1609	1612	1619	1634	1640
Russian, Baltic and North Sea ports	29	23	25	24	22
Spanish, African and Mediterranean ports	46	55	59	65	65

those other exports meant, above all else, the growth of trade
with Spain and the Mediterranean.

Finally, from Table 4 it will be seen that most of the goods
which paid subsidy were themselves woollen textiles. The
differences between them and those goods classified as shortcloths and therefore paying custom was one of degree rather

[1] For the commercial trends of the later sixteenth century, see L. Stone, 'Eliza-
bethan overseas trade', *Economic History Review*, 2nd series, II (1949), 30; and F. J.
Fisher, 'Commercial trends and policy in sixteenth-century England', *Economic
History Review*, x (1940), 95.
[2] Both tables have been compiled from the Port Books.

than of kind. The first half of the sixteenth century had seen a great expansion in the export of shortcloths; the first half of the nineteenth was to see an even greater expansion in the export of cotton goods; the most prominent feature of London's trade in the first half of the seventeenth century was the expansion in

Table 4 OFFICIAL VALUES OF COMMODITIES, OTHER THAN SHORTCLOTHS, EXPORTED FROM LONDON BY ENGLISH MERCHANTS IN 1640

	£
Woollen fabrics and hosiery	454,914
Other goods of English manufacture	26,973
Minerals	34,555
Agricultural produce	16,878
Re-exports	76,402
Total	609,722

the export of what were known to contemporaries as 'the new draperies' – fabrics made of combed, long-staple wool and characterized by their light weight and their wide range of patterns.

Thus the figures to be obtained from the Port Books and other sources suggest certain obvious and elementary conclusions as to the development of London's exports during the early seventeenth century. Those exports consisted almost entirely of woollen textiles of one kind or another. During the first fifteen years of the century they prospered greatly. Then, for the next twenty-five years, the trade in shortcloths – a trade carried on mainly with northern, central and eastern Europe – languished at a level, not merely below that which they had attained at the peak of the Jacobean boom, but even below that which had obtained when the century opened. Meanwhile the export of the new draperies – mainly to southern Europe – continued to expand until, by the eve of the Civil War, the pattern of London's commerce had been significantly altered. By that time, the trade in the newer fabrics almost equalled in value the trade in the old, and the ports of Spain and the Mediterranean were taking as large a share of London's exports as were those of Germany and the Low Countries. Sir George Clark no doubt did well to warn us against excessive reliance upon the accuracy of the Port Book entries.[1] It is obvious from internal evidence that the London volumes were sometimes carelessly compiled. But it would be

[1] G. N. Clark, *Guide to English commercial statistics, 1696–1782* (London, 1938), pp. 52–6.

carrying scepticism to the point of credulity to suppose that the
conclusions to which the London figures point were nothing but
statistical illusions; the other evidence pointing in the same
direction is too abundant. The preponderance of textiles among
English exports was a commonplace of contemporary economic
discussion. The opening years of the century have long been
recognized as a period of commercial prosperity.[1] The depression
in the cloth trade that followed Cockayne's disastrous scheme
has been described in detail by Professor Friis;[2] that of the early
'twenties has left a wealth of evidence in the proceedings of
Parliament and of the Privy Council in the State Papers, and in
the economic literature of the time; under Charles the complaints of distress in the cloth industry were sufficiently frequent
to make it clear that his reign saw nothing comparable to the
expansion with which that of his father opened. The history of
the new draperies has still to be written; but there can be little
doubt that their growth constituted the most important chapter
in the story of English industrial development under the early
Stuarts and little surprise that much of their output was sold
abroad. The new significance of the Spanish market – a market
made especially attractive by internal inflation and colonial purchases – was one cause of the revolution in Anglo-Spanish
political relations. The economic penetration of the central and
eastern Mediterranean by London merchants provides the major
theme of the Venetian State Papers. The change in the pattern
of London's overseas trade was reflected in the decline in the
relative prestige and importance of the Merchant Adventurers
and the rise in those of the Levant Company. By 1638 Lewis
Roberts could declare that the latter organization had 'growne
to that height that without comparison it is the most flourishing
and beneficiall Company to the commonwealth of any in England
of all other whatsoever'.[3] It is doubtful whether, even in 1638
that statement was strictly true; at the beginning of the century
it would have been ridiculous.

The real task of the historian is less that of defending than that
of explaining the conclusions to which the Port Books point. In

---

[1] W. R. Scott, *The constitution and finance of English, Scottish and Irish joint stock companies to 1720* (Cambridge, 1912), I, ch. vii.

[2] A. Friis, *Alderman Cockayne's project and the cloth trade* (Copenhagen, 1917).

[3] Quoted by A. C. Wood, *A history of the Levant Company* (London, 1935), p. 43.

some measure, no doubt, their explanation is to be found in the political history of the time. The expansion of trade with Spain and the Mediterranean was made possible by the peace of 1604; the sluggishness of the trade in shortcloths during the third and fourth decades of the century was partly the result of the Thirty Years War which impoverished some of its markets and broke the communications with others. In some measure, however, the explanation is to be found in more purely economic factors; one reason for accepting the evidence of the Port Books is that it coincides so closely with what might be theoretically deduced from the nature of English trade and industry in the early seventeenth century.

The outstanding feature of England's trade was that her exports consisted almost entirely of woollen textiles. The outstanding feature of her textile industry was that it operated under conditions of virtually fixed real costs. To say that is not, of course, to argue that seventeenth-century producers were not cost-conscious. 'The Cheapness of English cloth', declared the House of Commons in 1624, 'Together with the goodnes therof hath been in all tymes the true cawse that it hath bene so vendible.' In their efforts to keep money costs down clothiers and merchants protested vigorously against taxation, demanded that restrictions be placed upon the trade in raw materials, and cut wages until the sweating of labour in the textile industry became a major social problem. But, in the absence of real-cost-reducing inventions, reductions in money costs were necessarily limited and could not be continuous. Stuart finances were in no state to permit of considerable tax reliefs; interference with the trade in raw materials could have untoward results; wages could not be cut indefinitely. Moreover, pressure on money costs inevitably intensified the problem of adulteration; and in the debasement of materials and workmanship, to which both clothiers and their employees resorted in their struggle to keep costs low, lay one of the most vexatious problems of the time. The outcry against it filled a host of pamphlets and memoranda; the efforts to suppress it produced a not inconsiderable body of statutes, proclamations and council orders; the complications to which it gave rise were a constant source of embarrassment to the business world. In a theological age, it is true, men often ascribed that debasement to the peculiar wickedness that flourished in the hearts and minds of the manufacturing classes. But there were not wanting some shrewd enough to see that low prices and low wages were more to blame than any natural sinfulness of spinners and weavers.[1]

Thus the position of the seventeenth-century merchant was profoundly different from that of his nineteenth-century successor in so far as the expansion of his sales was not being constantly facilitated by cost reductions in the industry from which he drew his supplies. Even under such conditions, it is true, sales might on occasion be substantially increased even in well-established markets. Exchange depreciation, the difficulties of foreign competitors, unwonted interludes of peace in a world normally wracked by war, could all increase the demand for English cloth. But such conditions were of their nature temporary. Under normal conditions, the demand for English cloth in any area where the trade in it was well-established tended to grow but slowly. Under such conditions, the expansion of trade tended to be an extensive rather than an intensive process; a process of finding new markets rather than one of increasing sales in the old. The substitution of the export of cloth for that of wool had of itself introduced such a tendency in London trade, for it is an obvious truism that the demand for consumers' goods is geographically wider than that for raw materials. The former exists, at least potentially, wherever men of prosperity are to be found. The latter is of necessity confined to a comparatively few industrial areas. So long as wool had been the staple export, trade had perforce been directed to the few great manufacturing centres on the continent; above all to Flanders and northern Italy. When cloth took the place of wool there arose the possibility of finding new markets to be served directly from London, and much of the history of the later middle ages and of the sixteenth century was concerned with their exploitation. By the end of the sixteenth century the cost-structure of the cloth industry had made the finding of even newer markets essential to commercial progress. Few things stand out more clearly from the economic discussions under Elizabeth and the early Stuarts than the twin ideas that the old outlets for cloth were glutted and that new ones must be found; to impute those ideas entirely

[1] A. E. Bland, P. A. Brown and R. H. Tawney, *English economic history: select documents* (London, 1920), p. 337.

to theoretical naivety would be to overlook the technological conditions of which a realistic age was only too keenly aware.

Not unnaturally, in their search for new markets men's thoughts turned first to the regions made accessible by the great geographical discoveries, where English textiles were as yet unknown and where the possibility of new sales seemed therefore to be greatest. The hope of tapping a new demand for English cloth was a motive appealed to both by those who would found colonies on the American continent and by those who sought to open direct trade with the Far East. Yet, apart from purchases made in Spain for re-shipment to the Spanish colonies, neither the New World nor the Far East contributed any immediate solution to the problems of English exporters. The nations of the latter were highly commercialized; but for them English broadcloth was too heavy. 'The English', wrote Sandys in 1610, 'have so ill-utterance for their warm cloths in these hot countries that I believe they will suffer their ships to rot in the river than continue that trade any longer.'[1] Sandys was writing of Egypt and the countries to the south rather than of the Far East itself; but the same cry came from India. 'English cloth', wrote Thomas Aldworth from Surat in 1614, 'will not sell; it was only bought at first by great men to cover their elephants and make saddles for their horses. But for garments they use none in these parts.'[2] The early history of the East India Company was to furnish repeated proof of those assertions. By contrast, although North America provided ideal climatic conditions for the wearing of heavy woollens, it as yet contained few communities sufficiently commercialized to purchase them. Until the middle of the seventeenth century, the new markets for English textiles were found in the Old World rather than in the New, in southern Europe and Asia Minor rather than in the Far East.

Spain and the Mediterranean countries also, as the quotation from Sandys shows, presented a climatic problem. Although they had long provided an outlet for a limited number of shortcloths, those fabrics were too warm and heavy for general wear. But it was a problem to which the English textile industry itself could offer a solution. For to think of that industry as technologically stagnant would be highly erroneous. The absence of

[1] Quoted Wood, *Levant Company*, p. 33.
[2] *Cal. SP Colonial, East Indies, 1513–1616*, p. 317.

labour-saving inventions meant, not that ingenuity was dead,
but that it operated through other channels. Like the commercial expansion of the time, as also like the agricultural expansion
of the time, it was extensive rather than intensive. Just as merchants sought to open new markets rather than more fully to
exploit the old, just as agriculturists sought to bring more land
under cultivation rather than to increase the yield of that which
they already farmed, so clothiers sought to devise new types of
cloth rather than to cheapen those which they were already
making; a situation that is hardly surprising at a time when
labour was cheap and capital scarce. Admittedly, with wool as
their material and with no assistance from power-driven machinery in their major processes, they were unable to produce anything fitted for the Indian market. But in the new draperies they
provided a range of fabrics admirably suited for the warm, but
non-tropical, Mediterranean. Tradition has it that the new
draperies were introduced by Protestant weavers from the
Netherlands. But although they undoubtedly owed much to
alien immigrants, by no means all came from abroad; and whatever their origin it is not unreasonable to see in their development an obvious and appropriate response on the part of the
textile industry to the opportunities opened by the re-establish-
ment of direct trade with the Mediterranean in the later sixteenth
century and by the Anglo-Spanish peace of 1604.

The striking difference between the trade in the old draperies
and that in the new suggests a relationship, not only with the
conditions which obtained in the textile industry from which
they both sprung, but also with the prevailing forms of commercial organization. Northern and central Europe, the area in
which the sales of the old draperies were languishing, was the
sphere of influence of the great regulated companies – the Russia,
the Eastland and the Merchant Adventurers. By contrast southern Europe, where the sales of the new draperies were flourishing,
was an area of relative freedom. For none of the seventeenth-
century attempts to establish a Spanish Company seems to have
been really effective, and the monopoly of the Levant Company
never extended to the west coast of Italy. Moreover, even in
Germany and the Netherlands, the trade in new draperies was
for a considerable period left open to merchants not free of the
Merchant Adventurers. The correlation between regulation and

stagnation, between freedom and expansion, is too clear to be dismissed as pure coincidence. Yet the exact nature of the relationship between those phenomena is far from obvious. It is tempting to argue that it was one of simple causation; that the trade in shortcloths was sluggish because it was regulated and that the trade in the new draperies expanded because it was comparatively free. Yet it is doubtful whether the facts will support so simple an interpretation. The business correspondence of Lionel Cranfield does not suggest that the Merchant Adventurers had any policy of controlling prices or sales; the experience of the opening years of the century shows that regulation and expansion were not necessarily incompatible; it has been the purpose of this article to suggest that other reasons can be adduced to explain the different behaviour of the two branches of London's trade. In fact, it might be argued with some plausibility that the process of causation worked to some extent in the opposite direction; that regulated companies flourished in the northern European trade because there the problem was one of selling a well-established commodity in an area where the equilibrium point between supply and demand had been established by long experience and was unlikely to change with any rapidity; that the arguments for regulation were rejected in the case of Spain and much of the Mediterranean since there it was clearly possible to expand the sales of the new fabrics at current prices. Certain it is that men thought in different terms about the old and the new draperies. Throughout the later sixteenth century men looked upon the old cloth industry with suspicion as a breeding-ground of unemployment and distress; by the early seventeenth century some were pinning their hopes of solving the problem of destitution on the development of the new draperies.

To think of the new draperies purely in terms of the trade to Spain and the Mediterranean would obviously be contrary to the evidence of the Port Books. A minor, but not unimportant, proportion of them were sold in northern Europe and may have contributed something to the falling off in the demand for shortcloths. To think of the expansion of London trade purely in terms of the new draperies would also be to ignore one of the most significant pieces of evidence that the Port Books yield. The problem of increasing sales under conditions of comparatively rigid industrial costs invited not one solution, but two. Men could find new markets in which to sell their accustomed commodities; or they could find new commodities to sell in their accustomed markets. With respect to the latter solution the Port Books are suggestive rather than conclusive; but what they suggest is of some interest. In 1640, remarkably few English commodities other than textiles were exported by London merchants from their own port. England was still primarily an agricultural country; yet the agricultural produce shipped out by the city merchants was officially valued at less than £20,000. Professor Nef has shown that the late sixteenth and early seventeenth centuries saw a considerable expansion of English manufacturing industry; yet in 1640 Londoners exported less than £30,000 worth of manufactured goods other than textiles. Professor Nef and others have also shown that the same period saw a boom in mining; yet in 1640 the minerals exported from London were valued at less than £40,000. To some extent Londoners may have shipped their more bulky commodities from provincial ports – they certainly seem to have shipped fish from Yarmouth – yet the impression left by the Port Books is that the city merchants supplemented their trade in textiles, less by dealing in other forms of native produce, than by trading in foreign commodities. Of all forms of England's produce her wool, whether raw or manufactured, was the only one in great demand overseas. Outside of the trade in textiles, it was re-exports rather than exports that opened a road to fortune.

By 1640 Londoners were re-shipping East Indian wares to Russia, Germany, the Netherlands and even to Italy and the Levant; Virginia tobacco to Hamburg; Mediterranean produce to the Netherlands; European manufactures to Africa and America. According to the official valuations their re-exports in that year were equal in value to their exports of all English goods other than textiles; and those re-exports constituted only a proportion of the foreign goods which they sold abroad. For, since goods re-shipped from London had to pay subsidy both inwards and outwards and in addition to suffer the delay of twice navigating the often wind-locked Thames, it was normally more convenient to trade directly between foreign countries without touching England. And so to these re-exports there was added a body of invisible exports for which the evidence is fragmentary but of which the importance is unmistakable. In both the Baltic and the Far East, Londoners bought local wares in one port to sell in another. London capital found its way into the African slave trade and into the commerce of the Caribbean. But, as in the case of visible exports, it was above all in Spain and the Mediterranean that the city merchants found their opportunity. To those regions they shipped directly the fish of Newfoundland; the hides, wax and fur of Russia; the corn, timber and hemp of the Baltic; the varied products of Germany and the Low Countries. And English ships were busily engaged in trade between different Mediterranean countries.

The significance of that trade in foreign commodities should not be underrated. Although its volume must remain a matter for conjecture, it may have contributed substantially to the wealth of the London merchant classes. It certainly provided the foundation for two of the most characteristic developments of the middle and later years of the century. On the one hand, it gave the London merchants their interest in colonial expansion and shaped their attitude to colonial policy. In the seventeenth century, as in the nineteenth, the merchant looked upon colonies less as markets in which it might one day be possible to make substantial sales than as sources from which primary commodities might be speedily obtained for resale elsewhere. From that point of view, the desirable colonial policy was obvious. It was the policy of confining sales of colonial produce to English merchants; the policy that was to be enshrined in the 'enumerated commodity' clauses of the Navigation Acts. On the other hand, it was this trade in foreign produce which supplied a major cause of Anglo-Dutch rivalry. To contemporary observers, at least in this country, few nations differed more widely than England and Holland. The latter was poor to the extent of lacking not only articles for export but also the basic commodities for subsistence. The former, to eyes dazzled with national pride, was rich in both manufactured goods and raw materials. But to the historian, disabused of the idea that the fish of the North Sea belonged peculiarly to this country and that self-sufficiency is conducive to success in foreign trade, the similarity between the two countries is more striking than the differences. Each occupied a geographical position admirably suited for maritime expansion; each produced only a narrow range of commodities that could be exported in any considerable quantity; each sought to solve the dilemma by carrying and trading in the produce of other places. Even during the early seventeenth century, colonial policy and Anglo-Dutch rivalry were taking shape under the pressure of those circumstances. The later years of the century saw little more than the intensification of trends already apparent before the Civil War.

2 English Foreign Trade, 1660-1700

RALPH DAVIS

[This article was first published in *The Economic History Review*, 2nd series, Vol. VI (1954).]

I

Until the seventeenth century, changes in the character of English foreign trade always left untouched its central feature; from the days of the Angevin kings to the time of the Cromwellian Protectorate, wool or woollen cloth constituted almost the whole of English exports. As late as 1640, 80–90 per cent of exports from London were woollen cloth.[1]

Sixty years later, English commerce had taken on a new character. Woollens still led the list of exports, but no longer came near to concluding it as well; in 1699–1701, only 47 per cent of English exports were of woollen cloth. The new development on the export side, hardly foreshadowed before the Civil War, was the growth of a re-export trade[2] mainly in American or Eastern products, constituting some 30 per cent of total exports. This reflects an enormous growth in imports from America and the East; English trade as a whole now depended to a great extent upon the extra-European world.

If trade with Europe in the products of Europe, as shown in the table, be considered, the continuation of an old pattern is apparent. Imports are, in the main, of those textile products from north-west Europe which have always been complained of as unnecessary, frivolous and worthless; of luxury foodstuffs such as wine and fruits from Spain, Portugal and the Mediterranean; and of raw materials for the textile industries from the Mediterranean, and for the metallurgical, building and shipbuilding industries from the northern countries. Exports are still domin-

[1] F. J. Fisher, 'London's export trade in the early seventeenth century', above, pp. 66–8.
[2] Re-exports in 1640 do not appear to be more than 3 or 4 per cent of total exports. Fisher, 'London's export trade', p. 68.

Table 1 ANALYSIS OF ENGLISH FOREIGN TRADE BY COMMODITIES AND
AREAS, AVERAGE OF 1699–1701. (£000)*

		Total	Europe including Turkey and North Africa	West Africa, America and the East
A.	Imports:			
	Manufactures			
	Textiles	1,597	1,123	474
	Other	247	169	78
	Foodstuffs, etc.	1,969	910	1,059
	Raw materials	2,036	1,784	252
	Total	5,849	3,986	1,863
B.	Exports:			
	Manufactures			
	Textiles	3,125	2,815	310
	Other	458	182	276
	Foodstuffs, etc.	488	431	57
	Raw materials	362	344	18
	Total	4,433	3,772	661
C.	Re-exports:			
	Manufactures			
	Textiles	672	456	216
	Other	74	35	39
	Foodstuffs, etc.	941	898	43
	Raw materials	299	271	28
	Total	1,986	1,660	326
D.	Total of Exports and Re-exports	6,419	5,432	987

* These figures are derived from the Customs Ledgers in the PRO (Customs
3–3/5). They summarize the detailed table in the Appendix (p. 95–8).

ated, overwhelmingly, by woollen cloth (£2,771,000 out of
£2,815,000 textile exports; almost three-quarters of all exports
to Europe); it is supported, as it was a century before, by fish
(principally Yarmouth herrings) and minerals – above all, lead
and tin. The growth of the relative importance of south European markets for woollens, noted by Professor Fisher as occurring during the first four decades of the century, has been consolidated.[1] Only when we turn to the remainder of the table does

[1] Fisher, 'London's export trade', *passim*. This development is much more
marked in the London statistics than in those for the whole country which are
available at the end of the century. It is possible that, throughout the century, it
reflects to some extent the growing relative importance of the outports in the
North Sea trades, and the growing interest of London in the Iberian trades which
were already important to western merchants.

great change become apparent. Nearly a third of imports come from outside Europe; 40 per cent of exports are either re-exports of non-European commodities, or exports to India and America.

Why was it possible so to expand these distant trades – above all, the trade in the products of the Western plantations? Why, to take the most striking example, could England consume at the end of the century 13 million lbs of tobacco, as against 50,000 lbs in 1615 – and re-export a further 25 million lbs to Europe? The answer is usually assumed simply to be that vast new sources of supply were being opened up in the West. But the equally significant corollary must not be overlooked; vast new sources of demand were being opened up in England and Europe – demand created by sudden cheapness when these English plantation goods brought a collapse in prices which introduced the middle classes and the poor to novel habits of consumption; demand which, once realized, was not shaken by subsequent vicissitudes in prices, but continued to grow rapidly throughout the century.

Tobacco was a luxury at the end of the sixteenth century, obtainable by the generality at threepence a pipeful.[1] Less than a century later it was the general solace of all classes. Before 1619, twenty to forty shillings a lb was being paid for tobacco in England;[2] in the 1670s it retailed for a shilling or less. Virginia and the British West Indies had found a market with almost limitless potentiality; there was a rapid expansion of production in the plantations which by 1630 had driven the plantation price down to less than a penny a pound[3] – a temporary overproduction crisis which impelled the West Indian planters to turn to new products. Production more than once overtook demand in this way[4] but these intermittent setbacks were trifling when set against the enormous and continuing growth of output throughout the century. From 20,000 lbs in 1619, and just over a million lbs in the 1630s, the Virginia and Maryland export to London rose to 7 million lbs in 1662–3 and 9 million lbs in 1668–9,[5] to 12

---

[1] N. Curtis-Bennett, *The food of the people* (London, 1949), p. 81.

[2] G. L. Beer, *The origins of the British colonial system, 1578–1660* (New York, 1922), p. 86.

[3] *Cal. SP Colonial, America and West Indies, 1574–1660*, p. 117

[4] E.g. in the early 1680s. 'Tobacco, our sole manufacture, is through overproduction so underfoot that it will be impossible for the inhabitants to support themselves.' *Cal. SP Colonial, America and West Indies, 1681–5*, p. 104.

[5] BM Add. MSS. 36785.

million lbs in the late 1680s[1] and to 22 million lbs in 1699–1701. In the post-Restoration period, the normal peace-time price was not much above the disaster price of 1630, but producers continuously extended the supply. After 1685, tobacco bore a tax of some three times its plantation cost, but demand continued to rise as the smoking habit spread. The huge market thus opened for Virginia tobacco was not, of course, confined to this country; it was a European market, and two-thirds of imports were re-exported to Europe at the end of the century.

The case of sugar is similar, though less startling. The development of English production was part of an international movement which brought prices down. At the beginning of the seventeenth century Portuguese (i.e. Brazilian) production was already growing fast and reducing prices sharply[2] and the English West Indian islands, when they turned to sugar production, had this large established New World producer to contend with. They came late into the field – Barbados in the 1640s, Jamaica, as a substantial grower, after 1660 – and in the early 1660s they were still contending with the Portuguese even for the English market. But already their competition had caused a considerable decline in prices[3] and prices continued to fall, on the whole, until about 1685, by which time the English product had driven Brazilian sugar from the north European as well as from the English market. West Indies sugar imports to London, negligible before the Civil War, rose from 148,000 cwt in 1663/69[4] to 371,000 cwt in 1699–1701 – and a third of this latter total was re-exported. The plantation price of sugar reached a low point in 1685 of 12s. 6d. per cwt;[5] the retail price was halved between 1630 and 1680.[6]

---

[1] *Cal. SP Colonial, America and West Indies, 1689–92*, pp. 184–5.

[2] N. Deerr, *The history of sugar* (London, 1949), I, 102–10.

[3] J. Child, *A new discourse of trade* (1669), p. 220: 'In my time we have beat their Muscovado and Paneal sugars quite out of use in Europe, their Whites we have brought down in all these parts of Europe in price from seven or eight pound per lb [*sic*] to fifty shillings and three pound per lb [*sic*] and in quantity, whereas formerly their Brazil fleets consisted of 100 to 120 thousand chests of sugar, they are now reduced to about 30 thousand chests, since the great encrease of Barbadoes.' See also HMC House of Lords MSS. 1695–7, pp. 19–20.

[4] BM Add. MSS. 36785.

[5] C. S. S. Higham, *The Leeward Islands, 1660–1688* (Cambridge, 1921), pp. 191–2.

[6] Thorold Rogers's figures, whatever their general defects, here show unmistakably the falling trend in sugar prices; in 1634–5 sugar was sold at 1s. 2d. to 1s. 3d. per lb (a considerable reduction on late sixteenth-century prices); in 1684–9,

Calicoes appear to have entered the English and European market in a similar way. The complaints of pamphleteers in the last quarter of the seventeenth century of the impossibility of English competition with Indian labour at a halfpenny a day are well known.[1] Here, too, cheapness must have opened up new markets for textiles, as well as competing in old ones. Imports of calicoes, hardly heard of before the Restoration, rose from 240,000 in 1663/69[2] to 861,000 in 1699–1701; two-thirds of the latter were exported.

These three commodities comprise in value two-thirds of the imports to England from outside Europe[3] and almost two-thirds of English re-exports to Europe. Indian silks and mixed fabrics, Indian pepper and some minor commodities can be shown to have similar histories of greatly expanded sales associated with sharply falling prices. Thus the new type of English trade expansion, though dependent on the creation of English settlements and trading centres outside Europe, made its way by the cheapness of the supply drawn from them, creating new mass markets. In this respect it bears a striking similarity to the technological revolution which, getting under way a century later, developed new consumption habits in English and foreign populations with the cheap product of the machine. Both these phenomena contrast sharply with the continuous but slow growth of the cloth trade, based on a relatively static technique and stable costs.

It was the profits of this trade, a trade which seemed to have limitless possibilities for growth, which English merchants were determined to keep to themselves, along with its corollaries of export trade to the plantations and a shipping industry to carry their products. The Navigation Acts of 1651 and 1660 are attempts to keep the Dutch from exploiting

---

despite extra customs duties, at 6d. to 7d. J. T. Rogers, *A history of agriculture and prices in England* (Oxford, 1887), VI, 421–48.

[1] See, for example, the quotations in E. Baines, *History of the cotton manufacture* (1835), pp. 77–81. The benefits of cheap Indian textiles are discussed in 'Considerations on the East India trade' (1701; reproduced in J. R. McCulloch, *Early tracts on commerce*, 1856).

[2] BM Add. MSS. 36785.

[3] I.e. outside 'Europe including Turkey and North Africa', as shown in Table 1 (p. 79).

these new trades, as they had done during the Civil War years.[1]

The trade statistics under-state the magnitude of English interests beyond Europe. Two important supplementary fields of English activity are not revealed by them; the slave trade and the Newfoundland fishery. The fishery itself was increasingly carried on, after the Restoration, from small settlements in Newfoundland; but the fish were collected by ships sent by English merchants, and sold by them in the Mediterranean or the West Indies; the settlers' participation is indicated by the tiny exports to Newfoundland which are recorded. The Africa slave trade was of exactly the same nature, substituting Africans for fish; Africans were caught (on land) and sold in exchange for small quantities of goods to ships sent out from England, which took them to America for sale. It is difficult to estimate the annual value of these catches, but immediately before the Revolution they may well have exceeded half a million pounds a year.

Finally, the influence of transatlantic producers may be noted in another development, not very important in the seventeenth century, but pointing the way which trade expansion would take in the first half of the next century. This development was the growth of manufactured exports other than woollens. Though before 1700 the total of these miscellaneous manufactures was small, it was growing very fast – after 1660, hardly less rapidly than the growth of re-exports. In 1699–1701 miscellaneous manufactures constituted 8 per cent of English exports, and their value (London only) had risen from £222,000 in 1663/69[2] to £420,000 in 1699–1701. In this early stage, the growth of these exports was directly connected with the re-export trade; for it was, above all, an increasing demand from the English plantations.[3] The colonies provided a market in which English manufactures were protected, in which they had little native

---

[1] The plantation trade was opened to Dutch ships when the royal proclamation barring them lost force in 1642; and from 1643 to 1650 they participated on a large scale. (Beer, *Origins*, ch. xi. The war conditions, of course, hampered English trading. But Child considered that, if the trade were open, the Dutch would drive the English right out of it. Child, *New discourse*, p. xxix. For a general discussion on this point, see L. A. Harper, *The English Navigation Laws* (New York, 1939), pp. 242–5.

[2] BM Add. MSS. 36785.

[3] There is a similar rapid growth in the re-export of one class of Continental manufactures – linens – to the plantations.

competition, and which had an absorptive capacity rapidly
extending as colonial exports grew.

Table 2 EXPORTS OF MISCELLANEOUS MANUFACTURES
(LONDON ONLY) (£000)

	1663/69	1699–1701
West Africa, America and the East	86	259
Europe, etc.	136	161

Thus in the seventeenth century the English brass-, copper-
and ironware, silk and linen, hat-making and tailoring, glass-
and earthen-ware, paper, cordage and leather industries, and
others, were being fostered by their protected market across the
Atlantic, gaining strength with which they would later emerge
into competition with Europe and further modify the structure
of English trade.

II

The outstanding new features of English foreign trade after
the Restoration have been indicated. It is now proposed to
examine in some detail the trade statistics of the forty years after
1660, to analyse the structure of English trade[1] and to attempt
an estimate of overall changes.[2] During this period the growing
desire to have exact information on foreign trade, which led to
the beginning of regular trade returns after 1696, brought also a
scattering of information on earlier years. But the figures need
careful interpretation before comparisons are made.

The earliest and most valuable of the surviving statistics are
those for the years Michaelmas–Michaelmas 1662–3 and 1668–9,
contained in the well-known 'Book of Tables' in the British
Museum (Add. MSS. 36785). This book contains figures (for
London only) of exports of home produce, and imports. The
quantities were extracted, by order of the House of Lords, from
the books of the Customs in 1669–70;[3] the Colonial Office
records contain documents which may be the original extracts.[4]
But the 'Book of Tables' itself was probably compiled some years
later, and the valuations then added. The frequent quotations,
in the State Papers and elsewhere of the early 1670s, of trade

[1] For this general analysis, see Appendix (pp. 95,98).   [2] See pp. 91–2.
[3] HMC House of Lords MSS. 1665–70, p. 135.
[4] In the Public Record Office: CO 388–2.

figures for 1662–3 and 1668–9 clearly derive from this investigation,[1] but they refer only to quantities of commodities; if values had already been calculated, surely they would have been used in such references? Moreover, the valuations of French, German and Spanish wines correspond with the proclaimed prices of those wines which came into force in January 1675 and remained operative until the French wine import was prohibited in 1678.[2] Since a return of customs revenue for 1676–7 is included at the end of the volume, it seems likely that in their final form, with valuations, the tables date from 1678.

Some statistics were prepared for a few years in the early 1680s, but these have left little trace. They may be the basis of some calculations by Davenant;[3] just conceivably of an estimate of foreign trade in 1688 made by Gregory King;[4] and perhaps of a fairly precise quantitative statement of cloth exports for the year 1687–8.[5] Apart from this, and the details of trade with a few particular countries and in certain commodities[6] the 1670s and 1680s are statistically blank,[7] and the blank can only be filled by modern work on the Port Books on the lines which, it was said in 1696, would require the full-time work of four men to deal with London alone each year.[8]

[1] E.g. State Papers, Domestic (SPD) Charles II, 287–20/21; 288–25/27; HMC House of Lords MSS. 1670–8, p. 141.

[2] *Tudor and Stuart proclamations*, ed. R. Steele (Oxford, 1910); proclamation on the prizing of wine in January of each year.

[3] C. Davenant, *Works* (ed. Whitworth, 1771), II, 16.

[4] Gregory King, *The naval trade of England* (1688). King's statistics are hardly credible; he sets import trade in 1688, at the end he says, of eleven prosperous years, at £4,020,000 – not much more than the London import alone of 1669. Chalmers's estimate for 1688 is arrived at by doubling the average of 1663/69 London exports–which he mistakes for English exports. G. Chalmers, *Estimate of the comparative strength of Great Britain* (1794), p. 60.

[5] BM Harleian MSS. 1898–66.

[6] Listed in G. N. Clark, *Guide to English commercial statistics* (London, 1938), pp. 156–60. Figures of trade with Holland, Hamburg, Portugal and Italy for 1685–6, recently produced in House of Lords Manuscripts, 1712–14, pp. 516–43, contain serious errors. The London statistics are probably more reliable than those of the outports.

[7] SPD Charles II, 417–99/102 is a draft form for the compilation of trade statistics, not resembling that later adopted. There is an argument on the feasibility of preparing such statistics in SPD Charles II, 418–39, 94, 107.

[8] HMC House of Lords MSS. 1695–6, p. 24. This, and similar estimates in SPD Charles II, 418–107, and Davenant, *Works*, II, 351, need not be taken too seriously. Civil Service standards of industry and efficiency were clearly much lower then than they are today. But the task is enormous.

Serious and continued collection of data began in the 1690s. In 1696 detailed statistics of trade were prepared for the years 1693–4, 1694–5 and 1695–6, apparently on the same basis that was used subsequently for the Inspector-General's ledgers; but these statistics have disappeared.[1] Chalmers quotes some figures for these years, based, he says, on Sir Philip Meadows's calculations; and since Meadows was an original Commissioner for Trade and Plantations from 1696, these calculations probably come from the lost Custom House accounts.[2] This experiment led, in 1696, to the appointment of an Inspector-General of the Customs, and the beginning of the permanent series of Customs Ledgers, detailing trade by country and commodity.[3]

The problem is to find means of comparing the partial information afforded by the 'Book of Tables' for 1662–3 and 1668–9 with the fuller and more accurate figures available at the end of the century. These two years were peace years, moderately prosperous, and no more affected by war or war scares than any other two years of the 1660s. The three years 1699–1701, chosen for comparison, were also peace years, the period beginning sufficiently long after the Peace of Ryswick (September 1697) for most post-war adjustments to have worked themselves out.[4]

A detailed judgement on the valuations used in compiling the statistics cannot be attempted here; it is not essential if the main interest is in movements rather than in absolute amounts of trade. But large errors in the valuations of important commodities, and substantial differences between the valuations of 1663/69 and 1699–1701 must be indicated.

The existing Customs valuations of most commodities are to be found in the 'Book of Rates', the last revision of which was in 1660;[5] the schedule on which the general *ad valorem* duty of 5

[1] HMC House of Lords MSS. 1695–7, p. 221; Davenant, *Works*, I, 95.

[2] Chalmers, *Estimate*, p. 211. Average imports for the years 1694–6 are given as £3,050,000, and exports as £3,124,000, excluding imports from and exports to the plantations. This information should be reliable; the figures seem too large to apply to London only (cf. 1696–7 English imports £3,483,000, exports £3,526,000 *including* plantation trade).

[3] Clark, *Guide* has a detailed discussion of these records. They are in the PRO series, Customs 3. Dr W. Schlote appears to have been unaware of the existence of these ledgers when he wrote his *British overseas trade from 1700 to the 1930s* (English trans., Oxford, 1952). See pp. 3–4.

[4] Re-export of East India products was rather low in 1699, possibly reflecting the limited sailings to the East in the last year of the war.

[5] In a schedule to 12 Charles II, c.4.

per cent (later 10 per cent) was based. It attempts to list and value all commodities of importance, except the specially important 'Old Draperies' and wines – both these groups of commodities bearing specific duties. But the officials preparing the 1663/69 statistics and the Customs Ledgers disregarded these and made fresh valuations; it might be supposed that these revised values would be as accurate as near-contemporaries in close contact with the world of commerce could achieve.[1]

But what is the 'correct' valuation of goods passing through the ports? The basis used in the Inspector-General's Ledgers is clear; 'upon all the respective goods exported from hence, according to their current price here at home, and, in imported goods, according to their current price abroad'.[2] This almost corresponds with modern practice so far as exports are concerned, but imports are today valued at cost up to the point of landing – i.e. including insurance and freight.

The basis used for import valuations in 1663/69 was apparently quite different from that followed in 1699 or today. Three items of considerable size have very large manifest errors in their valuation – tobacco, wine and brandy. Tobacco was valued at 6d. per lb. This was probably near the merchant's price for poorer qualities[3] but was certainly far removed from 'first cost' in Virginia, which was usually under 2d. at this time. French wine was valued at £36 per ton, Rhenish at £54 and Spanish at £60, and French brandy at £48. But these were the London bulk selling prices[4] and, again, were far removed from first cost, which Child put at £6 to £7, and Davenant at £8, for French wine.[5]

It is noteworthy that these large errors in valuation occur for all the commodities which bore heavy import duties. Wine bore a specific duty – in 1663 £7 10s. per ton, roughly 100 per cent of first cost, and brandy was also heavily taxed. Colonial tobacco had the absurd Customs valuation of 1s. 8d. per lb, so that the 5 per cent duty came to a penny, and there was an imposition of a further penny; this total duty of 2d. per lb was over 100 per

---

[1] Child considered the Customs valuations too low on English drapery (i.e. the 'new draperies') silks and haberdashery, too high on lead and tin (*New discourse*, p. 166). The valuations of the first three are higher, and of the last two lower, in the 1663/69 figures than in the 'Book of Rates'. As to the valuations of 1699–1701, see the observations in Davenant, *Works*, v, 350 *et seq.*

[2] Davenant, *Works*, v, 350.   [3] Beer, *Origins*, I, 130–4.

[4] See pp. 84–5.   [5] Child, *New discourse*, p. vi; Davenant, *Works*, v, 366.

D

cent of first cost. All other imported commodities bore duties of only 5 per cent based on valuations which, at their worst, were far more reasonable than that of tobacco. It seems, therefore, that the compilers of the 1663/69 tables based their import valuations throughout on London selling prices – inflated by duty, freight and merchants' profits on the costs so inflated – and that this is not apparent to cursory inspection only because no other goods important to trade bore very heavy duties.[1] In other words, it is likely that all imported goods are valued at something considerably above the 'first cost' of the Customs ledgers but not 300–400 per cent above, as are tobacco, wine and brandy.[2] Exports, on the other hand, should be comparable as between the two periods; no accumulations of error can distort the valuations of goods between merchant and waterside as import values are distorted by the addition of duty and freight.[3] Comparison of actual valuations at the two dates shows that usually import valuations are lower at the later date than at the earlier, as might be expected from the preceding argument; exports show varying small changes, on the whole upward.[4]

It seems clear, then, that there was a general over-valuation of imports in 1663/69, but it is not possible to estimate its magnitude. However, the ascertained errors in wine, brandy and tobacco, large and fairly definite, should be corrected; and some arithmetical errors call for adjustment.[5]

The 'Book of Tables' when corrected as in Table 3, provides a basis from which to build an estimate of total foreign trade for the years 1663/69. Given London imports, and London exports

[1] Davenant, who observed the over-valuations of wine and other French goods imported, came to the conclusion that the import valuations included 'prime cost, commission, customs, freight, merchants' and retailers' profit' (*Works*, v, 366).
[2] The valuations of wine in 1699–1701 are much higher than those suggested for 1663/69, but this was due to a genuine rise in prices. Davenant, *Works*, v, 367.
[3] If the dating of these valuations at 1678 is correct (pp. 84–5), there remains the question whether 1663 prices were then known accurately.
[4] It is not always possible to equate valuations of 1663/69 and 1699–1701, as units of measurement, and descriptions and sub-classifications of goods change. But of nineteen commodities whose valuations can be compared (representing approximately half the value of 1699–1701 imports) fourteen show lowered and five increased valuations. Cloth exports show varying changes in valuation, but the general tendency is upward.
[5] The compiler of the 'Book of Tables' could not add up. His most serious error makes imports from Spain in 1669 £449,000 instead of £649,000.

of English produce, data on two further items are required – re-exports, and outport trade. These can only be roughly estimated.

The total of re-exports in 1699–1701 was £1,986,000 nearly two-thirds of which is made up by the three items tobacco £421,000, linens and calicoes £522,000 and sugar £287,000. The outports had little share in this trade, except in tobacco, of which they exported £152,000. The growth of re-exports from

Table 3 MAJOR ERRORS IN THE 'BOOK OF TABLES'

	Error per ton	*Tons 1663*	*Total error 1663 (£000)*	*Tons 1669*	*Total error 1669 (£000)*
Wine:					
France	£29	7,465	216	5,726	166
Spain	£48	6,575	316	6,343	304
Holland	£43	924	40	735	32
Brandy	£36	1,059	38	333	12
Tobacco (lb)	4d. per lb	7,367,140	123	9,026,046	150
Total to be deducted			733		664
Arithmetical errors			− 16		− 190
Net overstatement of imports			749		474

insignificance has been traced; much of that growth certainly took place after 1669. Tobacco and sugar re-export in the 1660s cannot have been of very large dimensions as compared with the 1699–1701 figures. Two-thirds of 'linens' re-exported were Indian calicoes; though it was said that the import of calicoes was insignificant before the 1670s, the figures belie this.[1] There must have been some re-export of calicoes in the 1660s; in 1676 Williamson wrote '100000 pieces of calecut sent yearly into Holland from hence.'[2] The remaining linen re-exports are almost entirely Dutch and German linens going to the American plantations, and the movement of these probably corresponded with the rise in exports of English manufactures to the colonies.

Consideration of the import figures, and of re-exports in 1699–1701, suggests that the re-export of these three groups of commodities at least trebled in the period 1660–1700; the increase

[1] Of the goods classified simply as 'calicoes' numbers imported rose from 241,874 in 1663/69 to 861,133 in 1699–1701; of the latter total, 507,039 were re-exported.

[2] SPD Charles II, 379–53.

may have been considerably more. This kind of expansion, or a greater, also characterizes some minor re-exports – Indian silks, little known in England in the 1660s; dyestuffs from the West Indies (logwood and indigo particularly) whose import to London grew from £3,000 to £71,000, and a few others. In all, nearly £1,600,000 of 1699–1701 re-exports are of these plantation or Indian products, or exports to plantations, which underwent growth of this order. Putting re-exports of these in 1663/69 at about £500,000, and assuming that other re-exports totalling nearly £400,000 in 1699–1701 had shown little change[1] it is suggested that re-exports in 1663/69 were not more than £900,000, and possibly considerably less.[2]

Exports from the outports in the 1660s can likewise be estimated within reasonable limits. These, though more varied than London exports, were also dominated by woollens; and the outports were particularly interested in varieties which were gaining ground during the period. Thus 40 per cent of outport cloth exports in 1700 was serges going out of Exeter;[3] and Exeter's direct foreign trade in serges was the product of the previous decade or so.[4] Another 20 per cent of outport cloth exports was Norwich stuffs (worsted, manufactured increasingly in the West Riding). Though London traded in these cloths, two-thirds of her trade was bound up with other varieties of cloth. It is probable, then, that outports cloth exports showed a faster rate of increase than those of London. Other outport exports showed moderate change, except grain, the export of which was negligible in 1663/69.

It is suggested then, that outport exports in 1663/69 may have been £1,100–1,200,000, i.e. woollens under £700,000 (rising to £1,032,000 in 1699–1701); fish £150–200,000, other exports £250–300,000. This again, is likely to be an over- rather than an underestimate.

[1] The principal items were raw and thrown silk, pepper and drugs; the value of imports of these into London showed little change over the period.

[2] Davenant (*Works*, II, 16) values 're-export' of American and East Indian products, on the average of 1682–8, at £1,400,000. Little confidence can be placed in these figures; but in any case they relate to the height of the pre-war boom, when trade may have reached the levels of 1699–1701.

[3] W. G. Hoskins, *Industry, people and trade in Exeter, 1688–1800* (Manchester, 1935; Exeter, 1968), p. 154. Exeter exports of serges were £392,000, total woollen exports from outports £979,000.

[4] Hoskins, *Industry*, pp. 14–19, 37, 70.

Inexact as these estimates are, they cannot be paralleled when outport imports have to be considered. The only possible course is to assume that the import/export relation was much the same in the 1660s as at the end of the century. There is some evidence of the general truth of this view. Sixty per cent of outport exports in 1699-1701 went to Holland, Hamburg and Bremen. Omitting Exeter (which, as shown above, was of relatively small importance in the 1660s) the two great ports in this trade were Hull and Newcastle, and both of these were, in the 1660s as in 1700, overwhelmingly exporting rather than importing centres.[1] Irish trade, mainly carried on from outports, may have stagnated as a result of import restrictions imposed after 1669;[2] but on the other hand the plantation trade grew rapidly,[3] and there is no reason to suppose that the relations of imports and exports changed markedly in trade with countries so closely bound commercially to England.

Outport imports in 1699-1701 were 72 per cent of exports; the same percentage, applied to the suggested export total for 1663/69 of £1,100-1,200,000, gives imports of £800-900,000.

It may be asked whether estimates which are so tentative are worth making. One answer is that this kind of estimate, perhaps improved upon, is all we can have for a very long time to come. The other is that a whole series of distinguished writers up to our own time – Charles King, Anderson, Chalmers, Cunningham – have fallen into the trap of comparing London figures for 1663/69 with English trade figures for 1696 onward, producing absurdly distorted and exaggerated pictures of the development

---

[1] The inward trade of Hull was small in 1668, consisting of such things as pantiles, pots and frying pans (SPD Charles II, 235-178). Newcastle's trade with Holland was mainly an export trade in 1651 (Surtees Society, *Newcastle Merchant Adventurers* (1895), I, 179).

[2] It is far from certain that it did. *Total* Irish exports in 1669 were £481,000 of which the principal constituents were wool £95,000, butter £73,000, tallow £53,000, beef £47,000 (R. Dunlop, 'A note on the export trade of Ireland', *English Historical Review*, XXII (1907), 775). In 1699-1701 *English* imports from Ireland were £307,000 (outports £294,000) of which wool was £122,000, tallow £84,000. Beef and butter were prohibited imports.

[3] These were the years in which Liverpool and Whitehaven were transformed into great centres of the transatlantic trade. See C. N. Parkinson, *The rise of the port of Liverpool* (Liverpool, 1952), chs. V, VI; P. Ford, 'Tobacco and coal; a note on the economic history of Whitehaven', *Economica*, IX (1929), 192-3. At Bristol, the tonnage of shipping entered from the West Indies rose from 1,900 in 1670 (PRO Port Books, Bristol) to 5,200 in 1700 (BM Add. MSS. 9764-116).

Table 4 AN ESTIMATE OF ENGLISH FOREIGN TRADE

	1663/69 (£000)	1699–1701 (£000)
London exports	2,039	2,773
Outport exports	1,200	1,660
Re-exports	900	1,986
Total exports (say)	4,100	6,419
London imports*	3,495	4,667
Outport imports	900	1,182
Total imports (say)	4,400	5,849

9 London imports for 1663/69 are probably somewhat overvalued; see pp. 87–8. The whole of the 1663/69 figures, with the possible exception of London cloth exports, are more likely to be too high than too low.

of English trade.[1] Davenant, when attempting to estimate the total trade of 1663/69, saw the difficulty, and solved it by adding a flat 28 per cent to London imports and exports to represent the outport trade of those years.[2] But outport imports were in reality rather small, and outport exports very large in relation to London trade (and, of course, this ignored re-exports). So there arises from Davenant's method his plausible explanations of the reasons for an enormous increase in exports to Holland – an increase which never occurred.[3] Late seventeenth-century trade cannot be seriously discussed until the temptation to make erroneous comparisons has been removed by the provision of some basis for a true one.

On our calculations, then, imports increased by just a third, and exports by rather more than half, in the period 1663–1701, the faster growth of exports being due to the growth of the re-export trade from the negligible proportions of the 1630s.

There is not, of course, a steady expansion of trade between the two dates. They are both within a long stretch of history which is characterized, at home and abroad, by exceptional dis-

[1] Today, the most generally accessible summary of English foreign trade before 1700 is probably in W. Cunningham, *The growth of English industry and commerce* (Cambridge, 1907), III, 931; it perpetuates this error.

[2] Davenant, *Works*, v, 401–42.

[3] If, for instance, this addition of 28 per cent were applied to 1699 London exports to Holland, it would give a total of £328,000 for English exports. But English exports were actually £1,766,000 – i.e. London exports £256,000, outport exports £746,000, re-exports £764,000.

turbances to trade. The Civil Wars were followed rapidly by war with Holland, war with Spain, and the unsettlement at home which followed the Protector's death. The Restoration period started well, but soon England was plunged into the second and third Dutch wars, the Plague and the Fire of London. Peace for England in 1674 was not accompanied by European peace, and for a further four years, while English shipping and distant trades prospered, England's most important markets were troubled.[1] The one period of good trade runs from the lifting of depression in 1677 to the Revolution of 1688. War-time trade depression followed, lifting somewhat in 1695[2] and was replaced by a few years of good trade in 1698–1701. Then war came down again, though with less disastrous effects on commerce than in the 1690s, and was followed by uncertainties over the Succession, only cleared up in 1715. The statistics reveal little of this, but they throw some light on one important point. The boom of 1698–1701 did not push English foreign trade to a new peak; it may not even have recovered positions reached immediately before the war, in the years 1686–8 when our foreign business was at its height.[3]

The view of an expansion of trade continuing beyond 1688 to 1702 is largely based on confused deductions from the 1663/69 London figures – e.g. the doubling of these figures to arrive at 1688 trade; describing this as *English* trade; and comparing the results with 1699–1701 English trade which, naturally enough, is larger.[4]

III

The change in the character of English trade in this period has an important implication. The total of foreign trade was not growing exceptionally fast; but it seems likely that in the years 1660–1701, which have been considered here, the rate of new investment in commerce (as contrasted with industry) was abnormally high. Much the most important reason for this was the

[1] The middle 1670s see many complaints of depression in the cloth trade, e.g. SPD Charles II, 361–132/3; 373–21; 378–43; all in 1674–6. Gregory King's view was that depression lifted in 1677.

[2] HMC House of Lords MSS. 1695–7, p. 25.

[3] Davenant, *Works*, 1, 149.

[4] See Chalmers, *Estimate*, table facing p. 235.

sudden and rapid development of re-export trade from negligible proportions to nearly a third of total exports in 1699–1701 (and the corresponding growth in import trade), for reasons already discussed. This was a revolution in trade. But it had effects on the whole economic structure quite different from those produced by past and future trade expansions.

For whereas expansion of exports would ordinarily be accompanied by increased investment in export industries, true re-exports – re-exports of goods in unaltered state – call for no investment at all in home industry. But merchants need capital to finance the trade, inward and outward. The development of the English entrepôt in these decades involved large investment in commerce not accompanied by industrial investment.

Other factors were operating in the same direction. The relative importance of trade to more distant places continued to grow. Apart from the East India trade, with its own peculiar finances, nearly all trade early in the century had been with Europe; and though voyages to the Mediterranean or the Baltic were longer than those to Holland or Hamburg, remittances for goods sold or freight earned could be, and were, sent by overland routes long before the ships carrying the goods returned home. After the Restoration, trade with the Americas flourished; a trade at the end of long ocean routes, and in which, if exports were relatively small, imports were commonly given credit for in advance. The new long voyage had to be financed from its beginning to its end – and beyond – and investment was continuing in English trading stations abroad. Both required further trading capital, and little industrial investment.

So far as foreign trade was an influence on the direction of the flow of capital, then, it was in this period making exceptionally small demands for new industrial investment in relation to its requirements for its own financing. And in this respect, the decades round 1700 are peculiar, for by that date the growth of re-export and of extra-European trade in general was beginning to slow down. The growth of docks and shipping, the great wealth of London merchant families, the preoccupation of writers of the period with problems of trade are familiar. The foregoing argument indicates that this was probably not accidental; that mercantile activity is conspicuous because it was for a time exceptionally important, requiring for its support an unusually large proportion of the nation's resources.[1]

Before the diversification of industry had made a substantial impact on foreign trade, and four generations before technical changes created an entirely new basis for commercial expansion, the English merchant class was able to grow rich, to accumulate capital, on middlemen's profits and on the growing shipping industry which was needed to carry cheap sugar and tobacco, pepper and saltpetre on the ocean routes. Because these sources made their great contribution to English foreign trade in the century after 1660, and in that century made great demands on the nation's capital, perhaps we should look with a little more favour on those historians of the past who dubbed this century with the title of 'The Commercial Revolution'.

APPENDIX

The following tables, derived from Add MSS 36785 for averages of years 1663 and 1669 (corrected as indicated on pp. 88–9) and from the Customs Ledgers (PRO Customs 3–3/5) for the average of the three years 1699–1701, present a detailed picture of the structure of English foreign trade in 1699–1701, with some opportunity for comparison with 1663/69.

The totals of trade for 1699–1701 differ slightly from those commonly quoted which are derived from C. Whitworth, *State of the trade of Great Britain* (1776). Whitworth's adjustments for foreign coin and bullion exported contain small errors.

Areas are made up as follows:

I   N.W. Europe – Germany, Holland, Flanders, France.
II   The North – Norway, Denmark and the Baltic.

[1] Professor K. G. Davies has an interesting discussion of commercial developments in this period. ('Joint stock investment in the late seventeenth century', *Economic History Review*, 2nd series, IV (1952), 283–301). He reminds us that the demand of foreign trade for new capital has in this period its reverse side in the accumulation of capital from the profits of foreign trade. He has, perhaps, underestimated the extent to which contemporary writings on trade show doubt and depression; the gloom of 'Britannia Languens' is by no means untypical. Professor Davies's statistics greatly overstate the growth of London trade. He says (p. 286) that London exports rose from £2,023,000 in 1662–3 to £3,577,000 in 1698–1701; but the latter figure includes foreign coin and bullion exported. The true increase is from £2,023,000 to £2,773,000.

ANALYSIS OF FOREIGN TRADE, 1663/69 AND 1699–1701 (£000)

(i) London, average of 1663 and 1669; (ii) London, average of 1699, 1700 and 1701; (iii) England, average of 1699, 1700 and 1701

	Total			Area I			Area II			Area III			Area IV			Area V			Area VI		
IMPORTS	(i)	(ii)	(iii)	(i)	(ii)	(iii)	(i)	(ii)	(iii)	(i)	(ii)	(iii)	(i)	(ii)	(iii)	(i)	(ii)	(iii)	(i)	(ii)	(iii)
Linens	582	755	903	570	678	798	6	45	48	—	—	—	6	32	57	—	—	—	—	—	—
Calicoes	182	367	367	—	—	—	—	—	—	—	—	—	—	—	—	—	—	—	182	367	367
Silks, etc.	215	208	208	81	18	18	—	—	—	105	83	83	—	—	—	—	—	—	29	107	107
Thread	141	74	79	141	74	79	—	—	—	—	—	—	—	—	—	—	—	—	—	—	—
Metal manufactures	73	55	72	70	47	63	3	8	9	—	—	—	—	—	—	—	—	—	—	—	—
Misc. manufactures	99	158	215	74	47	57	4	2	2	17	26	28	—	5	50	—	—	—	4	78	78
Total manufactures	1,292	1,617	1,844	936	864	1,015	13	55	59	122	109	111	6	37	107	—	—	—	215	552	552
Wine and brandy	144	467	546	64	41	48	—	—	—	80	426	496	—	—	—	—	—	—	—	—	—
Sugar and molasses	292	526	630	—	—	—	—	—	—	36	—	—	—	—	—	256	526	630	—	—	—
Tobacco	70	161	249	—	—	—	—	—	—	1	—	—	—	—	—	69	161	249	—	—	—
Fruit	196	135	174	3	6	9	—	—	—	193	129	165	—	—	—	—	—	—	—	—	—
Pepper	80	103	103	—	—	—	—	—	—	—	—	—	—	—	—	—	—	—	80	103	103
Misc. foodstuffs	163	191	267	74	40	51	4	8	9	31	76	86	6	—	44	22	36	46	26	31	31
Total foods	945	1,583	1,969	141	87	108	4	8	9	341	631	747	6	—	46	347	723	925	106	134	134
Silk, raw and thrown	263	344	346	—	1	1	—	—	—	262	301	302	—	—	—	—	—	1	1	42	42
Flax and hemp	86	116	194	26	3	8	56	112	185	4	1	1	—	—	—	—	—	—	—	—	—
Wool	29	67	200	2	—	—	1	2	2	26	62	73	3	1	122	—	—	—	—	—	—
Textile yarns	83	169	232	17	124	141	—	3	3	55	37	37	—	—	47	—	—	—	8	3	3
Dyes	146	203	226	36	34	41	—	—	—	91	90	92	—	—	—	3	71	85	16	4	4
Iron and steel	67	118	182	19	3	8	42	103	149	6	12	24	—	—	1	—	—	—	—	8	8
Timber	106	96	138	6	19	26	97	64	96	—	1	1	3	—	1	—	12	14	—	—	—
Oil	151	105	141	20	1	1	—	4	4	131	94	117	—	—	—	—	6	19	—	—	—
Tallow	1	10	85	—	—	—	—	1	1	—	—	—	1	9	84	—	—	—	—	—	—
Misc. materials	326	239	292	78	59	69	59	62	75	47	46	50	8	8	22	71	51	63	63	13	13
Total raw materials	1,258	1,467	2,036	204	244	295	255	351	515	622	644	697	15	18	277	74	140	182	88	70	70
TOTAL IMPORTS	3,495	4,667	5,849	1,281	1,195	1,418	272	414	583	1,085	1,384	1,555	27	55	430	421	863	1,107	409	756	756

Woollens	1,512	2,013	3,045	480	553	1,354	83	115	190	854	1,109	1,201	6	5	26	70	142	185	19	89	89
Silks	51	60	80	12	12	14	1	1	1	28	10	10	4	4	19	7	33	36	—	10	10
Metalwares	44	88	114	8	8	9	2	3	3	3	7	7	3	2	12	29	58	73	—	12	12
Misc. manufactures	127	272	344	36	47	58	—	7	8	33	48	56	6	12	29	47	146	181	3	—	—
Total manufactures	1,734	2,433	3,583	536	620	1,435	86	126	202	918	1,174	1,274	19	23	86	153	379	475	22	111	111
Grain	1	59	147	—	34	105	—	1	9	1	17	23	—	—	2	—	7	8	—	—	—
Fish	—	4	190	—	—	92	—	—	2	—	4	80	—	7	7	—	—	9	—	—	—
Misc. foods	61	75	151	43	11	35	1	11	18	4	22	25	6	4	33	7	18	38	—	2	2
Total foods	62	138	488	43	45	232	1	12	29	5	43	128	6	11	42	7	25	55	—	2	2
Lead	165	59	128	132	21	70	—	1	9	27	28	35	1	—	4	1	1	2	4	8	8
Tin	18	72	97	5	29	46	—	10	10	10	29	35	—	4	6	—	—	—	3	1	1
Misc. materials	60	71	137	30	48	76	2	2	5	14	10	12	11	5	36	2	5	7	1	—	—
Total raw materials	243	202	362	167	98	192	2	13	24	51	67	82	12	9	46	3	6	9	8	9	9
TOTAL EXPORTS	2,039	2,773	4,433	746	763	1,859	89	151	255	974	1,284	1,484	37	43	174	163	410	539	30	122	122
RE-EXPORTS																					
Linens	142	182	—	—	3	3	—	—	—	—	12	13	—	1	9	—	126	157	—	—	—
Calicoes	326	340	—	—	239	239	—	2	2	—	36	36	—	5	18	—	44	45	—	—	—
Silks	138	150	—	—	116	116	—	1	1	—	5	5	—	2	14	—	14	14	—	—	—
Misc. manufactures	52	74	—	—	19	21	—	—	—	—	3	10	—	1	4	—	26	36	—	3	3
Total manufactures	658	746	—	—	377	379	—	3	3	—	56	64	—	9	45	—	210	252	—	3	3
Tobacco	269	421	—	—	184	232	—	50	56	—	24	41	—	10	91	—	—	—	—	—	—
Sugar	262	287	—	—	248	255	—	6	6	—	5	5	—	3	21	—	—	—	—	—	—
Pepper	93	93	—	—	29	29	—	—	—	—	63	63	—	—	—	—	1	1	—	—	—
Misc. foods	115	140	—	—	68	68	—	5	6	—	9	12	—	6	13	—	19	33	—	9	9
Total foods	739	941	—	—	529	584	—	61	68	—	101	121	—	19	125	—	20	34	—	9	9
Dyes	79	85	—	—	54	57	—	4	4	—	15	16	—	6	8	—	—	—	—	—	—
Silk, raw and thrown	56	63	—	—	51	51	—	—	—	—	4	4	—	1	8	—	—	—	—	—	—
Misc. materials	145	151	—	—	90	92	—	5	5	—	19	19	—	5	7	—	24	26	—	2	2
Total raw materials	280	299	—	—	195	200	—	9	9	—	38	39	—	12	23	—	24	26	—	2	2
TOTAL RE-EXPORTS	1,677	1,986	—	—	1,101	1,163	—	73	80	—	195	224	—	40	193	—	254	312	—	14	14
TOTAL OF EXPORTS AND RE-EXPORTS	4,450	6,419	—	—	1,864	3,022	—	224	335	—	1,479	1,708	—	83	367	—	664	851	—	136	136

III   The South – Spain and Portugal and their islands, the Mediterranean.
IV   British Islands – Scotland, Ireland, Channel Isles.
V   Plantations – North America and West Indies.
VI   East India.

Division into commodity groups is necessarily arbitrary at times – especially in the case of semi-manufactured goods, such as textile yarns, steel and sawn timber, which are treated as raw materials.

Notes to the tables. Figures in £000

IMPORTS

Calicoes: includes all cottons without silk admixture.

Miscellaneous manufactures, 1699–1701: includes diamonds £60 (from India); paper £32.

Fruit, 1699–1701: includes raisins £104 (mainly Spanish); currants £47 (Turkey).

Miscellaneous foodstuffs, 1699–1701: includes cattle £42 (Scotland); drugs £53 (mostly Mediterranean and India); tea and coffee £35 (tea from India, coffee mainly West Indies).

Textile yarns, 1699–1701: includes linen yarn £175 (£141 Germany, £31 Ireland); mohair yarn £32 (Turkey).

Dyes, 1699–1701: includes cochineal £67 (Spain); madder £37 (Holland); logwood £33 (West Indies).

Oil: includes train oil from North America.

Miscellaneous raw materials, 1699–1701; includes skins £57; cotton £44; potash £40; pitch and tar £27.

EXPORTS

Miscellaneous manufactures, 1699–1701: includes leather and leatherware £87; hats £45.

Grain, average of 1699–1701 is made up as follows: 1699, £1; 1700, £188; 1701, £251.

Miscellaneous foodstuffs, 1699–1701: includes sugar £32; butter £21.

Miscellaneous raw materials, 1699–1701: includes skins £24.

RE-EXPORTS

Miscellaneous foodstuffs, 1699–1701: includes drugs £48.
Miscellaneous raw materials, 1699–1701: includes iron £24.

3 English Foreign Trade, 1700–1774[1]

RALPH DAVIS

[This article was first published in *The Economic History Review*, 2nd series, Vol. XV (1962).]

Eighteenth-century Englishmen were less troubled about the mercantile future of their country than their forefathers had been. The doubt which had nagged for so many decades at men's minds, whether England could successfully meet Dutch competition, faded unperceived during the long wars between 1689 and 1713 in which the rivals fought side by side. The newer commercial threat from the France of Louis XIV appeared less menacing after the military defeat of the French and the accessions made to England's colonial territories. As in every age, there were propagators of gloom and prophets of catastrophe; but the general atmosphere was one of optimism. Yet widespread optimism was little better founded than the pessimism it replaced. The bounding growth that had characterized English overseas trade before these wars – at the very time when fears of Dutch competition were most intense – was not resumed when the wars were over; though the return of peace saw a quick recovery of the wartime drop in trade, there succeeded a long period in which development was painfully slow. Although overseas trade did eventually break through into another spell of headlong expansion, the eighteenth century was by no means the long success story for English merchants that its predecessor had been. It was a century of realignment of trade – geographically and in terms of commodities – and not until towards mid-century could the swelling tide be seen unmistakably rolling in again.

This study of English trade up to the time when American

[1] I am grateful to Professor A. H. John for valuable criticisms. A version of this paper was read to Professor Habakkuk's seminar in Oxford and to Professor John's seminar in London in December 1961, and its present form shows, I hope, the benefit of the discussion and criticism it met on those occasions.

Independence and Industrial Revolution fundamentally changed
the conditions in which it was carried on, is based in the main on
the trade figures for 1699–1701, 1722–4, 1752–4 and 1772–4,
which are summarized in the Appendix.[1] It attempts to show
which were the lagging and which the dynamic elements in
English trade, and to suggest their relation to general economic
development.

No year is 'normal', but these groups of three, with slightly
irregular intervals, avoid war and major convulsions and contain reasonably mixed conditions. 1699–1701 was a period of
growth in renewed peace towards good trade, though not of
high boom. 1722–4 saw emergence into fair prosperity from the
slump which following the South Sea Bubble. 1752–4 was
marked by a turn down towards depression from a beginning in
high prosperity. 1772–4 spans a very brief if intense commercial
crisis, but compensates for this by including good years on either
side. None of these periods shows unrelieved depression or
unclouded prosperity;[2] their comparison should give a fair illustration of the long-term development of trade, but it is not suggested that the intervening years saw uninterrupted and even
processes of change.

[1] These are derived from the Inspector-General's returns in the PRO (Customs
3). Some doubt has been thrown by historians on the value of these statistics, but
I do not believe the revision of them, if it were possible, would very seriously
alter the general picture shown here. Much error in important detail is evident,
and some of the necessary modifications are indicated below; but the most serious
(and most carefully studied) errors in the statistics arise from the sharp advance
in the general price level which affects only the last decade or so of the century.
Professor T. S. Ashton has a lucid and temperate discussion of their use and
weaknesses in his introduction to E. B. Schumpeter, *English overseas trade statistics,
1697–1808* (Oxford, 1960), pp. 1–9.

This paper deals only with *English* trade. Despite the Union with Scotland in
1707, the customs records of Scotland were kept separately, and Scottish statistics are available regularly and in orderly form only from 1755. At that time, they
show Scotland's trade as having about 5 per cent of the value of England's. Large
quantities of Scottish goods were sent to London for export, and appear, therefore, only in the English trade statistics.

In analysing the statistical records a number of arithmetical errors have been
discovered, and the figures here consequently differ from the Inspector-General's
totals and others derived from them. The most important of these errors are:
over-addition of London exports to Spain, 1752, by £100 000; under-addition of
London exports to Virginia and Maryland, 1773, by £100,000; under-addition of
London imports from Russia, 1773, by £161,000.

[2] T. S. Ashton, *Economic fluctuations in England, 1700–1800* (Oxford, 1959), pp.
140–60.

For many centuries England's export trade consisted almost entirely of wool or woollen manufactures, and as late as 1700 the latter made up the sole considerable export of England's own produce. Supplemented during the later seventeenth century by growing re-exports of colonial and Indian wares, the constantly increasing export of woollens had with their help paid for more imported manufactures (chiefly linens) from the industrial areas of Europe, for more wine, fruit, sugar and tobacco from southern Europe and the Americas, and for a rising volume of industrial raw materials.[1] The English sheep had for so long carried most of the burden of English trade expansion on its back that at the opening of the eighteenth century its continuing success in this role (when the return of peace should permit) was taken for granted as the essential basis of English prosperity.

Yet woollen exports had already lost their momentum of growth, and they did not recover it. This is the more surprising when we observe the general tendency for the price of wool to fall from the Restoration until far into the eighteenth century;[2] the great extension of production of cloth in such low-wage areas as Devonshire, Lancashire and Yorkshire;[3] and the exploitation, in the first two of these areas at least, of the extraordinarily cheap wool and spinning labour of Ireland. There were strong reasons, even in the absence of technical innovation, why many grades of English cloth should have been produced much more cheaply around 1720 or 1750 than half a century earlier. Nevertheless the European market, which took 92 per cent of the woollen goods exported in 1699–1701, showed almost complete stagnation. The rapid advance of export to Spain and Portugal, which did continue, was balanced by decline elsewhere so the total of woollens exported to Europe remained almost unchanged (apart from short-term fluctuation) until 1750, and the brief burst of increased activity in the fifties was followed by decline. The growing contribution of other manufactured exports to the total English trade with Europe was on too small a

[1] R. Davis, 'English foreign trade, 1660–1700', above, pp. 78–98

[2] See J. R. McCulloch (ed.), *Early tracts on commerce* (1856), p. 321; *JHC*, 1737–42, p. 357; *A short view of the rise, progress and establishment of the woollen manufacture* (1753).

[3] This intense industrial activity ultimately contributed to rises in wages both in Devonshire and in the north of England; but for some decades these areas had advantages over, for example, East Anglia.

scale to compensate for this failure of the one great traditional product.

Industry was being developed and diversified rapidly not only in England but also through much of western and central Europe, to such a degree that for a time the effect was to discourage rather than stimulate mutual trade in manufactures. Industrial self-sufficiency was increasing; and neither England nor continental states had much chance of selling the products of new or small industries, without special cost advantages, across national frontiers and against the barriers of transport costs, customs duties and the national ties of merchants. At the same time, national self-sufficiency was checking international trade even in those manufactured textiles, produced by large highly-specialized industries, which had long circulated throughout Europe.

English woollen merchants, baffled by the effects of this general tendency towards self-sufficiency, might have seen illustrations of it on their own doorstep, in their own importing habits. The total English import of manufactures from Germany, Holland, Flanders and France fell from £1,015,000 to £471,000 per annum during the first three-quarters of the eighteenth century. Two groups of government measures contributed to bringing this about. The action taken by the ministers of Louis XIV to build up French political and economic power had produced a series of English responses in the mercantile field; prohibition of trade with France between 1678 and 1685 and again in wartime after 1689, and the imposition in 1693 and 1696 of special tariffs on French goods, virtually prohibitive so far as manufactures were concerned, which remained effective until the signing of the Eden Treaty in 1786. A wide variety of manufactures had been imported from France, many of them fine goods of which the coarser varieties were made in England. Quantities of them were still smuggled in; but behind the tariff barrier, with the aid of the technical skills of Huguenot refugees, industries were built up which went far towards replacing them.

Among manufactured imports, however, the most important category was that of coarse linens from Holland and Germany. Imports had grown fast in the seventeenth century, for England had no considerable industry to compete effectively or to clamour loudly for protection. In the new century the general heightening of tariff barriers in England was accompanied by steps which encouraged the bringing in of coarse linens from England's dependencies rather than from the continent. The import of linen wares from Ireland was aided by the removal of duties on them in 1697, while the Union of 1707 threw down all tariff barriers between England and Scotland. There were further measures to advance the Irish and Scottish linen industries; the abolition of the Irish export duty in 1705, the creation of a Board to encourage the growing of flax and the training of weavers and spinners in Scotland in 1727, and the provision in 1742 of a bounty on Scottish and Irish linen exported from England. With their natural advantages of cheap labour and lands suited to flax cultivation, their preference over continental goods in the English market, and presently the export bounty, the Irish and Scottish linen industries grew with mounting speed in the second and third quarters of the century;[1] by 1774 most of the linen used in England and her colonies came from within the British Islands and the import from Germany and Holland had been cut in half.[2]

Meanwhile continental development towards self-sufficiency nibbled in the same way at the market abroad for English woollens. France, of course, had built up her woollen industry and closed her gates to imports in the seventeenth century, and was becoming a serious competitor in south European markets. The growth of the German industry threatened many of the oldest English markets in central Europe, and it began to receive some measure of protection from the Imperial government.[3] English merchants engaged in the Hamburg trade never tired of explaining how the reduction of English linen imports caused a corresponding decline in woollen exports.[4] Sweden put a heavy duty

[1] Excellent accounts of these industries are C. Gill, *The rise of the Irish linen industry* (Oxford, 1925); H. Hamilton, *The industrial revolution in Scotland* (Oxford, 1932), ch. IV. There is no history of the English linen industry.

[2] A growing import of cheap Russian linen partly accounts for the decline of import through Hamburg or Amsterdam, but the total coming from continental sources was falling sharply by mid-century, and was already quite outstripped by Scottish and Irish supply.

[3] See the long report on the German industry and the prospects for Anglo-German trade (1716) in the papers of the Board of Trade in the PRO (CO 388–18–68).

[4] Petitions in *JHC, 1702–04*, p. 498; *1711–14*, p. 426; *1718–22*, p. 295; *1737–41* p. 121; *1741–45*, pp. 631, 817.

on imported woollens to protect her infant industry, and thereby practically ended their import from England. Even Spain and Portugal which, against the general European trend, took increasing quantities of English woollens throughout the first half of the century, began to foster their own industries in the 1750s and 1760s, and their demand for English manufactures at last slackened and fell away.[1]

English commercial relations with Europe were in fact becoming less and less concerned with its industrialized northwestern corner and increasingly with the Baltic and Mediterranean lands; a geographical shift associated with a long-term change in the character of English demands – not only with the declining demand for manufactured goods, but even more with the rising English need for raw materials for her growing industries. With every decade the imports of flax and hemp, textile yarns, iron, dyestuffs, oil, silk, timber and cotton showed a rise; and most of these things came from the Baltic or Scandinavian coasts or from the shores of the Mediterranean.[2]

IMPORTS FROM EUROPE (EXCLUDING IRELAND) (£000)

	1699–1701	*1722–4*	*1752–4*	*1772–4*
Manufactures:				
linens	846	922	853	594
other	339	220	100	101
Foodstuffs	864	843	659	1,141
Raw materials	1,507	1,748	2,200	2,834

In the seventeenth century there had been an approximate balance between the three classes of imports – manufactures, foodstuffs and raw materials – but this was now being tipped sharply, in European trade, towards the last of these.[3]

If English manufactures failed to expand their European market significantly, why did they need this fast-growing supply of raw materials? In part it was to replace some imported goods

[1] R. Herr, *The eighteenth century revolution in Spain* (Princeton, 1958), pp. 123–44; A. Christelow, 'The economic background of the Anglo-Spanish war of 1762', *Journal of Modern History*, XVIII (1946), 22–36; V. M. Shillington and A. B. W. Chapman, *The commercial relations of England and Portugal* (London, 1907), pp. 260–4, 277–9.

[2] In these analyses trade with Turkey is included as 'European'. It was a branch of the Mediterranean trade, altogether distinct from the other Asian trade carried on, via the Cape of Good Hope, by the East India Company.

[3] The growth of smuggling modifies the picture presented by these statistics, since it was chiefly concerned with wine, brandy and fine manufactured goods.

by their counterparts made at home. Moreover, the demand for manufactured goods was growing as the English became more prosperous or, more accurately, had an increasing surplus of money to spend during a half-century in which basic foodstuffs were becoming cheaper.[1] Expanding fleets, naval and mercantile, required great quantities of imported 'naval stores'. But to a significant degree English industrial growth now served an entirely new field of overseas trade – the demand for manufactures from the fast-multiplying population of the Americas.

The spreading of industry on the continent of Europe had set limits to the expansion of English cloth markets there. No such limits yet existed to the demand for all kinds of English goods on the other side of the Atlantic. In the northern colonies land was endless and men were few; the wage-earner could command very high payment, and only those craftsmen whose work had to be carried out on the spot were employed in large numbers. English artisans were reluctant to go to the slave islands of the Caribbean, and the essential workmen were attracted only in small numbers and by high wages. Until almost the end of our period the colonies had little industry of their own apart from some household production of coarse woollens and linens; and this is not because of repressive measures of the home government, but simply because colonial labour costs were far higher than those in England. Only in such a case as that of ship-building, where local needs were great and an abundance of cheap raw materials set off the high wages, was local industry able to exclude English products. The colonists had to import their requirements of manufactures; and they were accustomed by long habit, as they were compelled by the Navigation Acts, to deal with English merchants and to take their imported requirements from England, Nearly all these goods were made in England, Scotland or Ireland; German and Dutch linens were the only important exceptions, and they were being replaced from British sources by mid-century, Moreover, colonial population, small as it was by comparison with that of European countries, was growing at a tremendous pace, from a few hundred thousand in 1700 to approach three millions in 1774, and wealth and income were evidently growing faster. The protected Anglo-

[1] A. H. John, 'Aspects of English economic growth in the first half of the eighteenth century', below, pp. 71–9.

Scottish market of some eight or nine million people in 1774 had acquired a very useful colonial supplement.

The principal dynamic element in English export trade during all the middle decades of the eighteenth century was, therefore, colonial trade. This is well known. More than this; colonial trade introduced to English industry the quite new possibility of exporting in great quantities manufactures other than woollen goods, to markets where there was no question of the exchange of manufactures for other manufactures. At last in these protected markets outlets were appearing for English metalwares, Scottish linens, and a host of other things, in quantities which by the eve of the American Revolution had come to rival the whole export of the woollen industry itself. Moreover, so rapidly was American expansion proceeding after mid-century that even woollens began to go to the colonies in a volume that usefully supplemented the declining European demand. The process of industrialization in England from the second quarter of the eighteenth century was to an important extent a response to colonial demands for nails, axes, firearms, buckets, coaches, clocks, saddles, handkerchiefs, buttons, cordage and a thousand other things; a variety of goods becoming so wide that the compilers of the Customs records tired of further extending their long schedules of commodities and lumped an increasing proportion of these exports under the heading of 'Goods, several sorts'.[1] I have taken it for granted that these were nearly all manufactures. In the iron and brass industries and all the metalworking crafts dependent on them, colonial demands made an important supplement to those of the growing home market, and must have played a considerable part in encouraging the new methods of organization, the new forms of division of labour and the improved techniques, through which the metal industries were to make a major contribution to industrial revolution in England. Other industries, smaller and

[1] For this reason the totals of particular kinds of trade in Schumpeter, *Overseas trade statistics*, cannot be used in this kind of analysis. Mrs Schumpeter listed and totalled the values of some of the more important commodities, but her selected commodities form a rapidly declining proportion of non-woollen exports. Thus of manufactured goods exported, other than woollens, she covers some two-thirds (in value) in 1699–1701, and some one-third of the much greater total of 1772–4. The table in John, 'English economic growth', below, p. 168, is therefore not comparable with the figures used in this paper.

with less familiar histories, may well have been similarly affected.

The colonial market was only one – though much the most important one – of a group in which English goods had special advantages of a character they could not secure in continental Europe. Ireland was very much a dependency of the British crown. Its trade with Europe, though substantial, was limited by the ban on the export of Irish woollen cloth; its colonial trade was restricted by the Navigation Acts; the combination of these measures with the strong personal and political connections with England ensured that Ireland looked to England for nearly all its imported manufactures. In the course of the eighteenth century this Irish connection became of very great importance. Ireland's recovery from the extreme depression into which it had been beaten by the military campaigns of 1689–92 was at first very slow, but towards mid-century a rapid economic expansion was under way – in which the export trade in linen goods and livestock products played a great part – and the Irish market began to absorb considerable imports from England.[1] Like the American colonies, Ireland was ready to take a wide variety of manufactured goods. The strength of the native woollen industry made it impossible to sell English woollens in any quantity until the new West Riding products made their impact in the 1750s; but metalwares, silks, hats and other goods went in great and fast-growing volume. A new view of Ireland, not as a rival but as an aid to English expansion, began to appear. 'If we consider (apart from prejudices and particular interests) how greatly we are already Gainers by the Trade and Industry of that Country, poor as it is, we shall perhaps . . . begin to think that the Wealth and Prosperity of Ireland is not only compatible with that of England, but highly conducive also to its Riches, Grandeur and Power'.[2] Further afield, West African demand for English goods grew rapidly in the 1740s, providing a useful stimulus to the cotton industry in particular; a demand ultimately derived, of course, from the colonial import of slaves for the plantations. In Asia, the English merchant settlements which had always paid out great quantities of silver for the goods which

[1] On the growth of Irish prosperity from about 1725 onward, see D. Macpherson, *Annals of commerce* (1806), III, 181, 289; A. Dobbs, *An essay on the trade and improvement of Ireland* (Dublin, 1729).

[2] *A collection of tracts concerning the present state of Ireland with respect to its riches, revenue, trade and manufacture* (1729), p. 25.

they bought for England now began to develop a demand for English manufactures. The growth of military establishments and the securing of a firm grip on Bengal and Madras, with the trend towards English political dominance and all that this meant in terms of local revenue, was accompanied by a big expansion of English exports of all kinds to India, reaching substantial proportions after 1748.

EXPORTS OF MANUFACTURES FROM ENGLAND (£000)

	1699–1701	*1722–4*	*1752–4*	*1772–4*
Woollen goods:				
Continental Europe	2,745	2,592	3,279	2,630
Ireland and Channel Islands	26	19	47	219
America and Africa	185	303	374	1,148
India and Far East	89	72	230	189
Other manufactures:				
Continental Europe	456	367	647	987
Ireland and Channel Islands	60	40	168	280
America and Africa	290	376	1,197*	2,535
India and Far East	22	15	408	501

The principal dynamic element in English trade expansion during the second half of the seventeenth century had been the re-export of colonial goods. This branch of trade continued to be of great importance in the new century, kept its place with a little over a third of the growing total of exports throughout the period, still providing an important element in overall growth though now quite overshadowed in the *pace* of its expansion by the miscellaneous manufactures. Indeed, the rate of growth of the re-export trade slowed markedly in the early part of the century and was never fully recovered.

One other branch of export trade must be briefly mentioned. Not only was England nearly self-sufficient in manufactures; for a long time all needs of basic foodstuffs were produced at home. The appearance of corn surpluses late in the seventeenth century led to a system of bounties to encourage their export,[1] and this export reached a peak in the years round 1750 when it contributed quite significantly to the total English export trade. The new growth of population which was then beginning, while providing the labour force for accelerated industrial expansion,

[1] See D. G. Barnes, *A history of the English corn laws* (London, 1930), chs. I and II.

quickly absorbed the food surpluses and turned England in two decades from a large corn exporter to a substantial importer – the sharpest, most sudden large change in England's trading situation in our period. Legislation was introduced to discourage export and facilitate the import of corn, while the barriers which had long before been erected against the import of Irish meat and dairy produce were dismantled.[1] Despite the apparent panic over food supplies in the 1760s, however, the deficit was for a long time only a marginal one, as the surplus had been.

The sketch of export trade more or less explains developments in imports as well. By mid-century, more variegated foodstuffs came from the colonies, more raw materials from Europe; the

SUMMARY TABLE OF ENGLISH FOREIGN TRADE
(PERCENTAGES OF TOTAL EXPORTS AND IMPORTS)

	Total		Europe*		Asia, Africa and America	
	1699–1701	*1772–4*	*1699–1701*	*1772–4*	*1699–1701*	*1772–4*
Exports						
Woollen mfrs.	47·5	26·7	43·2	18·2	4·3	8·5
Other mfrs.	8·4	27·4	3·5	6·2	4·8	21·2
Foodstuffs	7·6	3·7	6·7	2·7	·9	1·0
Raw materials	5·6	5·1	5·3	4·7	·3	·4
Total exports	69·1	62·9	58·7	31·8	10·3	31·1
Re-exports	30·9	37·1	25·9	30·5	5·0	6·6
Total of exports and re-exports	100·0	100·0	84·6	62·3	15·3	37·7
Imports						
Manufactures	31·7	16·9	22·1	10·7	9·5	6·2
Foodstuffs	33·6	50·9	15·5	12·0	18·1	38·9
Raw materials	34·7	32·2	30·5	24·7	4·3	7·5
Total imports	100·0	100·0	68·1	47·4	31·9	52·6

* In this table, Ireland and Turkey are both included in 'Europe'.

growing surplus of colonial foodstuffs over English needs went to Europe to pay for the rising purchases of raw materials, while America itself – to complete the circle of trade – was satisfied for her increasing supplies by receiving in exchange a deepening and extending stream of English manufactures.

[1] Barnes, *Corn laws*, pp. 31–45.

The general pattern of English export trade between 1700 and 1774 has been indicated. To understand its meaning, however, we must briefly adopt a wider perspective. The export trade had been growing for centuries, but its development had not been smooth. It had gone forward in a series of spurts, each touched off by some new factor which operated violently for a time and then lost its initial force. The first of these which is relevant to this discussion is the change in the nature of woollen cloth exports which had its origin late in the sixteenth century. The political troubles which at that time caused havoc in the cloth-finishing industries of Brabant, and destroyed Antwerp's international trading position, drove English merchants to seek a new centre to replace Antwerp as their chief market, and to sell cloth directly to many customers formerly supplied through Antwerp. During much the same period, Spanish and Mediterranean markets began to present new openings to English cloth, not merely because of Antwerp's troubles but also by reason of the increasing costs of Italian and Spanish production. So the English woollen industry expanded the value of its exports in two ways. It developed the dyeing and finishing branches in association with its traditional products,[1] so that the proportion exported in a finished and dyed state went up, in the course of the seventeenth century, from about one-third to almost 100 per cent.[2] The slowly declining number of these cloths of traditional type exported during the century therefore provided, until near its end, an increasing value in export trade.[3] Secondly, it created alongside the old industry a new one, chiefly engaged in the making of worsteds of various kinds, which found that its products could be sold in great and rapidly growing quantities in Spain and Portugal, and to a lesser extent in Italy.[4] With the older branch of the industry slowly increasing the value of its export, and a new branch burgeoning so vigorously that it soon out-

[1] The export to Antwerp had been principally of undyed, unfinished cloths, which were dyed and dressed there.

[2] The figures for the first decade of the seventeenth century can be found in A. Friis, *Alderman Cockayne's project and the cloth trade* (Copenhagen, 1927), pp. 61–8.

[3] The value added to a cloth by dyeing and dressing varied, according to the dye used, between about 30 and 100 per cent.

[4] For general discussion of these developments see F. J. Fisher, 'London's export trade in the early seventeenth century', above, pp. 64–77; R. Davis, 'England and the Mediterranean, 1570–1670', *Essays in the economic and social history of Tudor and Stuart England*, ed. F. J. Fisher (Cambridge, 1961).

rivalled the old, cloth exports as a whole were rapidly expanding during most of the seventeenth century. But difficulties began to appear. In the third quarter of the century, the export of the old types of cloth reached a position in which nearly all were going out dyed and finished, and as their numbers were slowly decreasing their total value began to fall well before the end of the century. Woollen industries were developing on the continent, and in some cases secured tariff protection against English competition.[1] A tendency was appearing for replacement of even the lightest woollens by cottons, linens and silks; above all, the use of Indian textiles in Europe leaped forward at an astonishing pace from the 1670s. Though their cheapness secured these Indian fabrics new customers who would not have bought the dearer woollens in the same quantity, it is certain that they made some inroads on the demand for woollen fabrics at home and abroad. In 1708 Defoe could write – no doubt with his customary exaggeration: 'Almost everything that used to be wool or silk, relating either to the dress of the women or the furniture of our houses, was supplied by the Indian trade'.[2] These various influences were combining, towards the end of the seventeenth century, not indeed to reduce woollen exports, but to give a check to their constant expansion. And the momentum once lost could not be recovered; the woollen export neither advanced nor retreated – it hung fire.

The export trade as a whole was not, however, destined to languish in these last decades of the seventeenth century. Its total was carried forward on the crest of another wave, this time of the re-exports of colonial and Indian goods. Before the Civil War, re-exports were trivial; by the 1760s they were making a notable addition to English native exports; by the end of the century they added to that total no less than 50 per cent. In this new spurt forward, cheapness was the factor that made possible the growth of trade. Tobacco and sugar produced under plantation conditions could be sold at prices that brought them within the reach of most of Europe's population, and calicoes were cheap because of the low earnings of their Indian producers. The explosive initial rate of expansion could not have been continued

[1] See pp. 103–4 and C. Wilson, 'Cloth production and international competition in the seventeenth century', *Economic History Review*, 2nd series, XIII (1960), 209–21.

[2] Defoe's *Review*, 3 January 1713.

indefinitely; but in fact the trade in each of the three chief re-export commodities met special difficulties in the early eighteenth century. First, sugar. The French development of the island of Hispaniola (present-day San Domingo), which they acquired from Spain in 1697, faced the small British West Indian islands and their overcropped soils with competition at prices they could not meet outside the protected British market. Sugar re-exports to continental Europe fell away to negligible proportions in less than two decades after the Peace of Utrecht; only the Irish market remained. Tobacco re-export continued to grow fast, but for some decades after 1707 its increase was channelled through Glasgow, and until this port had fully worked up the trading possibilities which the Act of Union gave it, the *English* tobacco trade could make little progress. The re-export of Indian textiles was checked by the prohibitions and discriminations against them set up by nearly every European government in the years round 1700, though the trade still expanded slowly. In the first quarter of the new century, therefore, the total of tobacco, sugar and calico re-exports, which had been growing so fast, remained virtually stable.[1]

Both the dynamic factors in seventeenth-century trade expansion – first the woollen export and then the new re-export – were therefore losing strength around 1700. The onset of war in 1689 brought a sharp check to all trade, but this merely crystallized at a particular point of time the ending of a phase. The long, rapid, exhilarating rise in English trade was at last steadying down, under a variety of influences. Two great waves of progress had nearly spent their force, and it was this fact, not merely the long wars of 1689–1713, that slowed the overall expansion of trade for nearly half a century. There had to be a pause, for the next wave had not yet gathered its strength. Such buoyancy as remained in the export trade in the first half of the eighteenth century, indeed, came from returning prosperity in Spain and Portugal; in the interval before they, too, developed autarchic ambitions, their growing demand for English manufactures offset the decline in export to other parts of Europe. But it did no more; the products of English industry in its old form had very nearly reached the saturation point in their European markets.

[1] R. Davis, 'English foreign trade, 1660–1700', above, pp. 78–98.

The third leap forward, as we have seen, resulted from the expanding demand for manufactured goods of all kinds, coming from the growing colonial population. It was a most vigorous leap, which carried forward the total of exports very strongly right up to the Industrial Revolution. Even before 1700, though still in an embryonic stage, this trade had been developing fast; its growth accelerated in the late 1720s and 1730s, and was then halted by the onset of war. Indeed, the war of 1739–48 appeared to nip in the bud unmistakable signs that exports as a whole were beginning to gather way once more. Wars always imposed painful setbacks upon foreign trade, and this one was no exception, but there were significant differences in the way trade responded to such handicaps. During 1689–1713 the state of war concealed a weakening of England's foreign trading position that would have occurred anyway, war or no war. In 1739–48, on the other hand, the armed conflict was holding back trade that had great expansive potentiality, damming up demand that waited hungrily to be fed. The peace of 1748, therefore, found England ripe for an extraordinary increase in the volume of export trade. The major and continuing influence was the now violently accelerating growth in the export of miscellaneous manufactures to the colonies, Ireland and India, which had brought their total to very large proportions. It was reinforced by the growth to maturity of new re-export trades; in mid-century Carolina rice and China tea were being sent out from England in very large quantities, and they were soon to be reinforced by West Indian coffee. The re-export trade, which had languished for so long, grew very fast during the third quarter of the century. Significant additions to the total of exports were made, during the first years after the peace of 1748, by more temporary influences: the release of Spanish demand which had been pent up by nine years of war with England, and the export of surplus corn which reached its peak in the years round 1750. All these factors working together pushed English exports forward at a tremendous pace before the onset of new war in 1756.

Trade expanded slowly in the early part of the century because there was cessation or slowing of growth in some directions without the emergence of important counterbalancing forces elsewhere. In the third quarter of the century, however, decline in certain branches did not prevent a rapid expansion of total exports. The corn export ceased abruptly in this period; trade with the Iberian peninsula – the one branch of European woollen export which had always retained some vigour – turned downward as the ministers of Spain and Portugal strove to encourage and protect their home industries. Yet the continuing rise of colonial, Irish and Indian markets for manufactures, which now outstripped those of Europe, supported by renewed advance in re-export trade, were by now more than enough to outweigh these depressive effects.

It remains to draw attention to a doubt about the healthiness of the sharp rise in exports to America. The period of most rapid growth was the Seven Years War itself; it was most marked in relation to the colonies which were the principal bases of military operations. Clearly, it represented in some degree the private shipments by contractors of army stores,[1] the supply of goods to meet the demands made from the pay of officers and soldiers sent out from England, and the spending on English-made goods of local earnings from supply and service to the armies. War conditions may be set aside as exceptional; but it may be wondered how much of the enhanced export to America in the postwar years resulted from the demands of the garrisons which were maintained on a much larger scale than before the war in the colonies; garrisons whose pay and provisions were paid for in England, drew funds from the pocket of the English taxpayer, and so artificially replaced a home demand for goods by one which drew the goods across frontiers at which Customs officers stood guard, noting them all down and so turning them into International Trade. The buoyancy of Anglo-American trade after 1783 suggests we should not overstress the importance of this; but it cannot be ignored in discussion of the last years of colonial trade.[2]

The seventeenth-century Navigation Laws, which were not seriously modified before 1786, gave English merchants and

---

[1] Goods sent out by government departments themselves do not appear in the Customs records.

[2] The trade with India similarly expanded when the English military forces were increased in the 1740s, and no doubt this accounts for some of the rise in exports. But these forces were not, like the army in America, paid for by the English taxpayer.

shipowners an almost complete monopoly of trade with the colonies. The overall effect of these laws has been the subject of much discussion, but it can hardly be doubted that if the colonies had been free, from the beginning, to send their products direct to their ultimate markets in the cheapest ships available, a good deal of the trade would not in fact have been carried on with English ports, nor in English ships. English goods secured their fast-growing sales in colonies which were politically directed from England in ways intended to serve English (and to some extent colonial) as opposed to foreign interests. The colonies had to send their most considerable export staples to England, whatever the ultimate destination; when a new colonial commodity was found to be acquiring a useful European market, it was promptly added to the list of these 'enumerated commodities'. The colonies took their requirements from England or from each other, in the first place, because the laws compelled them to earn pounds sterling rather than pieces of eight, rix dollars, livres or ducats from the sale of their own goods; and because the Navigation Acts required that goods be brought to them only from English ports. They bought British rather than continental goods in the early decades of colonization because (except in the case of linens) continental goods could not bear the price of re-shipment plus the small part of English customs duties that was not refunded on re-export. The restrictions imposed by law were vitally important to England in the early decades of colonial development; they excluded, as they were designed to exclude, the exercise of Dutch commercial, financial and maritime skills which were well fitted to engross a large part of transatlantic trade. In time, changing conditions reduced the practical importance of the Navigation Laws, for they moulded the infant colonial trade so effectively that it developed the required character, and eventually matured in a form which was largely independent of the legal strait-jacket. Most of the colonial population, and nearly all the well-to-do of the merchant and planter and professional classes, were of British origin. The merchant houses, if they were not simply agencies of Liverpool and Glasgow firms, were English or Scots. Generation after generation the population of the colonies had become accustomed to take manufactures from British sources and sell through British factors. If a demand arose in Boston or Savannah or Kingston for new commodities – military buttons or musical boxes – the traders turned first to England to meet it. The force of habit was, by the mid-eighteenth century, even stronger than the force of law in maintaining the Anglo-American commercial connection. Moreover, English industry which colonial demand had helped to foster had evolved, in many of its branches, new organization with greater efficiency and more advanced techniques, so that by 1774 some English manufactures probably had real advantages in cost over their European rivals. Finally, as wealth grew in England, her own market became particularly important to some colonial producers; the West Indian islands, above all, gained far more from the English tariff preferences for their sugar than they lost by being prevented from selling it directly in the savagely competitive markets of Hamburg or Amsterdam.

Nevertheless, right down to the American Revolution the Navigation Acts did impose some distortion on the pattern of trade. This is clearly illustrated by the records of the tobacco trade. In the years 1771–5 inclusive, England imported 278 million lbs of tobacco from America, and re-exported 230 million. In the years 1786–90 inclusive, an independent United States sent only 203 million lbs to England, of which 110 million lbs were re-exported.[1] Released by war from the bonds of the Navigation Acts, Americans at once began a large direct tobacco trade with their continental customers. On the other hand, the large tobacco trade which was still – in spite of the temper of the times – carried on through English intermediaries, is eloquent of the extent of America's continuing dependence on old ways.

It was only in the very long run that the United States broke completely free from this economic dependence; but from 1783 Americans did trade directly with continental Europe, on an increasing scale. If they had found there manufactures which out-classed England's in quality or price, it is unlikely that old habits would have ruled for long; but in fact English manufactures were, at this very point in time, beginning to acquire a genuine superiority. In 1783, however, this was not clearly apparent as it is now, and a serious loss of American trade appeared to face

[1] Schumpeter, *Overseas trade statistics*, p. 60, table XVIII.

English industry. The West Indies, Canada, a growing Indian dominion and Ireland remained in the English sphere. But the health of the West Indian economy was likely to be undermined by the ending of their special relation with the former northern colonies, while Ireland had already seized the opportunity of the American war to force great commercial concessions from the English government, and was in a state of ferment which seemed likely to lead to the breaking of this connection too.[1] The prospects for trade based on privilege and non-economic influences were becoming gloomy indeed during the last quarter of the eighteenth century.

All this time, at England's doorstep there lived a population of 200,000,000 Europeans (as compared with 3,000,000 Americans across the Atlantic). They were England's traditional customers, and until recently her only ones. Yet it was only the old woollen industry that seriously carried on – as it had always done – the 'hard sell' on the continent; the newer industries cut their teeth on easier, privileged markets, mostly far away. The privileges could not be held for ever. They did not need to be. By the time privilege was threatened, towards the end of the century, England's cotton and metal industries had transformed themselves out of all recognition; they were poised ready to invade not only the European but all other markets with their irresistible bundles of products of the Industrial Revolution. Our period, which had opened full of false hopes for the future of trades already doomed to stagnation, closed with equally unreasonable fears at the loss of artificial aids which English commerce had already outgrown.

Note to the tables

The areas are constituted as follows:

North-west Europe: Germany, Holland, Flanders, France.
Northern Europe: Norway, Denmark, Iceland, Greenland and
     the Baltic.

[1] Ireland attempted in 1780 to use the very weapon with which the American colonies had struck their first serious blow – the non-importation of English manufactures. See D. B. Horn, (ed.), *English historical documents, 1714–83* (London, 1957), p. 694.

Southern Europe: Spain and Portugal and their islands, the
    Mediterranean including Turkey and North Africa.
British Islands: Ireland, Channel Islands.
America: North America, British and foreign West Indies and
    Spanish America, West Africa.
East India: all lands bordering the Indian and Pacific Oceans.

4 Trends in Eighteenth-Century Smuggling[1]

W. A. COLE

[This article was first published in *The Economic History Review*, 2nd series, Vol. X (1958).]

One of the most serious, and certainly the most baffling, problems which confronts the student of eighteenth-century trade statistics is that of smuggling. It is well known that high tariffs and the complexity of their administration provided a constant stimulus to all kinds of evasion – fraudulent entries at the customs and the relanding of goods entered for re-export as well as direct import smuggling – until the incentive was at length removed by the triumph of free trade in the nineteenth century. But it has generally been held that although smuggling was certainly widespread, the problem of its precise extent, or even its probable order of magnitude, defies solution. If this view is accepted, it is difficult to escape the conclusion that, for the purpose of measuring the level and trends of eighteenth-century foreign trade, the official statistics – at any rate of imports and re-exports[2] – are virtually useless.[3] In this paper, therefore, I propose to try to make an estimate of the quantitative importance of smuggling which will help us to assess the possible margin of error involved in the use of the official statistics. Such an estimate is bound to be speculative and cannot be exact. But at

[1] This is the first of two articles on the growth of British foreign trade in the eighteenth century which have been prepared at the University of Cambridge Department of Applied Economics in connexion with an inquiry into the Economic Growth of the United Kingdom sponsored by the Committee on Economic Growth of the Social Science Research Council of the United States.

[2] Manufactured goods were exempt from duty for most of the century, so the figures for exports are not much affected by smuggling, although they are open to criticism on other grounds and the illegal export of raw wool continued until the outbreak of war with France in 1793. See G. N. Clark, *Guide to English commercial statistics, 1696–1782* (London, 1938), pp. 15–16, 34–5; W. D. Cooper, 'Smuggling in Sussex', *Sussex Archaeological Collections*, x (1858), 91.

[3] Cf. G. D. Ramsay, 'The smugglers' trade: a neglected aspect of English commercial development', *Transactions of the Royal Historical Society*, 5th series, II 1952), 157 n.

E

least it should make possible an advance on the dubious practice of using the official figures as if the acknowledged deficiencies in the series did not exist.

I

At this stage, we cannot investigate in detail all branches of the illicit trade. Instead, we shall deal first with the traffic in one commodity, tea, and then consider what light the fluctuations in tea smuggling cast on the history of smuggling as a whole. The high value of tea in proportion to its bulk, coupled with a rate of duty which often doubled the legal price, made this particular traffic exceptionally profitable; and for a large part of the eighteenth century, tea was the one of the staple goods of the 'free trader'.[1] In March 1745-6, this clandestine trade was the subject of a special report by a Parliamentary Committee, and the question was again reviewed in the First Report of the Committee on Illicit Practices in December 1783.[2] On both occasions the committees considered estimates of the probable extent of the traffic in tea, and it is these which will form the starting point of our inquiry.

The best known of these estimates is the one supplied on the latter occasion by the deputy accountant of the East India Company. The accountant reckoned that from 1773-82 the annual exports of tea from China to Europe had averaged over 13 million lbs, and since 'The best information procurable, estimates the Annual Consumption of Tea by Foreigners in Europe' at under $5\frac{1}{2}$ million lbs, he argued that at least $7\frac{1}{2}$ million lbs must have been smuggled into Great Britain and her dependencies each year. This guess was supported by another, and supposedly independent estimate made by the Commissioners of Excise: on the basis of returns from the officers at the outports of the number of ships engaged in smuggling, their size, and the number of

---

[1] Most of the smuggled tea was imported direct by the smugglers from European markets, although some was landed from homeward-bound East India ships with the collusion of the Company's officers. It is also probable that when drawbacks were allowed on tea, a considerable part of the tea entered for re-export was illegally relanded. See W. Milburn, *Oriental commerce* (1813), II, 536-7; 'First Report from the Committee appointed to enquire into the Illicit Practices used in Defrauding the Revenue', 24 December 1783, H of C Reports, XI (1782-99), 230.

[2] *JHC*, XXV (1745-50), 101-10; *H of C Reports*, XI, 228-62.

journeys they made each year they, too, reckoned that about seven million lbs of tea was smuggled into the country each year.[1] Another contemporary estimate, however, drawn up under the direction of William Pitt from sources similar to, if not identical with, those used by the Excise Commissioners, advanced the much more modest figure of three million lbs per annum.[2] Unfortunately, this estimate is undated, but it is clear from internal evidence that it relates to a period of three years after 1773, and the association with Pitt suggests that it was drawn up at about the same time as the Commissioners' return. It is difficult to see, therefore, how the three estimates could be reconciled, and one wonders whether the political influence of the East India Company helped to determine which figures finally appeared in the report of the Commons' Committee.

But whatever disagreements may have existed about the precise extent of smuggling, all parties were agreed that the problem was serious and could not be dealt with by repressive measures alone. Accordingly, in September 1784, the cumbersome tea duties of £55 15s. 10d. per cent and 1s. 1⅘d. per lb were abolished and replaced by a window-tax and a duty on tea of 12½ per cent.[3] Following this reform, the sales of tea by the East India Company at once doubled, and soon trebled, while the imports of tea by the rival European companies showed a corresponding decline. By the 1790s continental imports had fallen to about five million lbs per annum – a figure remarkably close to the estimate of European consumption which the East India Company's accountant had made ten years before.[4] At first sight, the increase in the English Company's sales seems no less significant: the accountant had reckoned that barely a third of the home demand had been met by these sales, and the threefold increase in legal consumption after the reduction of the duty apparently confirms his estimate.[5] But, as Professor Ashton points out, it should 'be remembered that the legal market for

[1] *H of C Reports*, XI, 231, 246–7.
[2] Printed in A. L. Cross, *Eighteenth century documents relating to the royal forests, the sheriffs and smuggling* (New York, 1928), pp. 237–41.
[3] 24 Geo. III, c. 38.
[4] D. Macpherson, *Annals of commerce* (1805), IV, 336–7.
[5] The accountant reckoned that apart from smuggled tea several million lbs of dyed leaves were fraudently sold as tea each year, making the total illicit sales over 12 million lbs, compared with the Company sales of under 5¾ millions. See Macpherson, *Annals*, IV, 49 n.

tea was controlled on the side of supply, and that the East India Company had a case to establish'.[1] Moreover, it is necessary to take into account the effect on prices of a drastic reduction of duty and the ending of a disastrous war. Clearly, therefore, before a convincing inference about smuggling can be drawn from the figures of legal consumption, we need to know much more about the character of consumer demand.

A similar reservation applies to the earlier estimates of smuggling given in the report of the Parliamentary Committee of 1745-6. On that occasion, the committee received evidence from excise officers, tea traders and ex-smugglers – some of whom claimed to know the quantity of tea being shipped to England from continental ports – and here again the published account suggests fairly general agreement about the probable extent of the illicit traffic. A few months before the presentation of the report, at midsummer, 1745, the excise duty on tea of four shillings per lb had been replaced by duties of one shilling per lb and 25 per cent *ad valorem*.[2] It was estimated that in the three years immediately preceding this reform, smuggling had reached a peak of three million lbs a year – or more than three times the legal sales – while in the months which followed illegal imports had fallen and now stood at about one million lbs per annum.[3] The only direct evidence advanced in favour of the view that there had been such a substantial reduction of smuggling was the fact that legal sales had greatly increased. But since it was apparently assumed that the total home demand could be regarded as fixed at about three or four million lbs a year, no attempt was made to consider the effect of price changes on the consumption of tea.

II

None of the estimates discussed can, therefore, be accepted without further enquiry, but the consideration of them does suggest a method by which they may be checked. For if we can trace the effect of price changes on the demand for legally imported tea

[1] T. S. Ashton, *An economic history of England: the 18th century* (Oxford, 1955), p. 165.

[2] 28 Geo. II, c. 26.

[3] Evidence of Abraham Walter, *JHC*, xxv, 104-5. Most other witnesses suggested figures of a similar magnitude.

we should be in a much better position to judge how far the increase in consumption after 1745 and again after 1784 may reasonably be attributed to a decline in smuggling, and how far it was simply due to changes in the price of tea. Moreover – and perhaps more important – such an analysis should give us some indication of the trends in the illicit traffic during the intervening period, which at present is statistically blank. Fortunately the necessary material for this enquiry is available for most of the eighteenth century. From 1706 onwards, figures have survived of the quantity and sale value of all tea sold by the East India Company each year,[1] and from 1740 we also have statistics of the quantities retained for home consumption and the average sale price of each kind of tea.[2] In addition, the excise accounts preserved in the Customs Library record the quantities delivered out of the warehouse for home consumption in each excise year ending at midsummer as far back as 1724–5; and after midsummer, 1745, they give the sale value of tea for home consumption and the amount of excise duty.[3]

From this information, we have constructed an index of the wholesale price of tea including duty[4] from 1724 to 1829, which is given below in an appendix. Since we are interested in the price of tea for home consumption the index was based mainly on the excise statistics.[5] But for the first twenty years, it was

[1] These are printed in R. Wissett, *A compendium of East India affairs* (1802), II (no pagination). See also, Milburn, *Oriental commerce*, II, 534; J. Macgregor, *Commercial statistics*, v (1850), 58. In Macgregor's table, the figures of sales are incorrectly described as the quantity imported.

[2] *Parl. Papers*, 1845 (191), XLVI, 593–7.

[3] I am greatly indebted to Dr S. J. Prais for his assistance and advice in carrying out the analysis which follows.

[4] It has sometimes been assumed that no duty was included in the price of tea sold at the East India Company's sales. This is true after 1784, but before that date the customs duty was paid by the Company and was therefore included in the sale price. The excise duty, on the other hand, was paid by the buyer when the tea was cleared for home consumption and has to be added to the sale price to obtain the wholesale price inclusive of duty.

[5] The fuller information given in the excise statistics also makes it possible to calculate the price more accurately in years when the duty changed. Unfortunately, there are some gaps in the series. The data for the excise years 1785 and 1786 are incomplete as no excise duty was levied on tea from 15 September 1784 to 1 August 1785. The series ends at midsummer 1814, and a new series begins in January 1816. Thereafter, it is possible to give figures for calendar years. The figures of quantities sold are also incomplete for the excise years 1768–72, when the duty of one shilling per lb on black and singlo teas was temporarily suspended, but for this period I have used the quantities given by Macpherson (*Annals*, IV,

necessary to use prices derived from the figures of all tea sold at the Company's sales, adjusted for differences in the years and the level of the two series.

If we wish to analyse the demand for tea over a long period, however, it is necessary to take into account the changes in population and the price of other consumer goods. For this reason, our analysis will be based on the 'real' prices of tea[1] and consumption per head of the population. Unfortunately, the available indices of the prices of consumer goods are difficult to use and much less reliable than the statistics of tea prices. Those constructed by Dr Gilboy[2] and Mrs Schumpeter[3] relate to harvest years, and are based to a large extent on contract prices, which were often insensitive to short-period fluctuations. Silberling's cost of living index,[4] on the other hand, which is not open to the latter objection, is for calendar years, and covers only a few years of the period of high duty before 1784. It therefore seemed best to use Mrs. Schumpeter's consumer goods' index, adjusted for the difference between harvest and excise years, for the whole of the period from 1724 to 1823, and to extend her series to 1829 on the basis of the Silberling index. This series was then used to deflate the tea index, and thus give us an index of the real prices of tea. As we have no population series for Great Britain as a whole in the eighteenth century, the figures of *per capita* consumption were calculated throughout on the basis of estimates of the population of England and Wales alone.[5] Finally, by taking five-yearly moving averages of both consumption per head and the index of real prices, some

---

336). Comparison of Macpherson's figures with those given in the excise records for other years reveals a few minor discrepancies, but they are not large enough to be significant.

[1] I.e. the prices of tea in relation to those of other consumer goods.

[2] E. W. Gilboy, 'The cost of living and real wages in eighteenth century England', *Review of Economic Statistics* XVIII (1936), 134–43.

[3] E. B. Schumpeter, 'English prices and public finance, 1660–1822', *Review of Economic Statistics* XX (1938), 21–37.

[4] N. J. Silberling, 'British prices and business cycles, 1779–1850', *Review of Economic Statistics* V (1923), 235.

[5] Until census data became available in 1801, I have relied for this purpose on the decennial estimates given in John Brownlee's, 'The history of the birth and death rates in England and Wales', *Public Health*, XXIX (1916), 211–22, 228–38. It has been assumed that population changed at constant rates during the intervening years.

allowance was made for the defects in the figures for individual years.

III

The relationship between the real prices of tea and the average legal consumption per head in each of these five-yearly periods has been plotted on a logarithmic scale in the accompanying diagram.[1] As we might expect, the arrangement of the points bears little resemblance to an orthodox demand curve except over relatively short periods of time: on the contrary, it suggests that the demand for legally imported tea was characterized by repeated and violent changes of level. To illustrate the behaviour of demand from year to year more clearly, the points have been linked up in chronological order within each of the periods specified. If we follow the sequence indicated by the arrows, we shall observe that at the beginning of our period in the 1720s, labelled (a) in the diagram, the legal consumption of tea was rapidly increasing although the price of tea was almost stationary. In the early 1730s, there was a sharp contraction in demand (b), and after a few years of comparative stability (c), there was a temporary increase in demand at the end of the decade (d). A much larger increase in 1745 was followed by another period of comparative stability (e), and a further upward movement during the Seven Years War (f). Then, after 1763, legal demand dropped sharply (g), and, with the exception of the excise years 1768–72, remained at a low level until 1784 when there was again an enormous increase.

What explanations can we find for these sudden changes in the level of demand? How far can they be attributed to changes in the incentives to, and opportunities for, smuggling? From the data summarized in Table 1 it will be noted that most of them were associated with variations in the rate of duty. The two largest increases in demand followed the tariff reforms of 1745 and 1784, while the temporary increase in the excise years 1768–72 coincides with a period when the excise duty of one shilling

[1] It has become conventional in economic diagrams to show the price level on the vertical axis. Since we are interested in the effect of price changes on the level of consumption, however, the procedure has been reversed here, so that an increase in demand at a given level of prices will appear as a movement upwards, rather than a movement to the right.

per lb was suspended on all black and singlo teas in an effort to reduce smuggling.[1] For twenty years before 1745 the rates of duty were unchanged, but since at that time most of the duty was levied at a flat rate of four shillings per lb the total amount,

Table 1 ESTIMATES OF THE REAL PRICE, CONSUMPTION PER HEAD, AND RATES OF DUTY ON TEA

Excise years ending at midsummer	Average real price of tea (1725=100)	Average annual consumption per head (lbs)	Rate of duty (percentage of the net cost)
1726–30	95	·10	84
1731–35	89	·11	110
1736–40	80	·17	125
1741–45	78	·13	119
1746–50	67	·41	76
1751–55	60	·51	84
1756–60	58	·62	84
1761–65	60	·68	93
1765–67	53	·64	95
1768–72	38	1·00	65
1773–75	41	·76	101
1776–80	43	·68	103
1780–84	45	·66	110
1787–91	25	2·09	12·5
1791–95	23	2·24	12·5
1796–1800	22	2·54	29
1801–05	24	2·33	62
1806–10	29	2·07	95
1810–14	27	2·02	96
Calendar Years			
1816–20	28	1·89	97
1821–25	38	1·91	100
1825–29	34	2·00	100

expressed as a percentage of the net cost, was related inversely to fluctuations in the price of tea. It is significant that the fall in legal demand in the early 1730s occurred at a time when tea prices were also falling sharply and when, in consequence, the rate of duty rose from 90 per cent in 1730 to 156 per cent in 1735.

This fits in with other evidence which suggests that smuggling

[1] 7 Geo. III, c. 56. In order to show the effect of these three major changes of duty on the demand more clearly, only the levels of consumption in the five-yearly periods immediately before and after the change have been marked in the diagram.

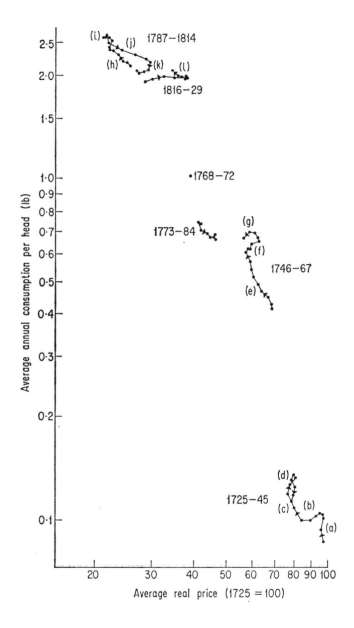

increased in the 1730s after a temporary fall in the late 1720s. Before 1724 it was believed that large quantities of tea were being exported from England in order to claim the drawback and were afterwards illegally relanded.[1] Accordingly, at midsummer in that year, the duty of four shillings per lb was made an inland duty and transferred from the customs to the excise.[2] This measure seems to have been successful in checking one form of fraud, since the quantity of tea entered for re-export, which in the years 1719–23 had averaged 380,000 lbs, fell by more than 70 per cent.[3] But as the duties still amounted to 84 per cent of the net cost the incentive to evasion was as great as ever. In 1728, the Danish East India Company enlarged its stock and three years later a Swedish company was formed from the ruins of the old Ostend company. Both these companies were believed to exist mainly to supply the illegal British demand for duty-free East India goods, and in the early 1730s the French and Dutch companies were also reported to be extending their activities.[4] It seems likely, therefore, that although the reform of 1724 may have resulted in a temporary increase in the revenue of the British government, in the long run its only effect was to extend the market of the East India Company's continental rivals.[5]

In two cases the reasons for the change in demand are somewhat less obvious. It is possible that the increase in legal demand in the late 1730s was in part due to the act of 1736 which offered an indemnity to all smugglers who turned King's evidence, provided they were not found guilty of subsequent offences.[6] Again, the outbreak of the Austrian Succession War in 1739 may have led to stock-piling by the 'fair' traders and to a temporary interruption of the continental supplies on which the 'free' trade depended. But whatever the cause, the movement was short-lived and in the early 1740s the legal demand dropped to the level of the mid-thirties. During the Seven Years War, on the other hand, when a similar increase occurred, it was main-

---

[1] Milburn, *Oriental commerce*, II, 536.   [2] 10 Geo. I, c. 10.

[3] See Milburn, *Oriental commerce*, II, 534.

[4] Milburn, *Oriental commerce*, II, 537; Macpherson, *Annals*, III, 143–4, 167–8, 183, 204–5.

[5] In 1721 European imports of tea from China had amounted to about 3,800,000 lbs, most of which was probably smuggled into Britain. By 1745 the figure was approaching nine millions. See Milburn, *Oriental commerce*, II, 536; *JHC*, xxv, 103.

[6] 9 Geo. II, c. 35.

tained until the return of peace, despite the fact that in 1759 the customs duty was increased by 5 per cent.[1]

Eighteenth-century wars were likely, of course, to affect the smugglers' trade in a variety of ways – indirectly through their effects on the legal trade of the combatants, and directly because, on the one hand, duties were usually increased in war-time and, on the other, the danger of impressment greatly increased the hazards of the illicit traffic. Most of these wars had a temporarily adverse effect on Britain's legal import trade, but from 1756–63 imports rose fairly steadily by about 2·3 per cent each year.[2] Tea imports fluctuated considerably, but in 1760 the East India Company's ships brought home over nine million lbs, nearly twice the previous record. During this period, French colonial power was undermined, the French East India Company entered into a period of decline,[3] the British Navy dominated the seas and heavy fighting raged on the continent of Europe. Such conditions must have made the smugglers' livelihood unusually precarious, and it is possible that the movement of prices was also against them. In England, the legal price of tea rose in the early years of the war, but fell again after 1760, and by 1763 was only 8 per cent higher than in 1756. In Amsterdam, on the other hand, the price of black Bohea tea, the variety most favoured by the smugglers, rose by more than 70 per cent in the course of the war.[4] Hence, it is quite possible that the relatively high demand for legally imported tea in Britain at this time was at least partially due to the temporary scarcity and unusually high price of smuggled supplies.

IV

In general, then, it seems reasonable to associate the major shifts in demand before 1784 with fluctuations in smuggling. But be-

[1] 32 Geo, II, c. 10.
[2] Based on figures extracted from PRO Customs 3.
[3] Macpherson, *Annals*, III, 402; E. Levasseur, *Histoire du commerce de la France* (Paris, 1911) 1,474 *et seq.*
[4] N. W. Posthumus, *Inquiry into the history of prices in Holland.* vol. I, *Wholesale prices at the exchange of Amsterdam, 1609–1914* (Leiden, 1946). At Nantes, in France, the price of green tea apparently increased by only 7 per cent during this period, although the series is unfortunately incomplete. The price of black tea is not given. See H. Hauser, *Recherches et documents sur l'histoire des prix en France de 1500 à 1800* (Paris, 1936), pp. 487, 509.

fore we consider the implications of this conclusion, something must be said about the influence of other factors. In this connexion the pattern of demand *after* 1784 is particularly suggestive. For eleven years after the passing of the Commutation Act the duty was much too low to make large-scale smuggling profitable, and we know that the long wars from 1793–1815 completed the ruin of the continental companies which had been the main suppliers of the free traders.[1] Yet the demand for tea was still far from stable. Admittedly, in the period of low duty after 1784, labelled (h) in the diagram, consumption rose fairly steadily as the price fell, but at the end of the century, when the fall in prices was arrested and heavier duties were re-imposed, there seems to have been a further, though erratic, *increase* in consumption (i), and in the period of rising prices and duties which followed (j) consumption proved increasingly higher than at corresponding prices at the end of the eighteenth century. In the latter part of the Napoleonic War, when the duty had again risen to nearly 100 per cent of the net cost, the demand fell to the level of the late eighteenth century (k), but in the 1820s, despite continued high duties, it gradually moved to the right until it recovered the level of the early 1800s (l). It is possible that this 'dip' was due to the temporary revival of illicit trading. But what about the rest of the period after 1800? How are we to account for such high sales in a time of rising prices and duties?[2]

The most probable explanation in this case is that consumers' habits had changed. At the beginning of the eighteenth century tea was a fashionable but expensive luxury enjoyed by comparatively few. By the end, according to the family budgets collected by Eden, it was in common use even in the households of the labouring poor, and the annual sales were sufficient to provide

[1] The Swedish East India Company survived until 1806, and was finally dissolved in 1813. Macgregor, *Commercial statistics*, v, 57; E. F. Hecksher, *An economic history of Sweden* (Cambridge, Mass., 1954), pp. 195–6.

[2] It is possible, of course, that our estimates of the real price of tea during the Napoleonic Wars are less reliable than those for the eighteenth century, owing to the difficulty of measuring changes in the value of money during this period. The available price indices may well overstate the rise in prices during the wars, and if so our estimates of the real price of tea will be too low. This might account for the fall in demand in the latter part of the wars, when the real price of tea was apparently falling, although the market price remained exceptionally high until the return of peace. It would not, however, explain the difference between the level of demand in the early 1800s and the late eighteenth century.

two-thirds of the population with a half pint of tea every day.[1]
Initially, of course, this change was made possible by the steady
fall in the real prices of tea. But it is also true that if the increased
consumption were maintained over a long period we should
expect it to become habitual: as a contemporary put it, though
tea 'may be deemed an artificial necessary, it becomes a necessary
that few would be disposed to relinquish'.[2] Indeed, we should
expect that as more people began to drink tea and gradually acquired a taste for it, the demand would tend to increase. Thus,
in a period of falling prices, consumption would rise both as a
result of a movement along the demand curve and because of the
effect of changing tastes on the level of demand. Or, to put the
matter another way, the actual levels of consumption shewn in
the diagram will represent points on a demand curve which is
constantly moving upwards and to the right. While prices continue to fall, of course, the extent of this shift will be difficult to
detect. But if prices begin to rise – as they did at the beginning
of the nineteenth century – it will at once become apparent,
since neither the consumption of individuals nor the number of
consumers will be likely to revert to their former level.

These considerations cannot be overlooked if we are to assess
the effect of smuggling on the legal demand before 1784. At that
time there was no period of rising tea prices comparable to the
first quarter of the nineteenth century. Nevertheless, the fall in
prices was by no means continuous, and it is possible, for example, that the sudden increases in the demand for legally imported tea about 1739, and again during the Seven Years War,
were in part due to the effect of changing tastes on the level of
consumption in years when prices were rising. Nor can we
ignore the influence of changing tastes on the trend of consumption when prices were falling. If the change in tastes was continuous we should expect consumption to increase fairly smoothly
so long as prices were also falling steadily. But if there were a
sudden, violent fall in the price level such as occurred in 1745,

[1] Sir F. M. Eden, *The state of the poor* (1797); Wissett, *East India affairs*, II.
Wissett reckoned that an ounce of tea gave an infusion of two quarts, and despite
change from China to Indian tea, the same is roughly true today. The branch
manageress of a well-known tea-shop tells me that she uses a pound of tea for
196 cups, or just over eight gallons.
[2] Henry Dundas, Viscount Melville, in a speech in March 1798, quoted by
Wissett, *East India affairs*, II; Milburn, *Oriental commerce*, II, 535.

1767 and again in 1784 as a result of changes in the rate of duty, although there would be an immediate increase in sales, some time might elapse before consumers' tastes became adjusted to the new price situation.[1]

Similar difficulties arise, if we consider the effect of changes in real incomes on the course of demand. If, for example, there was a secular rise in real incomes, consumption would tend to rise relatively rapidly when prices were falling, and to fall much more slowly when prices were rising. And if there was a sudden change in the price level which was not accompanied by a commensurate change in real incomes, there would be some alteration of the trend of demand quite apart from the possible effect of smuggling. It is unlikely that such considerations – and they could easily be multiplied – would completely invalidate inferences about smuggling drawn from the behaviour of consumer demand. For however great the long-term effects of changing tastes and real incomes, they would hardly account for fluctuations of the magnitude which occurred in this century.[2] But they do suggest that the reaction of consumers to price changes can give us only an approximate idea of the size of the problem with which we have to deal. Moreover, it should be remembered that our data will only indicate the effect on the legal demand of a given change in the legal price of tea. Since, however, smuggled tea sold for less than the legal market price, and the ratio between these prices was constantly changing, we cannot assume

[1] This might explain why, when prices were temporarily reduced in the excise years 1768–72, the demand was still relatively low compared with the level reached in the 1790s. Similarly, it would be unwise to base a judgement on the figures for the years immediately following the tariff reforms of 1745 and 1784 if we wish to assess the full effects of the change on the level of demand.

[2] Theoretically, it is possible to conceive of a situation in which the increase in legal consumption which took place in 1784 (when prices were reduced by about 40 per cent) might be explained without the assumption that there had been a considerable reduction in smuggling. If incomes were distributed very unequally the demand for tea might be elastic at very high prices and relatively inelastic as the price fell and the demand of the wealthy was satiated; then, if prices continued to fall, it would become elastic as tea came within reach of the poorer classes, and finally inelastic again as their demands were met. If the resulting 'dent' in the demand curve were large enough, and occurred at the right point, the increase in consumption after 1784 could be attributed to a movement *along* the curve. For these conditions to be satisfied, however, it would be necessary to assume, not only a wide gulf between the rich and poor, but also that tea was a luxury commodity in the 1770s. In fact, however, the latter supposition seems to be so much at variance with the contemporary evidence that it can be safely ignored.

that changes in the legal demand accurately reflect the real extent of fluctuations in smuggling. For these reasons, we shall not attempt to make detailed quantitative estimates of changes in the volume of smuggling in the course of the century. Instead, we shall simply try to determine whether the major shifts in demand which followed the tariff reforms of 1745 and 1784 were large enough to substantiate the contemporary estimates of smuggling which were discussed earlier.

V

It will be convenient to deal first with the change in demand after the passing of the Commutation Act, since we can assume that in the years which followed large-scale smuggling of tea virtually ceased. After the act came into effect, the index of the real prices of tea dropped by eighteen points, from an average of 43 in 1773–83 – the excise years to which the East India Company's estimate of smuggling most nearly relates – to 25 in the five-yearly periods *circa* 1789–90. Such a reduction in price might have been expected to produce an increase in consumption of roughly the same magnitude, i.e. from 0·7 to about 1·2 lbs per head of the population. This calculation is based, not simply on the somewhat erratic behaviour of legal demand in the American War period – when prices were rising – but on the long-term relationship between falling prices and the trend of consumption in the second half of the eighteenth century.[1] Yet, in fact, legal consumption rose to 2·1 lbs per head, which represents an increase in demand of 0·9 lbs or 75 per cent.

Now, according to the 1783 Report, smuggled goods sold for between half and two-thirds the legal price,[2] so it might be thought that the real price of legally imported tea after the

[1] Between c. 1789 and c. 1793 a reduction of 7·6 per cent in the real price of tea was associated with an increase in consumption of 6·4 per cent. For 1749–53, on the other hand, the corresponding figures are 11·5 and 16·5 per cent. In the 1770s, real prices were about midway between those obtaining in the early 1750s and 1790s. We might expect, therefore, that a small reduction in price in the 1770s would have produced a slightly greater proportional increase in consumption, but that 'elasticity' would gradually fall below unity if the price continued to fall towards the level of the early 1790s. It should be noted that in this, and the subsequent calculations, proportional changes have been measured as percentages of the upper values in the case of both quantity and price.

[2] *H of C Reports*, xi, 228.

Commutation Act was passed was about the same as smuggled tea before. Hence, if the whole of the increase in demand was due to a decline in smuggling, it could be argued that the illicit sales had averaged 0·9 lbs per head, or nearly seven million lbs each year. It should be noted, however, that the free traders usually found it more profitable to import the coarser varieties of tea, both because the excise duty weighed more heavily on cheap teas and because good quality tea required greater care in packing and transport.[1] And whereas the *average* price of tea fell by about 40 per cent as a result of the reduction of duty, the price of the cheapest black tea dropped 60 per cent. Moreover, it is possible that consumers would tend to buy more when they could obtain tea in the open market without the difficulties and risks involved in dealing with the free traders. It seems likely, therefore, that the total illicit sales before 1784 were a good deal less than seven million lbs. On the other hand, if we reverse the procedure outlined above and calculate the expected consumption in the period 1773–83 on the basis of the observed level of demand after 1784, we shall find that, at the legal prices then prevailing, the actual figure falls short of the expected by just under four million lbs a year. And since at that time smuggled tea could undoubtedly be bought for considerably less than the market price, it seems probable that the actual volume of contraband sales was greater than this difference implies.

We may conclude, then, that on the eve of the Commutation Act illegal sales of tea probably amounted to somewhere between four and six million lbs a year. If, as the East India Company's accountant asserted, large quantities of dyed leaves were being fraudulently sold as tea,[2] illegal imports of tea may well have been smaller than these figures suggest – unless the frauds continued on the same scale after the duty was reduced. Certainly, our calculations do not support the Company's view that the legal sales of tea accounted for barely a third of the total consumption. But at least we must admit that during the American War smuggling may have reached greater heights than Pitt's advisers feared, if not quite the level claimed by the East India Company.

It is more difficult to apply the same technique in analysing the consequences of the tariff reform of 1745. Before that date the legal demand for tea was much too unstable to permit ac-

[1] Cf. *JHC*, xxv, 103.   [2] See above, p. 123 note 5.

curate measurement of the effect of price changes on the level of consumption. All that can be said is that demand tended to be much more elastic than it was later in the century. In the twenty years before 1745 the increase in consumption was two or three times greater than the reduction in the real price, but by the early 1750s the proportion had already fallen to about 1·4: 1. Hence the fall in prices following the act of 1745 – which amounted to about 14 per cent – might have been expected to produce an increase in consumption of anything between 20 and 40 per cent. Even so, it is clear that the reduction in duty was accompanied by a substantial increase in demand. For on this basis the expected consumption after the act was passed would have been between 0·17 and 0·22 lbs per head, whereas the actual sales in the excise years 1747–51 averaged 0·43 lbs per head, which, with a population of about six millions, represents a difference of $1\frac{1}{4}$–$1\frac{1}{2}$ million lbs.

Since the price of smuggled tea was still slightly below the legal price of the cheapest black tea even after the act became law,[1] it seems reasonable to suppose that the decline in smuggling was at least as great as this increase in demand suggests. It seems equally clear, however, that the illicit trade in tea continued on a significant scale for some years after 1745. In the early 1760s the legal sales of tea were about a million pounds greater than they had been a decade earlier, although the real price of tea was almost exactly the same at the two dates. Since this represents an increase in demand of nearly 40 per cent in one decade, it would clearly be unreasonable to attribute the change solely to the effect of changing tastes or real incomes. It seems, therefore, that between the early 1740s and the end of the Seven Years War the average annual imports of tea by the free traders must have declined by about two million lbs. If this was so, it follows that the contemporary view that before 1745 about three million pounds of tea had been smuggled each year cannot have been a wild exaggeration. Whether it could have been a serious under-estimate, it is impossible to say on the evidence of the legal demand alone.[2] But it is difficult to believe that illegal imports of tea at

[1] The retail price of the cheapest black tea in London was about five shillings a lb, while the price of smuggled tea was variously estimated as between four and five shillings. *JHC*, xxv, 103–5.

[2] It would be possible, of course, to estimate the expected demand at the prices prevailing in the early 1740s, by a questionable process of extrapolation based on

that time could have reached the levels attained during the American War, if only because the total European imports were smaller.[1] Moreover, it is unlikely that the witnesses called by the Commons' Committee would have been guilty of minimizing the extent of the problem. As we have already noted, several of them were smugglers, and most of them were traders, interested in demonstrating that high duties had meant extensive smuggling and that only a further reduction would ensure the elimination of the evil. In other words, like the East India Company nearly forty years later, they had a case to establish.

We may conclude, then, that contemporaries were not seriously misinformed about the probable magnitude of smuggling, although some of them had good reasons for erring on the high side in their estimates of the extent of the traffic. In the early 1740s, the tea legally sold by the East India Company almost certainly represented only a small fraction of the total consumption, and it seems likely that at least two million lbs, and probably more, was annually sold by the free traders. Thereafter, tea smuggling never assumed the same relative importance, and for a time it seems to have suffered an absolute decline. In the mid-1760s, however, and still more during the American War, there was a renewed expansion of the illegal traffic, until by 1784 the smugglers' sales probably equalled, if they did not surpass, the quantities sold by the East India Company, and were almost certainly substantially greater in absolute terms than they had been forty years before.

VI

What light does this survey cast on the history of smuggling as a whole? Unfortunately, the scarcity of reliable price data would make it difficult to subject other branches of the contraband trade to the type of analysis attempted here. But the history of one other major commodity, tobacco, suggests that the apparent

---

the observed level of demand at the end of the century, but since the bulk of the tea consumed in the earlier period must have been sold by the smugglers at considerably less than the market price, such a calculation would be virtually meaningless.

[1] See pp. 123, 130 note 5.

decline in tea smuggling in the middle of the eighteenth century may not have been exceptional. There is abundant evidence that in the early part of the century large quantities of tobacco were brought into Britain without payment of duty either by direct smuggling or by fraudulent entries at the customs.[1] At the beginning of the century, according to Davenant, the retained imports of tobacco averaged over 11 million lbs a year, whereas between 1730 and the mid-1740s they seem to have fluctuated between five and seven million pounds.[2] No doubt this fall was partly due to the apparent decline in the popularity of smoking in the eighteenth century.[3] But if so it is remarkable that by the early 1760s net imports had climbed back to over 10·6 million lbs, or about 1·6 lbs per head – a figure which was not surpassed until the last decade of the nineteenth century.[4] Moreover, it has been pointed out that the total exports of tobacco from America after 1791 barely equalled the quantities which were officially recorded as passing through Britain in the period from 1761 to 1775.[5]

There are, indeed, grounds for the view that in the middle decades of the century there was a causal relationship between fluctuations in tea smuggling and movements in the illicit trade as a whole. Contemporaries believed that the profitability of smuggling other commodities depended to some extent on the possibility of running them with tea, and bulky goods, such as brandy, were often used as ballast in ships which were mainly employed in the lucrative traffic in tea. Thus, a witness before the Commons' Committee in 1745–6 argued that a reduction of the duty on tea, which was 'by far the most considerable Commodity that is run', would lead to a general decline in smuggling; and forty years later a similar view inspired the great reform of 1784.[6] This theory is supported by the available evidence of goods

[1] Cf. T. C. Barker, 'Smuggling in the eighteenth century; the evidence of the Scottish tobacco trade', *Virginia Magazine of History and Biography*, LXII (1954), 387–99; Alfred Rive, 'A short history of tobacco smuggling', *Economic History*, I (1929), 554–69.

[2] Alfred Rive, 'The consumption of tobacco since 1600', *Economic History*, I (1926), 61–2.

[3] Rive, 'The consumption of tobacco', pp. 63–4.

[4] See Macpherson, *Annals*, III, 583; Rive, 'The consumption of tobacco', pp. 72–3.

[5] L. A. Harper, *The English navigation laws: a seventeenth-century experiment in social engineering* (New York, 1939), p. 262.

[6] *JHC*, XXV, 108; *H of C Reports*, XI, 230, 286; Macpherson, *Annals*, IV, 49–50.

seized by the customs and excise officers. Such records tell us little or nothing about changes in the volume of smuggling, but they probably indicated fairly accurately variations in the importance of different commodities. Unfortunately, there are no figures of seizures available for the 1740s and 1750s, and it is possible that after the reduction of tea duty in 1745 tea smuggling lost the pre-eminence which was claimed for it at that time. Nevertheless, the records which have survived show that in 1764–6 seizures of tea were not much smaller in value than those of all foreign spirits combined.[1] Nor did the relationship vary much in the next fifteen years despite fluctuations in the tea duty.[2] Admittedly, tea and foreign spirits did not exhaust the list of smuggled goods (though they probably accounted for about half), but the fuller records of seizures for 1769–73 and 1778–82 suggest that in the 1770s, at any rate, there was little change in the importance of tea in the contraband trade as a whole. Although there were fluctuations in the seizures of other goods, tea seems to have represented about a quarter or a fifth of the total at both periods.[3]

After 1784, of course, the enterprising free trader tended to look elsewhere for easy profits, and although the virtual abolition of the tea duty probably contributed to a general decline in smuggling, there is no reason to suppose that it came to an end. Seizures of contraband goods, and armed clashes between the smugglers and the revenue officers continued well into the nineteenth century, but despite the reimposition of heavy tea duties, tea smuggling never regained its former importance. The official value of tea seized in 1822–4, for example, works out at a mere £1,900, compared with about £15,000 for tobacco, and £17,000 for brandy and gin.[4] Similarly, evidence of tea smuggling

[1] Figures of seizures in 1764–6, 1769–73 and 1778–82 are given in Appendix No. 4 of the 1783 Report. *H of C Reports*, XI, 240–3.

[2] At the official rates of valuation of imports, seizures of tea averaged about £11,000 in 1764–6, £12,000 in 1769–71 and £15,000 in 1778–82. The corresponding figures for foreign spirits work out at about £14,000 in 1764–6 and 1769–71, and £18,000 in 1778–82. At market prices tea would probably represent a smaller and fluctuating proportion of the total.

[3] This can only be a rough estimate, since the figures of seizures may not be complete and East India goods were not all valued at constant prices in the official trade statistics. It should be remembered, too, that tea was easier to conceal than many other smuggled commodities.

[4] Based on a return cited by H. N. S. Teignmouth and C. G. Harper, *The smugglers* (London, 1923), II, 222.

tells us relatively little about the fortunes of other branches of the illicit trade in the years before 1745. At the beginning of the century, tea was a newcomer to European commerce and can have played only a minor part in the smugglers' trade. An official return in May 1733, of the quantity of goods seized and con- demned during the previous ten years, suggests that even at that time seizures of brandy were worth three times as much as those of tea.[1] Clearly, therefore, illegal imports of tea must have grown relatively rapidly to acquire the predominance which they apparently enjoyed by the 1740s.

Nevertheless, if fluctuations in tea smuggling provide us with an index, however crude, of the fortunes of the rest of the illicit traffic during the critical period from 1745–84, it should be pos- sible to suggest the probable trends in smuggling during the century as a whole. We can probably assume that there was a general increase in smuggling in the years before 1745, even if in magnitude and phasing it did not correspond with the expansion of tea smuggling. The complaints of contemporaries and the re- peated attempts to prevent smuggling by legislation both sug- gest that the problem became more serious as the tariffs grew more burdensome and complicated. We know that the 1740s were the heyday of armed bands of smugglers, such as the Hawk- hurst gang, and it has been suggested that the organization of the contraband trade reached its full development only in the reign of George II 'when there was a systematic and permanent traffic in contraband, sympathized with by the bulk of the population of the maritime counties'.[2] Again it seems reasonable to accept the view that smuggling was increasing in the 1770s and that the decline in its importance may be dated from Pitt's reform of the customs in the 1780s.[3] But our evidence suggests that its growth had not been continuous: after reaching a peak in the 1730s and 1740s, it apparently declined in the latter part of George II's reign before rising again to its fullest extent in the late 1770s.

If this was so, it would appear that the legal and illegal branches of England's import trade tended to move in opposite

[1] 'The Report of the Committee appointed to inquire into the Frauds and Abuses in the Customs . . .' *H of C Reports*, 1 (1715–35), 610. It should be noted, however, that judging by the fuller returns preserved in PRO T64/143–5, tea may already have taken second place by this time.

[2] H. Atton and H. H. Holland, *The King's customs*, 1 (London, 1908), 134.

[3] Cf. Cross, *Eighteenth century documents*, pp. 27–8.

directions in the eighteenth century. In the early part of the century, the legal trade was comparatively stagnant, and in the 1730s and early 1740s there was a period of absolute decline. After 1745, on the other hand, legal imports rapidly increased, fell sharply during the American War, and then rose again at the end of the century. But it now seems likely that an allowance for smuggling would tend to damp down these fluctuations. We still cannot determine, of course, the precise extent of the margin of error involved in the use of the official statistics. But at least we can make a reasonable guess at the probable order of magnitude of the contraband trade. We have suggested that the illicit sales of tea averaged between four and six million pounds annually during the American War; and if, as the figures of seizures imply, illegal imports of tea represented about a quarter or a fifth of the total quantity of smuggled goods, valued at constant official prices, it seems possible that £2 or £3 million worth of goods may have been smuggled into Britain each year.[1] In the same period, total legal imports did not amount to much more than £12 million per annum. Clearly, therefore, fluctuations in smuggling must have had a significant influence on the trends in legal trade. Admittedly, the estimate of smuggling might be reduced by about a third if, as the East India Company's accountant suggested, part of the illicit sales of tea were in fact accounted for by fraudulent substitutes made at home rather than by illegal imports of real tea. On the other hand, since smuggled goods represented a net addition to home consumption, estimates of their value should be compared with the values of officially retained imports. At present figures of net imports are not available, but we hope to meet this deficiency in a subsequent article on the official statistics of legal trade.

[1] For what it is worth, it may be noted that a witness before the Commons' Committee in 1746, when the official rates of valuation probably still bore some relation to actual prices, reckoned that over £1 million was annually exported in specie to pay for smuggled goods, apart from illegal exports of raw wool. Another witness gave a figure of £200,000, apparently for tea alone. Before 1736, when the price of tea on the Continent was much higher, it was said that payments for tea were as high as £800,000. See *JHC*, xxv, 102, 104.

APPENDIX

AN INDEX OF THE AVERAGE WHOLESALE PRICE OF TEA
FOR HOME CONSUMPTION, INCLUSIVE OF DUTY

$(1725 = 100)$

Year ending at midsummer

Year	Index	Year	Index	Year	Index
1725	100	1759	65	1794	31
1726	95	1760	66	1795	32
1727	106	1761	61	1796	33
1728	105	1762	63	1797	33
1729	98	1763	61	1798	36
1730	95	1764	62	1799	40
1731	95	1765	61	1800	39
1732	92	1766	59	1801	41
1733	88	1767	56	1802	41
1734	68	1768	43	1803	44
1735	67	1769	38	1804	45
1736	71	1770	38	1805	54
1737	74	1771	45	1806	56
1738	73	1772	46	1807	59
1739	78	1773	56	1808	60
1740	84	1774	50	1809	59
1741	80	1775	48	1810	63
1742	80	1776	49	1811	59
1743	85	1777	49	1812	61
1744	73	1778	50	1813	60
1745	74	1779	51	1814	63
1746	60	1780	55	*Calendar year*	
1747	64	1781	53	1816	54
1748	72	1782	57	1817	54
1749	65	1783	57	1818	56
1750	65	1784	57	1819	53
1751	63	1785	—	1820	51
1752	57	1786	31	1821	53
1753	57	1787	32	1823	53
1754	55	1788	31	1824	53
1755	54	1789	33	1825	52
1756	57	1790	31	1826	48
1757	60	1791	32	1827	46
1758	60	1792	31	1828	44
		1793	31	1829	42

5 *Anglo-Portuguese Trade 1700–1770*[1]

H. E. S. FISHER

[This article was first published in *The Economic History Review*, 2nd series, Vol. XVI (1963).]

In his later article Professor Davis makes clear that some three-quarters of the growth which occurred in the English export trade in manufactures between 1699–1701 and 1752–4 depended about equally on increased shipments to two regions alone, southern Europe – very largely Spain and Portugal – and the English empire in America.[2] This, however, overrates the European demand for English manufactures in the first half of the eighteenth century, since the trades to Spain and Portugal both notably depended on these countries' colonial connections with Central and South America. Miss McLachlan has indicated that the goods shipped to Spain at this time were to a considerable extent destined for re-export to Spanish America, and although she did not consider if an expansion of such re-exports underlay the growth of Anglo-Spanish trade this was probably a significant factor.[3] While, as will be shown below, the expansion of English exports to Portugal was closely linked to the flourishing Portuguese connection with Brazil, which led to a growing re-export of foreign manufactures from Lisbon across the Atlantic and also enhanced metropolitan Portuguese demands for foreign products. The business that English merchants drove to the English colonies in this period was in fact complemented by substantial if indirect trades to the Iberian empires in America.[4]

[1] This article is based on part of my unpublished University of London PhD thesis, 'Anglo-Portuguese trade, 1700–1770' (1961). I am grateful to Professor A. H. John for valuable criticism.

[2] R. Davis, 'English foreign trade, 1700–1774', above, pp. 99–120

[3] J. O. McLachlan, *Trade and peace with old Spain, 1667–1750* (Cambridge, 1940).

[4] The Spanish empire was tapped as a market in other ways, through the South Sea Company's 'annual ship' concession for a direct general trade which was irregularly resorted to between 1713 and 1739, and especially through the illicit trades conducted from Jamaica and the other English West Indian islands. See McLachlan, *Trade and peace*.

It seems clear that full understanding of the growth of English commerce in the years 1700 to 1750 needs to be sought in a wider context, to include the Americas as a whole.

I

This paper examines the trade between England and Portugal in the years 1700 to 1770: the trade with Madeira has been excluded together with that between Portugal and the English possessions in North America.[1] These years saw remarkable developments in Anglo-Portuguese commerce, developments closely bound up with the important changes concurrently occurring in Portuguese commerce and general economic life, which have been recently considered anew by V. Magalhães Godinho in a seminal article published in 1950.[2] In the mid-seventeenth century, as far as can be seen, the trade between England and Portugal was comparatively moderate. London's exports alone to Portugal in the two years Michaelmas 1662–Michaelmas 1663 and Michaelmas 1668–Michaelmas 1669, for instance, averaged some £156,000, a level well below the trades with Spain, France and Germany; while imports into London from Portugal came to only £77,000. The exchange consisted essentially of the lighter woollen and worsted manufactures, especially serges and bays, for sugar, oil and fruit.[3] In the 1670s and 1680s English exports to Portugal may well have fallen away to some extent as a result of the serious commercial depression in Brazil and Portugal brought about mainly by the rise of West Indian sugar production, and the import restrictions and attempts to develop home industries which Magalhães Godinho argues were inspired

[1] Anglo-Portuguese trading relations in these years are studied in V. M. Shillington and A. B. W. Chapman, *The commercial relations of England and Portugal* (London, 1907), pp. 205–95. This work is still of considerable value for the political background and institutional and treaty questions, but does not bring out the full significance of general movements in the trade while it naturally lacks the insight to be gained from recent studies by Portuguese historians.
[2] 'Flottes de sucre et flottes de l'or (1670–1770)', *Annales, Economies, Sociétés, Civilisations*, v (1950), 184–97. A good discussion of the Portuguese Atlantic economy between 1570 and 1670 is found in F. Mauro, *Le Portugal et l'Atlantique au XVIIe siècle (1570–1670)* (Paris, 1960), while Portuguese commerce and economic life more generally in the mid-eighteenth century is well treated in J. de Macedo, *A situação económica no tempo de Pombal* (Porto, 1951).
[3] BM Add. MSS. 36785. The outports, however, undoubtedly had quite substantial dealings with Portugal.

by the depression. But the later 1690s saw the revival of Brazilian commerce, based largely on the discovery of gold, and for the next sixty years or so Portugal enjoyed a period of remarkable commercial prosperity. Largely because of this English exports to Portugal expanded strikingly, and the 'Portugal Trade' became a leading branch of England's foreign trade. The 1760s, however, witnessed the ebbing of the tide of Brazilian wealth, and, as a result, a marked slump in England's export trade to Portugal.

The only extant series of figures for the trade between England and Portugal in the years 1700–70 are the official English statistics compiled by the Inspectors-General.[1] These best measure changes in the volume of transactions, but there are reasons for thinking they offer some guide to long-term movements in the value of this trade. It is true that the official valuations of English exports to Portugal remained virtually unchanged after 1715. On general grounds, however, it seems probable that the prices of the major woollen textile exports tended to fall between about 1715 and the mid-century, and that this trend was reversed either before or during the Seven Years War. The official figures thus probably over-estimate the actual value of exports to Portugal between about 1715 and 1750 and under-estimate it afterwards. Import valuations too remained virtually unchanged, but the scattered prices available for wines, the chief recorded import from Portugal, suggest a general stability of prices in the period. Moreover, the composition of both exports and imports remained essentially the same throughout, so that like can be compared with like. There are, of course, other sources of error in the official statistics, the practice among exporters of over-stating their shipments, the exclusion of freight and insurance payments on imports, and the smuggling which occurred: undoubtedly, for example, Portuguese wines were illegally run into England although this was probably more than compensated by the French wines coming from the Channel Islands and elsewhere entered as Portuguese.[2] These points suggest the official statistics have a further tendency rather to exaggerate actual

[1] PRO Customs 3.

[2] On the use of the Inspectors'-General figures see G. N. Clark, *Guide to English commercial statistics, 1696–1782* (London, 1938), pp. 33–42, and the introduction by T. S. Ashton to E. B. Schumpeter, *English overseas trade statistics, 1697–1808* (Oxford, 1960), pp. 1–9.

export values and to under-state actual import values. Nevertheless, with these reservations in mind, the official figures can be
used as a broad, approximate guide to general movements in the
trade.

Table 1 THE TRADE BETWEEN ENGLAND AND PORTUGAL, 1698–1775
(£000 ANNUAL AVERAGE)

	Exports to Portugal	*Imports from Portugal*	*Export surplus*
1698–1702	355	200	155
1700–4	514	254	260
1701–5	610	242	368
1706–10	652	240	413
1711–15	638	252	385
1716–20	695	349	346
1721–5	811	387	424
1726–30	914	359	555
1731–5	1,024	326	698
1736–40	1,164	301	864
1741–5	1,115	429	687
1746–50	1,114	324	790
1751–5	1,098	272	826
1756–60	1,301	257	1,044
1761–5	965	314	650
1766–70	595	356	239
1771–5	613	365	248

Source: C. Whitworth, *State of trade of Great Britain* (1776), part II, pp. 27–8. His
1713 export figure has been corrected to £628,000.

Table 1 indicates that the course of English exports to Portugal changed much in these years, a doubling or so of trade by
1740 being followed by a period of comparative stability ending
in a burst of renewed growth in the late 1750s, and then, in the
1760s, by absolute decline. The period of overall growth to 1760
will be examined first, and then the years of decline.

Down to 1760 the re-export to Portugal of foreign goods and
English colonial products remained small, annual shipments
averaging £29,000 in 1706–10 and £22,000 in 1756–60,[1] with
German and Dutch linen, pipe staves, and dried Newfoundland
cod most prominent. The increase in exports to Portugal thus
depended entirely on shipments of English produce and manufactures, of which textiles composed by far the most important

[1] The official values from PRO Customs 3 have been used here and below to
indicate the relative importance of particular products or groups of products, but
it should be remembered they offer no more than broad approximations to the
actual values.

group, their share of total exports ranging between 71 per cent in 1706–10 and 83 per cent in the late 1750s. Predominant among the textiles shipped were woollen and worsted cloths, especially the lighter and more moderately priced. Shipments of bays, a semi-worsted fabric, were most valuable of all, rising from an annual average of £159,000 in 1706–10 to £443,000 in 1756–60. In the early years of the century perpetuanas and serges ranked second but by the early 1720s had been overtaken by worsted stuffs, whose shipments averaged £167,000 annually in the late 1750s. Down to 1740 the finer quality woollen cloths remained distinctly secondary, exports of short, long and Spanish cloths together in most years being well below £100,000; afterwards shipments of the first two grew somewhat and between 1756 and 1760 respectively averaged £155,000 and £100,000 annually. Shipments of worsted stockings and hats made from felt, beaver and castor also grew markedly over the period, at its end averaging £80,000 and £89,000 respectively. Minor consignments of silk goods, linens and cottons were also made to Portugal, together with a great miscellany of non-textile manufactures, the most important being wrought iron wares whose value, however, had risen to only £20,000 by 1756–60. Lead and lead shot, tin and coal were also exported, but again only in minor quantities throughout. Notable shipments of foodstuffs were also made, particularly grainstuffs; of these wheat cargoes invariably had the greatest value, normally varying between 5 and 12 per cent of all exports, but experiencing no overall growth.

On the other hand, officially recorded imports from Portugal (which excluded bullion) followed a quite different course to 1760. Broad stability to 1715 was followed by a more expansive period lasting until the late 1740s after which a decline set in. Primary products of Portuguese growth were pre-eminent, in particular wine which regularly accounted for over 80 per cent of the total trade. Oranges, figs, shumach, oil, cork, and salt were also shipped, but in modest quantities throughout; sugar imports, formerly so important, had ceased.

According to the official statistics every year between 1700 and 1760 saw the balance of visible trade in England's favour; over the period as a whole it grew decidedly and averaged over a million pounds annually at its greatest in 1756–60. It is probable that before 1750 these official surpluses were larger than the real surpluses, because of the tendency for English export prices to fall and the other weaknesses of the official figures discussed above, and that whenever the official surplus was small, as in 1700, 1701 and 1718, a visible trade deficit was in fact incurred. However, considerable sums accrued to England each year from her 'invisible trades' with Portugal, principally the sale of cod caught off Newfoundland by west of England fishermen,[1] the use of English ships and marine insurance facilities in Portugal's colonial and foreign commerce,[2] the employment of a growing volume of capital by English merchants in the long credit commonly granted to textile purchasers in Portugal,[3] and the English merchants' varied interests as principals in other branches of Portuguese trade and economic life.[4] These earnings would have gone far towards compensating the exaggeration of the official surplus down to 1750,[5] so that on current trade account as a whole England may well have enjoyed surpluses not very much different from the official figures. These recurrent surpluses could have been settled in three main ways, through English investment, by payments made through a third country, or in bullion. Some English investment in vineyards and shipping did occur but in a small way only:[6] probably more important was the likely employment of part of the English trade balances each year in expanding the amount of commercial credit granted to

[1] In 1729 an English merchant's survey of Portugal's foreign trade put the yearly sale of Newfoundland cod by the English at about £55,000. Attachment to Tirawley to Newcastle, 26 June 1729, PRO SP 89/35. A copy is in the Biblioteca Nacional of Lisbon, Colecção Pombalina, Cod. 638, ff. 461–2. Another merchant at this time considered a figure of £88,000 more in order. Attachment to Compton to Newcastle, 6 Aug. 1729, n.s., PRO SP 89/35.

[2] For details see my thesis, pp. 258–61, and A. H. John, 'The London Assurance Company and the marine insurance market of the eighteenth century', *Economica*, n.s. xxv (1958), 132–3.

[3] Throughout English merchants dominated the supply of textiles to Portugal: with sales for the metropolitan market payment was normally deferred about six months, while for the Brazil trade longer credits were common extending to as much as two or three years. In 1758 some London Portugal merchants thought the extent of Portuguese commercial indebtedness relating to the English export trade as a whole never less than 'the full amount of above Two Years Importations', at that time a sum in the region of £2,500,000 and probably a quite realistic assessment. See my thesis, pp. 97–9, 106–11.

[4] See my thesis, pp. 254–8, 261–3.

[5] Imports from Portugal were mostly carried in English vessels and insured in London which also reduces the significance of the official exclusion of freight and insurance payments on imports.

[6] See my thesis, pp. 261–3.

the Portuguese and in financing English interests in other branches of Portuguese commerce. There is no evidence of substantial payments made via a third country – Portugal in fact seems to have had visible trade deficits with all the chief European nations.[1] In consequence the English surpluses were, in the main, regularly settled in bullion, an arrangement as much deplored by contemporary Portuguese observers as it was extolled by Englishmen. The exchange-rate of a nation habitually exporting gold should be normally at gold export point and this is borne out in Portugal's case in these years by reference to the London rate on Lisbon[2] (unfortunately the Lisbon rates on London are not available). If gold export point is taken as 5s. 5¾d.,[3] then in all but twenty years between 1700 and 1760 the yearly London rate of exchange (average of the first rate quoted each month) stood at this level or below, and in only eight years, 1700–6 and 1717, did no first-monthly rate fail to do so. In 1700 and 1701 England's trade may have been in deficit, but in 1702–6 the official surplus ranged from £266,000 to £596,000. This discrepancy probably sprang from the abnormal conditions in the bullion and exchange markets during the War of the Spanish Succession, in particular from the subsidies paid to Portugal and the English military expenditures there. Special circumstances must also have applied in 1717.

Such English commercial remittances did not comprise the entire bullion trade to England from Portugal at this time. Shipments based on Dutch, German and other European nations' trading surpluses with Portugal were initially made to England because of the frequent availability of English ships at Lisbon bound for England which were both armed and possessed diplomatic immunity from search,[4] and the special bullion dealing services offered by English houses. In 1729, for instance, an English merchant in Lisbon declared that part of the bullion outflow settling Portugal's trading debts with other European

---

[1] *Mercator's Letters on Portugal and its commerce* (1754), pp. 11–15. See also the survey of Portugal's trade, PRO SP 89/35.

[2] J. Castaing, *Course of the exchange*.

[3] *The British merchant* [ed. 1721] quoted without correction in the early 1750s by M. Postlethwayt, *The universal dictionary of trade and commerce* (1751–5), put the gold export point at under 5s. 6d. See L. S. Sutherland, *A London merchant, 1695–1774* (Oxford, 1933), p. 30. Other sources, probably later, put it at 5s. 6·01d., par being 5s. 7½d., Sutherland, *London merchant*.

[4] The Falmouth–Lisbon packet-boats as well as men-of-war.

countries went directly to Italy, and 'the Rest for the most part
by the way of England on account of the Conveniences of the
Exchange and of Shipping'.[1] This may exaggerate England's role
as an entrepôt, but it seems clear a very considerable part of continental European bullion balances in Portugal were remitted
homewards in this way.[2] Another contemporary in fact thought
these foreign transfers composed the 'greatest part' of all the
bullion exported to England,[3] while others stressed the value of
shipments based on Dutch and German trade.[4] All these observers were interested, however, in minimizing English responsibility for the drain of bullion from Portugal, and it seems likely
that in most years English commercial remittances remained by
far the larger element because of England's much greater trade
with Portugal compared to other countries.[5] Some figures
survive of the bullion brought by the packet-boats to Falmouth
from Lisbon: between 25 March 1740 and 8 June 1741 its value
came to £447,347,[6] while in the calendar years 1759 and 1760
it totalled £787,290 and £1,085,559 respectively.[7] This certainly
underestimates the total bullion flow to England in these years,
since in wartime warships were much resorted to for safer
carriage, while merchant ships were also employed. Throughout
the period the transfers were principally made in gold, chiefly
Portuguese coin.

The dramatic growth of English exports to Portugal between
1700 and 1760 was due primarily to an impressive secular expansion of the Portuguese market for foreign manufactures. This
was itself closely related to the return of a high level of prosperity
in Portuguese commerce which Magalhães Godinho has shown
began in the 1690s and continued down to about 1760.[8] In
Portugal itself the development from about 1690 of wine

[1] Attachment to Tirawley to Newcastle, 26 June 1729, PRO SP 89/35; Col.
Pombalina, Cod. 638, f. 461.
[2] See *Mercator*, pp. 37–8, and *Description de la ville de Lisbonne* (Paris, 1730), pp.
267–8.
[3] *Mercator*, p. 38.
[4] Sir Matthew Decker, *An essay on the causes o, the decline of foreign trade* (1744),
p. 89; A. Anderson, *An historical and chronological deduction of the origin of commerce*
(1764), I, x; N. Magens, *The universal merchant* (1753), p. 67.
[5] See below, p. 155.
[6] University Library, Cambridge, Cholmondeley (Houghton) MSS. P. 44, 50
and P. 89, 17/1.
[7] Col. Pombalina, Cod. 635, f. 445.
[8] Godinho, 'Flottes de sucre', pp. 188–94.

producing and exporting industries in the Douro and Tagus regions and elsewhere[1] gave a strong impulse to the existing metropolitan demand for foreign manufactures. Expanding wine exports, largely in response to increasing English demands,[2] meant employment and incomes were stimulated in the regions concerned, and a larger market for manufactures, especially textiles, created and sustained. Moreover, with the revival of Portuguese commercial prosperity in the 1690s the policy of home industrial expansion was abandoned,[3] and for the next sixty years Portuguese manufacturing interests, with few exceptions, remained little developed.[4] Increased resort was thus made to foreign supplies of manufactured goods, financed by the foreign balances earned from the expanding wine trade.[5]

More important, however, was the remarkable expansion of demand for foreign manufactures in Brazil during the first sixty years or so of the century, due to its rapid internal economic development and in particular the phenomenal rise of gold mining.[6] About 1690 settlement there was largely confined to the coastal regions of the northern captaincies, with agriculture, especially the plantation cultivation of sugar and to a lesser extent tobacco, the predominant economic activity. The total population at this time has been estimated at between 184,000 and 300,000.[7] In the 1690s gold was discovered in the interior, in what became known as the captaincy of Minas Gerais, and subsequently discoveries were made in other regions. Total output

[1] Godinho, 'Flottes de sucre', pp. 188–9, and Macedo, *Tempo de Pombal*, pp. 73–8.

[2] On the substitution of Portuguese for French wines in English imports at this time, see my thesis, pp. 53–8.

[3] Godinho, 'Flottes de sucre', pp. 188–9.

[4] Macedo, *Tempo de Pombal*, pp. 207–10. See also A. Anderson, *Origin*, II, 94, and J. Cary, *An essay towards regulating the trades of this kingdom* (1719), p. 69.

[5] The process at the end of the seventeenth century was well observed by an Englishman writing in 1699: 'Its plain y[t] during the [recent] War y[e] Planters & Vineyard dressers in Portugal finding greater request of their Wine, sedulously multiplied y[e] Planting of Vines, & employ'd far greater numbers of people in it than formerly: by wch means there hath been a far greater Exportation of our English Manufactures', PRO SP 100/37, f. 47.

[6] Brazilian economic life at this time is usefully examined in R. C. Simonsen, *Historia economica do Brasil, 1500–1820* (2 vols. São Paulo, 1937); for a good general account of life in Brazil see C. R. Boxer, *The golden age of Brazil, 1695–1750* (Berkeley and Los Angeles, 1962).

[7] Estimate published by Contreira Rodrigues and quoted by Simonsen, *Brasil*, II, 51 n.

grew quickly: available estimates put it at an annual average of 1,500 kg between 1691 and 1700, between 1701 and 1720 it had risen to 2,750 kg annually, in the following twenty years to 8,850 kg and between 1741 and 1760 attained an overall peak of 14,600 kg annually.[1] Diamonds were also found in quantity in Minas Gerais from 1723 onwards. The discovery and working of the gold deposits, and to a still notable if far less significant extent, the diamond fields, gave a great impetus to Brazilian economic growth. Boom conditions and an acute labour scarcity led to heavy immigration from Portugal and the large-scale transportation of negro slaves from Africa. Many new settlements were established in the interior, a strong impulse was given to internal trade and it was not long before Rio de Janeiro rivalled Bahia in opulence and importance. By the 1760s the colony's population had grown impressively, perhaps to about one and a half millions.[2]

These changed circumstances explain the revival in the value of Brazil's exports to Portugal, which had been in decline since about 1670 following the rise of West Indian sugar production. Extant figures for the trade are poor and sparse but those reported by Professor Simonsen indicate the colony's total exports to Portugal rose from about £2,400,000 in 1700 and £2,500,000 in 1710 to about £4,800,000 in 1760.[3] This was chiefly due to increased gold shipments whose approximate annual value at these three dates was £350,000, £600,000 and £2,200,000 respectively. At the last date gold exports were running at a level not much below sugar exports. Additional evidence for greatly expanding gold shipments is provided by Magalhães Godinho,[4] while the reports (incomplete though they are) of the Brazilian trading fleets' cargoes scattered through the correspondence of the English envoys and consuls in Lisbon during this period offer further evidence of a general commercial expansion.[5] The growth of Brazil's population, primary output and exports to Portugal greatly enlarged the effective demand in the colony

---

[1] A. Soetbeer, *Edelmetall-Production und Werthverhältnis zwischen Gold und Silber* (Gotha, 1879), p. 92, quoted by J. F. Normano, *Brazil: a study of economic types* (Chapel Hill, 1935), p. 31.

[2] Estimate published by Thomas Ewbank, *Life in Brazil* (New York, 1856), and quoted by Simonsen, *Brasil*, II, 51 n.

[3] Simonsen, *Brasil*, II, graph opposite p. 222.

[4] Godinho, 'Flottes de sucre', pp. 192–3.   [5] See PRO SP 89/16–92, *passim*.

F

for manufactured consumer goods, especially textiles. Since Portugal forbade her colonists to set up their own manufacturing industries and yet was unable to meet all their demands herself, considerable recourse was necessarily had to foreign supplies. The Portuguese officially required all trade with Brazil to be carried on from Portuguese ports alone, and to a very great extent this was observed. The resultant greatly increased flow of foreign manufactures to Brazil from Lisbon was financed partly from the sale of Brazilian sugar, tobacco and other agricultural products to European countries, with the balance settled in gold.

Furthermore, the exploitation of Brazil's gold resources and the great revival of her commerce made Lisbon again one of the wealthiest cities in Europe, enriching the Crown and Court, and providing profits and employment for a large mercantile class. Other commercial centres with interests in the Brazil trades, particularly Oporto, also benefited. The expenditures of the Crown, the merchants, and others, tended to transmit the commercial prosperity of the period more widely through the Portuguese economy, providing some stimulus to economic activity in general and raising the level of aggregate demand in the country for manufactured goods as well as other commodities. A further stimulus was thus given to imports of manufactures from abroad, largely paid for in gold and other products derived from Brazil. The remaining major cause of the Portuguese market's expansion was also South American in origin. This was the rise of a contraband trade between southern Brazil and Buenos Aires, a gateway to the extensive Spanish markets in Chile and Peru, which became especially active after 1713 following Spain's return to Portugal of Nova Colonia do Sacramento on the north bank of the River Plate.[1] It consisted mainly in the exchange of manufactures for silver, and about 1760 was thought to exceed £200,000 annually in value.[2] In 1761 the Rio de Janeiro fleet's cargoes in fact included 'about Four Millions of Crusades in Silver [about £500,000] the produce of the Trade at Nova Colonia ... conveyed with the greatest secrecy in order not to give umbrage to the Court of Spain'.[3]

[1] See Godinho, 'Flottes de sucre', pp. 190–1.

[2] Walpole to Rochford, Attachment C, 4 July 1774, PRO SP 89/77.

[3] Hay to Pitt, 29 Aug. 1761, PRO SP 89/54. Although the Portuguese trading system called for annual fleets, sometimes they sailed only once every two or even three years.

The key role of Brazilian developments, particularly in gold mining, in the growth of English exports to Portugal down to 1760 was clearly recognized by the English domiciled in Portugal. In 1706, for instance, the Consul at Lisbon wrote that the English woollen manufactures trade 'improves every day, and will doe more as their country grows richer which itt must necessarily do if they can continue the importation of so much gold from ye Rio every year'.[1] In 1711 the Lisbon Factory ascribed their growing business principally to the 'Improvement of the Portuguese Trade to the Braziles and the great Quantity of Gold that is brought from thence', and added, 'as that trade does go on Encreasing our Woollen Trade will also probably Encrease proportionably'.[2] And in 1715 they tersely declared the Brazil trade the 'Basis and Foundation' of their whole trade.[3]

Of the European manufacturing nations it is clear England benefited most from the Portuguese market's buoyancy in this period. In 1716 the English Factory in Lisbon considered their trade to Brazil exceeded the combined French and Dutch trades, and that British commodities made up the 'chief part' of all trade with the colony,[4] while in 1730 a French writer remarked 'le Commerce des Anglois à Lisbonne est le plus considérable de tous; même selon bien des gens, il y est aussi fort que celui des autres Nations ensemble'.[5] And two years later, Lord Tirawley, the English envoy to Portugal, declared 'the English are the Nation here of most Considerable Figure by far, both from our Numbers settled here, our Shipping and Trade'.[6] How did England come so to dominate the supply of manufactures to Portugal in this period? It is unlikely the Anglo-Portuguese commercial treaties of 1642, 1654, 1661 and the Methuen treaty of 1703 which regulated their mutual trade had much effect in this connection.[7] They set out the detailed legal and commercial guarantees essential if a trade carried on largely by Protestant merchants and involving much capital was to flourish with an autocratic

---

[1] Milner to Hedges, 28 Aug. 1706, PRO SP 89/19.
[2] Memorial of 1 Oct. 1711, PRO CO 388/15 M 123.
[3] Memorial of 31 July 1715, PRO CO 388/20 P 71.
[4] Memorial of 20 Oct. 1716, PRO CO 388/18 O 117.
[5] *Description de la ville de Lisbonne*, p. 224.
[6] Tirawley to Newcastle, 6 June 1732, PRO SP 89/37.
[7] For these treaties see Shillington and Chapman, *Commercial relations*, part II, chs. III and IV.

and Catholic country. But by and large the other nations enjoyed similar privileges: in 1712, for example, the English Consul in Lisbon pointed out 'ours was the first treaty of Commerce & by subsequent treaties w:th France, Holland, Spain, Sweden &c: they have granted the same priviledges to them as wee have'.[1] The English merchants' principal competitors, the French, however, were at various times seriously impeded in their trade with Portugal. The *Pragmatica* of 1677 and subsequent late seventeenth-century Portuguese edicts prohibiting the use and importation of certain luxury-type goods, and the attempts to build up home production in Portugal, were felt most particularly by them: England's trade was far less affected, and in any case by the Methuen treaty it again secured full legal recognition[2]. Moreover, during the War of the Spanish Succession, when England and Portugal were actively allied against France, French commerce with Portugal virtually ceased altogether, which much favoured the sale of English wares, and was further seriously hampered by English naval action during the later Anglo-French wars of the period.[3]

English merchants also had certain economic advantages over their foreign competitors. The increasing Portuguese demand for manufactures came from peoples living in countries with warm climates, and was chiefly for light woollen and worsted textiles in the low to medium price range, suitable for their clothing and furnishing needs. At the end of the seventeenth century England was far more specialized in the production of such fabrics than either France, Holland or the German states, and consequently better placed to exploit an expanding market.[4] Moreover, the fall in English textile prices relative to the generally stable prices of Douro wines and Brazilian gold, Portugal's chief commercial returns to England, probably meant the terms of trade between the two countries were moving in Portugal's favour from about 1715 to 1750, thus enabling her to purchase

[1] Milner to Lewes, 14 May 1712, PRO SP 89/22.

[2] See Miss M. E. Turner's unpublished University of Oxford DPhil thesis, 'Anglo-Portuguese relations and the war of the Spanish succession' (1952), pp. 112–13 *et seq.*, and Godinho, 'Flottes de sucre', pp. 186–8.

[3] On the decline of French commerce with Portugal around 1700 see *Description de la ville de Lisbonne*, pp. 256–62.

[4] On the earlier decline of the important Dutch worsted industry see C. Wilson, 'Cloth production and international competition in the seventeenth century', *Economic History Review* 2nd series, XIII (1960), 213–19.

more English textiles than would otherwise have been the case. Further advantages were derived from the Portuguese wine trade to England. The English merchants in Portugal controlled both the purchase and shipment of the wines sent to England,[1] and their extensive business connections with the various wine-producing and trading regions, particularly in the more populous northern provinces, greatly helped their business in imported manufactures. In 1758 some London Portugal merchants commented 'the Vintagers have always considered the English as their chief Benefactors and Support; and . . . the Trade of British Commodities at Oporto is intimately connected with and dependent upon That of the Wines'.[2] And in 1773 the Superintendent-General of Customs for northern Portugal rather bitterly wrote of Oporto as 'a city with an English heart where this Nation [the English] has much power and where nothing pleases except that which comes from England'.[3] English businessmen could probably also ship their goods to Portugal more cheaply than their principal competitors. France, with her own wine production and colonial plantations, imported very little from Portugal, and while a substantial trade in sugar, tobacco and salt was carried on from Portugal with Amsterdam and Hamburg,[4] much less shipping space was probably required than in the wine trade with England. The likelihood of return cargoes from Portugal for English vessels was consequently greater than for French, Dutch or German vessels, which made for lower freight charges for English exports. The advantage may have been even greater: in 1713 certain London merchants observed 'in times of peace ships have often carried out cargoes of goods freight free [to Portugal and Italy] only obliging the persons to lade them home with wines'.[5] Finally, a large and expanding trade with Portugal and her colonies, as with all the contemporary less-developed countries, demanded the ability to provide long credit and a plentiful supply of it. This was probably the most serious factor handicapping French merchants. Lacking a single great commercial and financial centre they were unable to compete on equal terms with the English, who could

---

[1] See my thesis, pp. 156–61.
[2] Memorial of 12 July 1758, PRO SP 89/51.
[3] Col. Pombalina, Cod. 631, f. 113.   [4] See *Mercator*, pp. 11–15.
[5] *Calendar of House o fLords MSS.* x (1712–14), 109.

draw on the concentrated mercantile wealth of London[1] and also benefited from the long chain of credit extending back into the manufacturing areas. The Dutch, on the other hand, suffered no such handicap, but the force of their financial bargaining power was much lessened by their limited manufacturing capacity.

II

In the 1760s, in decided contrast to the preceding decades, English exports to Portugal contracted: from an annual average of £1,301,000 in 1756–60 official shipments fell to £965,000 in 1761–5 and £595,000 in 1766–70. The yearly figures show the decline beginning in 1762 and continuing until the end of the decade. In the 1770s exports remained comparatively stable about this much lower level. The value of the textiles shipped, which had averaged over a million pounds annually in the late 1750s, slumped to £709,000 in 1761–5 and £459,000 in 1766–70, although in both periods they still accounted for over 70 per cent of total export values. Woollen and worsted cloths, especially the lighter and more moderately priced, still remained most important. Of the individual products the slump in the shipments of worsted stockings and hats was particularly striking, the former's average annual value in 1766–70 falling to £20,000, and the latter's to as low as £5,000. Of the other manufactures wrought iron wares continued to stand out, and in contrast to the general tendency their exports increased during the decade.[2] English grain shipments to Portugal remained quite large down to 1766, but then virtually ceased altogether.

Official imports into England from Portugal, however, showed relatively little change in the 1760s from their earlier level. Among them wines remained dominant, accounting for over 80 per cent of total import values during the decade. The contraction in English exports thus resulted in a sharp fall in the official English trade surplus; by 1766–70 it had declined to £239,000 annually, but the rise in textile prices at this time probably means the official figures exaggerate the real fall. The 'invisible' earnings from the Newfoundland cod trade and other activities, moreover, must have substantially improved the English trade position, so that on current account as a whole the actual sur-

[1] See John, 'The London Assurance Company', pp. 135–6.
[2] To £29,000 annually by 1766–70.

pluses were probably greater than the official surpluses. There is again no evidence of significant Portuguese payments through a third country, or of substantial English investment in fixed assets in Portugal, while the volume of English commercial capital in the country was probably falling with the decline in English trade, so that the English surpluses continued to be regularly settled by an outflow of bullion. Although bullion shipments for English merchants must have fallen away quite appreciably compared to earlier decades, this was in part at least compensated by the growing remittances made to England on the account of North American colonial merchants, whose trade with Portugal expanded quite strikingly at this time.[1] Down to 1765 the yearly London rate of exchange on Lisbon, as would be expected, stood below gold export point (taken as 5s. 6·01d.) except for 1762 and 1763 when, however, export rates ruled in a number of months. But between 1766 and 1770 the London rate fell to gold export point in four months only, in 1766. These were rather exceptional years, however: the London market price for gold was unusually high, the yearly price (average of the first price quoted each month by Castaing) ranging from £3 19s. 0⅜d. per ounce in 1766 to £4 os. 2⅜d. in 1769, and bullion export points on the exchanges would have been higher too.

As before, bullion was also shipped to England on the account of Dutch, German and other continental European merchants. The proportion of the foreign merchants' total shipments from Portugal which went first to England probably fell during the Seven Years War, when Dutch and other neutral warships were preferred to English warships because of the risk of attack by French privateers,[2] but became very high afterwards. In 1769, for instance, the English Envoy in Lisbon could write that the English vessels employed 'not only carry the Ballance due to British Subjects but also to those of France, Holland & other Countries of the North'.[3] In this decade annual figures of the Falmouth packets' cargoes are available.

The figures overleaf undoubtedly understate total bullion imports from Portugal, especially in wartime, owing to the other shipping employed. Bearing in mind the declining size of the

[1] See my thesis, pp. 78–80, 138–9, 148–9.
[2] *Occasional thoughts on the Portuguese trade* (1767), pp. 11–12.
[3] Attachment to Lyttelton to Weymouth, f. 48, 21 June 1769, PRO SP 89/69.

Table 2 BULLION IMPORTED INTO FALMOUTH FROM LISBON BY THE
PACKET-BOATS, 1761–9

	£		£
1761	548,532	1766	906,286
1762	286,099	1767	813,370
1763	693,676	1768	930,461
1764	1,186,714	1769	902,456
1765 (from 11 April)	631,081		

Source: Col. Pombalina, Cod. 635, f. 445, Cod. 636, f. 10.

English trade surpluses and allowing for colonial American remittances to England, the continuing great size of the packets' imports in these years suggests shipments on foreign merchants' accounts must have been quite noteworthy, possibly amounting to about one-third of total imports at the end of the decade. Such an estimate is very uncertain, however; it is also possible, in view of their declining interests, that English merchants were repatriating large sums of commercial capital from Portugal to England at this time.

Why did English exports to Portugal contract so precipitately in the 1760s? The ending of grain shipments after 1766 stemmed directly from the growth of English domestic demands for grain-stuffs and the consequent rise in prices, which not only reduced the trade's profitability but in some years led to a general prohibition on corn exports. On the other hand, the decline in the English manufactures trade largely occurred because of the ending of the long period of Brazilian prosperity and the onset of a severe and protracted depression in Portuguese trade which, according to its principal historian, Jorge de Macedo, reached its nadir in 1768–71 and remained serious until 1779.[1] The depression began with Portugal's unwilling entry into the Seven Years War in January 1762, when, in addition to losing the commercial benefits accruing to her as a neutral nation, her own foreign commerce became subject to disturbance. Far more serious though was the absolute decline which began in Brazil's gold output and trade. From an average of 14,600 kg annually in 1741–60 the output of the mines is estimated to have fallen to 10,350 kg annually in 1761–80,[2] while Professor Simonsen's figures suggest gold shipments to Portugal from being worth about £2,200,000 in 1760 had fallen back to about £750,000 in

[1] See Macedo, *Tempo de Pombal*, ch. IV, for a general account of the depression.
[2] Soetbeer, *Edelmetall-Production*, p. 92, quoted by Normano, *Brazil*, p. 31.

1776.[1] This is supported by Magalhães Godinho's observation that the gold brought to Lisbon from Brazil had begun to diminish before 1765, and did so especially after that year.[2] These years also witnessed a marked slump in the value of Brazil's sugar trade.[3] Altogether Brazil's total exports seem to have fallen from about £4,800,000 to about £3,000,000 between 1760 and 1776.[4] This depression in important sectors of Brazilian production and trade from about 1762 onwards substantially reduced the colony's effective demand for manufactures, and caused a notable contraction in foreign imports from Portugal, including products coming from England.

The decline of Brazil's prosperity also had a serious depressing effect on the income of both the Portuguese Crown and the mercantile communities in Lisbon and Oporto. The yield of the *quinto*, the main tax levied on Brazilian gold production, for example, fell away from an annual average of about 102 *arrobas* in 1751–60 to 97 in 1761–5, 86 in 1766–70 and 78 in 1771–5, and other leading branches of the royal revenue were markedly diminished during the 1760s.[5] Falling Crown and mercantile incomes tended to dampen the general level of purchasing power in Portugal, reducing the demand for foreign textiles as well as other products. The ending in 1762 of the hitherto large Brazilian contraband trade with Buenos Aires was a further blow. According to a Portuguese minister this 'was put a stop to by the Spaniards who had blockaded Nova Colonia ... which occasioned a great diminution in the Remittances of Gold from the Rio de Janeiro & in the consumption of English Goods'.[6] In 1773 the check to the trade still existed.[7] It is probable, too, at this time that the terms of trade between England and Portugal were shifting in England's favour with the rise in her textile prices. This movement may well have begun in the 1750s but then Portugal's prosperity was still sufficiently expansive to more than absorb the English price increases; in the 1760s,

---

[1] Simonsen, *Brasil*, II, graph opposite p. 222.
[2] Godinho, 'Flottes de sucre', p. 195.
[3] Simonsen, *Brasil*, I, table opposite p. 170. See also Macedo, *Tempo de Pombal*, pp. 169–70.
[4] Simonsen, *Brasil*, II, graph opposite p. 222.
[5] See Macedo, *Tempo de Pombal*, ch. IV.
[6] Attachment to Lyttelton to Shelburne, 1 Sept. 1767, PRO SP 89/63.
[7] Walpole to Rochford, 19 June 1773, PRO SP 89/75.

however, the fall in Portuguese incomes would have made its depressing influence on imports from England far more evident.

Whereas the Englishmen resident in Portugal had recognized the prime significance of developments in Brazilian gold mining for their trade's expansion to 1760, they failed in general to appreciate their contrary significance in the 1760s, and mainly attributed the contraction in trade to various measures taken by the Portuguese government about this time. Some of these measures did adversely affect imports from England, in particular the raising of import duties to finance Lisbon's rebuilding after the 1755 earthquake, which bore especially heavily when Portuguese incomes began falling, and the establishment of two companies in 1755 and 1759, the *Companhia do Grão Pará e Maranhão* and the *Companhia de Pernambuco e Parabaía*, with exclusive rights to the trade with large areas of Brazil.[1] Most serious though were the fresh attempts made in the 1760s to develop native Portuguese industries, once again in response to the pressures of commercial depression. English trade in hats and silk goods clearly suffered from such ventures,[2] as probably did other products in the 1760s although this policy was not in fact fully implemented by the Portuguese until 1769 and after.[3] The merchants in Lisbon also complained of a revival in French competition. In 1765 they reported the 'Crape Trade is entirely lost . . . owing to the French having introduced their Druggets' and that the French were also importing large quantities of long ells and stuffs. The French had also introduced their long bays but until then with little success.[4]

From the early 1780s until the first years of the nineteenth century Portugal's foreign commerce experienced a new phase of prosperity, resting largely on the development of trade with Asia and the re-export of Brazilian cotton to England.[5] English exports to Portugal, however, did not revive appreciably until the late 1790s, mainly because of the advances which had been

---

[1] See Lisbon Factory memorials 6 June 1760 and 29 Nov. 1764, PRO CO 388/53 Ll 20 and Ll 24, no. 16, and memorial of 24 July 1765, PRO CO 388/95 I2.

[2] Lisbon Factory memorial, 24 July 1765, PRO CO 388/95 I2.

[3] See Macedo, *Tempo de Pombal*, ch. v.

[4] Memorial of 24 July 1765, PRO CO 388/95 I2.

[5] Godinho, 'Flottes de sucre', p. 196. See also his study, *Prix et monnaies au Portugal* (Paris, 1955), pp. 259–76.

made in Portuguese manufacturing industry, and for some years in this decade Portugal, officially at least, achieved a surplus in her visible trade with England. In 1808, following the French invasion of Portugal, occurred the end of an era in Anglo-Portuguese commercial relations, when Brazil, whose economic fortunes had been of such great influence for more than a century, was formally thrown open to direct trade from England.

III

Anglo-Portuguese trade in the years 1700 to 1760 has a particular interest in the light of observations contained in recent work. Professor Wilson has indicated how in the later seventeenth and early eighteenth centuries various branches of the woollen cloth industry on the Continent were developing apace and sales opportunities for similar types of English cloth were becoming more limited.[1] While Professor John has suggested that the relatively slow growth of English exports to the English American colonies in the eighteenth century before 1740 was linked to a movement of the terms of trade in England's favour in the 1720s and 1730s brought about by the sharp fall in tobacco and sugar prices.[2] Against this background the Portuguese trade proved of special value to England. It represented during the first half of the eighteenth century, after the English American colonial trade as a whole, England's most buoyant export outlet for her manufactures, essentially because of Portugal's industrial backwardness coupled with Brazil's rising prosperity in which the precious metals played such a great part. The terms of trade were probably moving in Portugal's favour from about 1715 until 1750, and although thereafter the movement was probably reversed Portugal's prosperity was still sufficiently expansive until the early 1760s to more than compensate this. Over the whole period to 1760 the trade made a substantial contribution to the maintenance of industrial employment in England. It also helped further the improvements taking place in commercial organization, while the gold inflow was crucial to the increasing gold circulation in the country and the establishment of the gold

[1] Wilson, 'Cloth production', pp. 219–20.
[2] A. H. John, 'Aspects of English economic growth in the first half of the eighteenth century', below p. 169.

standard, as well as facilitating trade with the 'hard currency' areas of Europe. Finally, the control of this bullion trade, the use by Portugal of English ships and marine insurance services, and the returns from the credit advanced to Portuguese merchants, notably aided London's rise in this period to the position of the leading European financial centre.

6 Aspects of English Economic Growth in the First Half of the Eighteenth Century[1]

A. H. JOHN

[This article was first published in *Economica*, No. 28 (1961).]

I

There exists a justifiable scepticism among many economists and historians as to the possibility of formulating a comprehensive theory of economic growth. This doubt, and the reasons which underlie it, have been admirably expressed by Mr Bensusan-Butt:[2]

> The complexity of economic progress is almost infinite. There are many dynamic factors and they operate in an environment of the most elaborate kind. A theory that sought at once to be precise and to accommodate all the dynamic and structural complications of reality under one dome of abstract argument could possibly not be constructed at all, and, if it could be, would be incomprehensible to the vast majority of those who are or would be interested in the subject.

To affirm such a view is not to adopt an attitude of defeatism: nor does it imply insistence upon the uniqueness of individual historical events. There can be no doubt about the value of the questions which considerations of economic progress raise, nor about the need to study particular cases both in time and space. But it does, however, call attention to the strange air of unreality which enshrouds even the most elaborate models discussed by economists, and also to the fact that the paths along which economic progress moves can be, and in fact are, extremely diverse.

The historian in particular, if not also the model-builder, is

---

[1] This paper in its original form was read at a seminar in the Department of Economic History, London School of Economics and I thank my colleagues and especially Professor F. J. Fisher and Professor T. S. Ashton for their helpful comments.

[2] D. M. Bensusan-Butt, *On economic growth: an essay in pure theory* (Oxford, 1960), p. 1.

confronted with the great difficulty of identifying and measuring economic progress. Economists are not entirely agreed among themselves as to how this should be done for present-day conditions; and historians, with scantier quantitative evidence, find their various suggestions less viable still. One form of measurement, and the basis of many others, is the rate of growth of the national income. To some extent this is a choice dictated by the nature of evidence, because it makes the assumption that, through time, political units are the appropriate bases of measurement. Even if, for the sake of convenience, this assumption is granted, the historian still faces the fact that diminishing returns rapidly set in when collecting evidence for national income calculations before the middle of the last century. In English history, the figures compiled for Excise purposes together with other miscellaneous statistics take us back to the beginning of the eighteenth century, but their coverage is partial and their validity not beyond question. Attempts to fill the gaps, such as that made by Professor W. Hoffman,[1] are courageous, but not convincing. There is, too, the intriguing and, during the eighteenth century, the increasingly important question of invisible imports and exports; and, since we are not dealing with closed economies, that of terms of trade. Further, there is the constant problem of assessing qualitative changes and the need to correct time series for variations in the value of money.

With the adoption of more abstract indices, such as *per capita* incomes, difficulties multiply rapidly. In the first place a new and formidable variable is introduced in the form of population. Different rates of change in numbers and national income, even when technical innovation is active, can produce some odd results. Rising aggregate output with a more rapidly rising population must mean a fall in real incomes per head. It is this difficulty which, fundamentally, underlies the 'optimist' and 'pessimist' schools of thought about the industrial revolution. Conversely, in certain situations, falling aggregate output, with a more rapidly falling population, must mean rising incomes per head. Again, with the need to ascertain pretty reliable population figures there is the question of its composition. For as Professor Hicks has pointed out, 'the fall in national income per

[1] W. G. Hoffman, *British industry, 1700–1950* (translated by W. O. Henderson and W. H. Chaloner, Oxford, 1955).

head of total population', where the size of families increases, 'would not indicate that the nation was economically going down hill'.[1] The significant factor is the working population, which excludes children below working age, women engaged at home and old people, but includes the unemployed. The difficulties involved in ascertaining the magnitude of such a factor require no elaboration and one has not to go very far back in time to encounter an evidential void.

The measurement of economic growth everywhere involves a degree of approximation. As one moves back in time this margin of error widens rapidly, and historians may justifiably wonder whether the new techniques will ever supersede the older impressionistic judgements.

II

One may take the first half of the eighteenth century to illustrate some of these points – the value of the questions raised by considering economic growth, the difficulties of empirical verification and the complexity of the factors involved. The choice of period is largely an arbitrary one, determined by the existence of statistical evidence; and but for this, 1670 or 1680 might be a far more appropriate starting point.

It is a convenient half-century to examine because it is possible, for practical purposes, to eliminate two of the most important variables in the measurement of economic growth as it would be reflected in changes in national incomes per head. The role of the state, in the first place, was not so large as to make any marked discrepancy between total output and the personal incomes of those who produced it. Indeed, it can be argued that state activity, as for example in the creation of a well-run national debt with its effects upon the development of financial institutions, tended to promote the average standard of living. There also existed a stable social structure already deeply imbued with economic freedom. Secondly, there is general agreement that although population continued to increase, the rate of growth was slower than in the periods immediately preceding the Restoration, or following the Seven Years War. Estimates

[1] J. R. Hicks, *The social framework: an introduction to economics* (2nd edition, Oxford, 1952), p. 188.

of population increase during the first half of the eighteenth century vary from 250,000 to 400,000; and it seems likely that much the same figures apply to the years from 1660 to 1700. This implies an addition of from 5 to 8,000 persons *per annum* to the inhabitants of England and Wales, which contrasts sharply with the 60,000 which, on average, were yearly added after 1760. And not only was the rate of growth moderate, but there is every reason to believe that the structure of the population remained unchanged throughout the period. The proportion of children to total numbers was high, there were high birth and death rates, and there were comparatively few in the ages of maximum efficiency. Hence it seems possible to argue that numbers did not exert any undue pressure upon the national income. For both these reasons, any increase in national output would tend to be reflected in an improved standard of living, although the position might well be accentuated or modified by movements in the terms of trade.

The half-century is also a convenient one to examine because the growth of foreign trade in English manufactures was not sufficiently spectacular to overshadow other factors. This is a characteristic which the period shares with the years 1669 to 1700, where a comparison of London's trade, uncorrected for changes in the value of money, suggests an increase of about one-third.[1] The figures given in the table[2] – not comparable with

THE AVERAGE ANNUAL VALUE OF ENGLISH EXPORTS OF MANUFACTURES
AND PRODUCE (EXCLUDING SPECIE) AND OF RE-EXPORTS (£m)

	Woollens (1)	Non-woollen textiles (2)	Major Non-textiles (3)	Total (1)+(2) +(3)	Other exports	Total exports	Re-exports
1706–10	3·83	·12	·63	4·58	·17	4·75	1·54
1711–20	3·79	·13	·77	4·69	·07	4·76	2·19
1721–30	3·59	·14	·87	4·60	·40	5·00	2·91
1731–40	4·15	·16	1·04	5·35	·49	5·84	3·20
1741–50	4·30	·27	1·27	5·84	1·15	6·99	3·59
1751–60	5·42	·56	1·54	7·52	1·38	8·90	3·55

those for the preceding period – show a very slow rate of growth in woollens until 1750 and a faster one for total exports of manufactures. The evidence for woollen textiles must, however, be

[1] R. Davis, 'English foreign trade, 1660–1700', above, pp. 78–98.
[2] The table has been compiled from E. B. Schumpeter, *English overseas trade statistics, 1697–1808* (Oxford, 1960).

treated with caution, because it masks a secular change in the composition of exports from the costlier and heavier cloths to the lighter and cheaper fabrics. During this half-century, shipments of Spanish cloth, serges, long and short cloths either stagnated or declined, while the weight of newer fabrics, the major item in woollen exports, doubled. In terms of employment, therefore, foreign trade may well have been more buoyant than its measurement in value suggests. The most significant increase, as shown in the table, is to be found in 'non-textile' and 'other' exports. The two categories are not necessarily exclusive because only the major non-textile items are listed; but it is fairly certain that the first reflects a rise in foreign demand for coal and metal products, and the second, to some extent, an increase in the exports of grain.

The figures for re-exports are interesting in that, as in the period 1660–1700, their rate of increase is quicker than that of exported manufactures until 1740; after that date it is slower. This places in clearer perspective the importance attached to the colonial trade by contemporaries. It also prompts another suggestion. The goods re-exported were acquired partly in exchange for services and slaves, partly for exports of English manufactures and produce. The quantity of the latter sent to the West Indies shows no significant increase until after 1740, while exports to America grow after 1726 but include shipments to the middle and northern colonies. Were it possible accurately to separate exports to the southern states, from which re-export goods were drawn, the pattern might well be the same as in the West Indian trade. If to these facts is added the sharp fall in tobacco and sugar prices in the 1720s and 1730s,[1] it is possible that the terms of trade moved significantly in England's favour between 1720 and 1740. In general, it cannot be said that the re-export trade had an important direct effect on English industrial growth; but the profits made in it added greatly to the country's financial strength and to the development of her financial institutions, especially in London.

Side by side with these characteristics of population and

---

[1] The average prices of Muscovado sugar in London per cwt were: 1706–16, 34s. 7d.; 1721–30, 24s. 1d.; 1731–40, 22s. 3d.; 1741–50, 32s. 9½d.; 1751–8, 15s. 11d. R. B. Sheridan, 'The sugar trade of the British West Indies, 1660–1756', an unpublished University of London PhD thesis.

G

exports went a large and sustained increase in agricultural output. Based primarily upon the use of clovers, artificial grasses and roots, this was the direct result of the more intensive use of land. The adoption of these new farming methods, it is true, varied considerably in different parts of the country, although it is worth noting that clovers were in use as far north as Worksop by 1692. What is certain is that their use was most marked in southern England, which, at the time, was the most populous and economically advanced part of the country. Their consequence was a rise in the size of the animal population and of the amount of crops taken from the land: and hence an increase of food and raw materials.

It is the conjuncture of a sluggish growth of population and of the export trade in English manufactures with a marked rise in agricultural output that is particularly interesting. What effects did this situation have upon the growth of the English economy during this period?

III

Agricultural innovation, associated as it was with land enclosure, implied a greater investment of capital. Farmers had to buy new seeds, to rear and maintain more animals, to carry a greater stock of implements: landowners were involved in the planting of hedges, in the building of roads and farms and in a more extensive policy of maintenance. Agricultural improvement also meant a re-deployment of resources in the form of land and labour. By permitting the lighter soils of southern England, hitherto mainly used for pasture, to be continuously cultivated there was a direct increase in the amount of labour required. To some extent this was balanced by the conversion of clay soils, particularly in the Midlands, to grass, which, with its accompanying enclosure, meant a movement of labour from the land into the neighbouring towns and industrial centres.

One of the major reasons for the continued growth of agricultural productivity in parts of southern England was the existence of an overseas market for grain. Between 1700 and 1760 the amounts exported rather more than doubled, and England became, for a time, the major surplus area in north-west Europe. Other consequences followed. Grain became an important bulk cargo, and between 1730 and 1763 about 110,000–130,000 tons were, on average, carried annually from English ports in ships which only occasionally exceeded a hundred tons burthen. This had its effect upon the more efficient use of shipping, upon investment in shipbuilding and upon the employment of dockside labour. Combined with the decline of Baltic supplies, which were largely handled by the Dutch, the same factor may well have contributed to the extension of our carrying trade: and so enabled this country to earn more from foreign freights and insurance.

'In years of abundance', writes Professor Ashton, 'the amount of cereals exported might be such as to lead to a favourable balance of trade and sometimes to a net import of bullion. Whether through the effect of this on credit, or, more directly, through its effect on the incomes of exporters and others there may well have been a tendency, at such times, to a rise of earnings and employment throughout the community.'[1] Though not entirely the result of grain exports, it is worth noting that interest rates in London showed a secular downward trend in the first half of the century, giving cheap money conditions from the early 1730s until the opening of the Seven Years War; and that this was reflected in the rise of bullion reserves in the Bank of England.

IV

Agricultural innovation in this period was also associated with the fall in the prices of foodstuffs, more especially grain. How far this movement of prices affected the entire country is not known with certainty: we lack, for example, information for the western and northern parts, where oats and barley, rather than wheat, were the staples of diet. But for southern England there is substantial evidence of the downward trend, although the extent of the fall may well have varied in different areas. Despite years of bad harvest, wheat prices in 1720–50, were, on average, about a quarter lower than they had been in 1660–80. As a consequence, given either stability or an increase of money wages – or even a fall at a slower pace – this must have

[1] T. S. Ashton, *An economic history of England: the 18th century* (Oxford, 1955), p. 61.

meant that many classes of people found themselves with surpluses which they could either save or spend on other things. Other types of goods also tended to fall in price but not to anything like the same extent as grains, so that terms of trade, moved in favour of manufactures.

This is, perhaps, a more sophisticated way of telling an oft-repeated tale: the material prosperity of early eighteenth-century England, seen at its best in the refinement of its architecture and domestic furnishings, and at its worst in the coarse insensitivity of much of its social life. The fall in food prices must have exercised a powerful influence on the middle income-groups of contemporary society, and we may trace some of its effects in the rise of daily and weekly newspapers and even in the large sale of Hogarth's prints. But this is by no means the whole story. Dr Coleman has written: 'The particular age structure and the expectation of life of the population kept low the numbers of the working force at the age of maximum efficiency; the continuing expansion of the economy in trade, industry and agriculture and the slow rate of population growth increased the demand for labour. There was thus generated a pressure to push up wages.'[1] Thorold Rogers, Mrs Gilboy and, lately, Professor Phelps Brown and Miss Hopkins have shown this to be true of certain kinds of work-people. The latter have, for example, demonstrated that the money wages of building craftsmen and labourers in south-eastern England increased by about a third between 1670 and 1736.[2] The absolute level of wages differed markedly in various parts of the country; but wherever economic activity was increasing the same trend can be traced. 'At the beginning of the century the normal rate of unskilled workers in Lancashire seems to have been about 8d. a day. It stood in sharp contrast to the 14d. paid in Oxford and the 20d. in London. By the middle of the century the Lancashire rate had risen to 12d.; the Oxford rate still stood at 14d. and the London rate was 24d'.[3] If one can assume that food prices also fell in the north and the west as well as in the south and southeast there were clearly large sections of the population for whom

[1] D. C. Coleman, 'Labour in the English economy of the seventeenth century', *Economic History Review* 2nd series, VIII (1956), 288.

[2] E. H. Phelps Brown and S. V. Hopkins, 'Seven centuries of building wages', *Economica*, XXII (1955), 195–206.

[3] Ashton, *The 18th century*, p. 232.

this coincided with rising money wages; and for whom, as a result, there was an increase in real incomes. 'The real quantities of the necessaries and conveniences of life which are given to the labourer,' wrote Adam Smith, have 'increased considerably during the course of the present century.'[1]

How far the potentialities of the situation were lessened by self-sufficiency in the production of grain and by an increased demand for leisure is difficult to say. In general, there were far more people buying their bread or bread-grain than were producing it, especially in southern England. There was certainly a good deal of complaint on the second score, but this might to some extent have been biased in origin: and the deeply ingrained tendency to irregular work need not necessarily be the same as increased leisure. It is impossible to reach a firm judgement on this matter. But in view of the steady townward drift both from enclosed villages and from areas unaffected by enclosures, it would seem that the attractions of higher wages were not totally obscured by traditional standards of living. In all, therefore, the effect of these two factors was probably to limit rather than to prevent the growth of the home market as a consequence of rising real wages.

What evidence is there then for an increased consumption and output arising from this situation? The easiest expression to trace, although from our point of view the least important, is the rise in the consumption of imported groceries. By 1700, the retained imports of sugar amounted to about 15,000 tons a year, representing approximately five lbs per head of the population. By the 1730s imports had doubled, and by the mid-1750s had almost trebled. Retained imports of rum went up even faster. Coffee, on the other hand, was an upper-class drink and, as a consequence, showed a much slower rate of growth. Tea and tobacco were subject to such extensive smuggling that official figures are more than doubtful, but imports – legal and illegal – certainly increased. Equally certain is the fact that they were bought by people well down in the ranks of the less well-to-do. In the 1730s, the substitution of tea for ale threatened a crisis in the payment of Scottish judges, whose salaries were paid from the duties on that drink. The authorities of that kingdom alleged that the 'meanest people', especially in the

[1] *The wealth of nations* (Cannan ed. Methuen, 1904), 1, 200.

boroughs, took tea with their morning meal. 'The same drink', it was said, 'supplies all the working women with their afternoons' entertainment to the exclusion of twopenny ale.' In the richer south, the Excise returns suggest that there was no such great switching of demand, and beer and gin, as well as tea, were freely imbibed. Although not in the category of imported goods, it is worth noting at this stage that the relatively stable prices for meat and dairy produce, compared with those for grain, also reflected their increased consumption. These dietary changes had their repercussions on employment in distilling, sugar-refining and especially pottery, which grew rapidly during these years.

The effect of increased real incomes upon other aspects of domestic industry is more difficult to trace if only because the State exercised less control for taxation purposes, and there are accordingly fewer statistics. It is the result, too, of the kind of goods bought and the nature of the industry which supplied them. Broadly speaking, the same features apply here as in the matter of diet: there is a broadening of the range of consumer goods and the substitution of new articles for older and cruder ones. There was better furniture, the lantern clock, cheap Birmingham products, wider ranges of textile fabrics and, at the mid-century, lace and Sheffield plate. Some of these goods were made locally by craftsmen, the increase in whose numbers is difficult to trace. The spread of clock-making in the provinces is a good illustration of this. Other goods were made more exclusively in areas which specialized in their production, and the growth in internal demand for them helped to break down regional autonomy.

One example of this may be seen in the developing metal trades of the period. By 1717 the Midlands and south Yorkshire consumed between them well over half the production of English bar-iron, as well as most of the brass. From these metals were made the growing output of buckles and toys at Wolverhampton, the great variety of 'Brummagem Pretences', the harness and stirrups at Walsall, and over the entire region brass locks, buttons, candlesticks and nails. In Sheffield, where there was a greater emphasis on the making of edge-tools, 'the first half of the eighteenth century was a period of rapid and accelerating expansion of trade. By 1750 the rate at which boys were

being apprenticed was more than four times as great as it had
been at the beginning of the century.'[1] Exports certainly made
some contribution to this activity, but the main impetus came
from home demand. As far as bar-iron is concerned, this can be
indicated by the construction of a crude index:[2]

	1715–19 *Tons*	*1734–38* *Tons*	*1748–52* *Tons*
English bar-iron production	13,300	12,190	18,800
Imported pig and bar-iron	15,468	29,275	29,652
Total	28,768	41,465	48,452
Weight of all iron exports	2,385	4,294	8,710

The table greatly underestimates home production of iron as a
whole because it omits the use of pig-iron in castings – an expanding branch of the industry: and these contemporary estimates of the output of bar-iron have themselves been recently
criticized as considerably below the probable level of production. But even as it stands, the table clearly shows the relative
importance of the home and foreign markets, because much the
same kind of article was sold in both. This growth of the west
Midland and Sheffield industries fits well into the pattern of a
widening range of consumer goods; but it would be wrong to
ascribe the prosperity of these areas entirely to the re-disposition of incomes. In a large measure it was also the result of
investment in agriculture and building. There was a close connection between agricultural improvement and the development of the Birmingham and Sheffield areas. 'The country
trade took off [in the 18th century] a considerable proportion of
the Midland industrial product', writes Professor Court. 'Its
importance can be imagined when a single ironmonger in a
deep country district like the Vale of Evesham held a stock of
three tons of nails at a time "for the country sales" as well as
ironmonger's and cutler's goods of all sorts.'[3]

[1] G. I. H. Lloyd, *The cutlery trades* (London, 1913), p. 118.

[2] The figures for bar-iron production are from E. W. Hulme, 'Statistical
history of the iron trade of England and Wales', *Transactions of the Newcomen
Society*, IX (1928–9), 12–35. The weights of imports and exports have been calculated from Schumpeter, *Overseas trade statistics*, and are averages for the years
mentioned. The estimates given above have been criticized by M. W. Flinn, 'The
growth of the iron industry, 1660–1760', *Economic History Review* 2nd series, XI
(1958), 144–53.

[3] W. H. B. Court, *The rise of the Midland industries, 1600–1800* (London, 1953),
p. 133.

After food there was no product more likely to reflect an increase in real wages than textiles: and there is no industry whose growth is more difficult to assess because of its ubiquity, its complexity and, in some respects, the importance of smuggling. As far as its major branch is concerned, we may put the statement of a 'well-informed and moderate contemporary observer' that 'the woolen trade of England hath in the thirty-five years last past to 1753 been progressively increasing' against the slow rise in the values of exports: and Miss Deane, working on different although equally tenuous evidence, came to the conclusion that 'home consumption per head was increasing' during the early decades of the century.[1] The case is clearer when some of the newer branches of the industry – worsted stockings, silk, linen and cotton – are considered. Silk, for example, expanded rapidly with the influx of French emigrés after 1686, and imports of raw and thrown silk rise to about 1730, dipping in the 1730s and 1740s; and, as a result, there was an extension of the industry in such places as Spitalfields and Coventry, and new centres established at Derby (1702 and 1717) Sherborne in 1740, Congleton in 1752 and Macclesfield in 1756. All this was accomplished in the face of an active smuggling trade. The early growth of the cotton industry is also explained largely in terms of domestic consumption, despite the use of cotton thread in mixed woollen cloths. The printing of East Indian calicoes, founded in this country towards the end of the seventeenth century, grew rapidly. Commenting on production figures in 1712–19, Miss Mann states 'The most striking fact . . . is the large home consumption. Over two million yards of printed calicoes and linens were used annually by a population of about six million.'[2] With the prohibition of imported calicoes in 1721, the production of English fustians and linens 'increased enormously'. 'The manufacture of cotton, mixed and plain, is arrived to so great perfection within these twenty years', wrote a contributor to the *Gentleman's Magazine* in 1739, 'that we not only make enough for our own Consumption, but supply our Colonies and many of the Nations of *Europe*. The Benefits

---

[1] P. Deane, 'The output of the British woolen industry in the 18th century', *Journal of Economic History* XVII (1957), 221–2.

[2] A. P. Wadsworth and J. de L. Mann, *The cotton trade and industrial Lancashire* (Manchester, 1931), p. 138.

arising from this Branch are such as to enable the Manufacturers of *Manchester* alone to lay out above thirty thousand
Pounds a year for many Years past on additional Buildings:
T'is computed that *two thousand new* Houses have been built in
that industrious Town within these twenty years.'[1] Export
statistics show that the importance ascribed to overseas markets
was exaggerated – understandably so in an export-conscious
age – but the period of growth was later substantiated by a
report of 1752. 'From the year 1730 to the year 1740 the linen
and cotton manufacture made the most rapid progress. Irish
yarn was to be purchased at the low rate of 20d. per spangle and
West Indian cotton wool from 8d. to 10d. a lb.'[2] An analysis of
the records of a Kendal manufacturer of cottons shows the
same conclusion; overseas markets play only a small role in his
business until the Seven Years War. The textile industry of
Lancashire grew up largely on the domestic market and was
nourished by terms of trade which favoured manufactured
products.[3]

Thus far the growth of the domestic market has been indicated by comparing our knowledge of industrial expansion
with that of exports. The same purpose can be achieved in
another way – by tracing changes in the methods of distribution.
As long as people had only small sums to spend on articles
other than food, especially those not made locally, their purchases were bound to be occasional; usually after the harvest,
in an economy so largely agricultural. While this seasonal
flow of money persisted well into the nineteenth century, the
periodic fair was already declining in importance by 1700. Its
place, as a method of distribution, was increasingly taken by
the weekly market and the shop. Buying was ceasing to be
marginal and intermittent and was becoming continuous.

In London, the shop was well established in the seventeenth
century; and by 1750 the use of printed bills for the sending out
of accounts was common, and a few tradesmen were experi-
menting with press advertising. It is rather to the emergence

[1] *The Gentleman's Magazine*, 1739, pp. 479–80.
[2] BM Add. MSS. 38342, ff. 232–6.
[3] Imports of linen and cotton yarns and raw materials were 70 per cent higher
in 1741–50 than in 1711–20. There were also substantial imports of Scottish linen
yarn and a marked rise in the retained imports of linen cloth: much of the latter
'for the wear of the common people'.

of the provincial shop from the welter of markets, fairs and hawkers that we must look. As early as 1675, the village of Clayworth, in the county of Nottingham, had its grocer, petty-grocer and butcher,[1] and other large villages may well have been similarly equipped. By the mid-eighteenth century, a thriving town like Wolverhampton could boast of a dozen drapers and almost the same number of grocers, apart from druggists, iron-mongers, stationers and a goldsmith. It was, as might be expected, a development which was most pronounced in the country town. But as today, such centres also served the needs of those who lived in the villages round about, and many town shopkeepers had their stalls in the smaller local markets. Samuel Johnson's father, whose book and stationers shop was at Lich-field, regularly visited Ashby-de-la-Zouche, Abbots Bromley, Burton and Uttoxeter for this purpose.

The growth of a steadier demand for goods, both by con-sumers and manufacturers, had its repercussions on the manner in which the wholesale market was organized. By the early decades of the eighteenth century, the hawkers, pedlars and packmen had, as their companions on the road, a large number of outriders, or commercial travellers. Inland iron merchants, like Reynolds of Bristol, made a six-monthly visit to their smith and founder customers, as did representatives of the London and Bristol drysalters. The Manchester warehouseman, the West of England clothier, the Birmingham hardware factor, and some of the wholesale grocers, all sent their travellers around the country. According to contemporary comment, the numbers of these outriders already constituted a nuisance in some trades by 1760, and two years later, when Scotland found itself with balance-of-payment problems, some Scottish bankers regarded them as a major channel through which gold had moved into England.

Both approaches, then, converge to show an expansion of the domestic market, already under way before the period be-gan, but which grew substantially after 1700. It is not possible,

[1] It must be remembered that the title by which a village (or even town) shop-keeper called himself was only a partial indication of the range of goods which he sold. 'My master then had a full trade for groceries, ironmongerware and several other goods', wrote William Stout of Lancaster in 1680 (*The autobiography of William Stout of Lancaster, 1665–1752*, ed. J. D. Marshall (Manchester, 1967), p. 74). The same is, of course, true today.

with the evidence available, to distinguish accurately how far it was the result of incomes and investment generated in foreign trade and how far it arose from other factors. But the character as well as the extent, of the expansion, when compared with the growth of overseas commerce between 1700 and 1750, suggest that other powerful forces were at work. In so far as this growth arose from internal factors, they in turn, made their contribution to the growth of real capital. There were, as a consequence, more spinning wheels, looms, forges and tools of all kinds. It was in the context of the domestic market that Darby first used coke for the smelting of iron, Huntsman perfected a new method of making steel, and the expansion of the iron industry in south Wales, Shropshire and Furness occurred. The same is true of the growth of the early tinplate industry and probably of copper and brass. Quantitatively the main streams of investment flowed, as for many years to come, into agriculture, transport and building. The increase of river and road improvement was designed to improve inter-regional communication as much as any other purpose. Reference has been made to building activity in Manchester as a result of industrial expansion, and there is a wealth of other examples. Similar activity can be traced, for example, in the Spitalfields area of London, in Leicestershire, the Black Country, and Sheffield. In the late sixteenth and early seventeenth century, when the terms of trade had favoured the farmer, there had been a great rebuilding of agricultural dwellings: now a reverse movement encouraged the extension of urban and industrial construction.

All these forms of investment had their secondary effects. Professor Hoskins observes that Leicestershire house-building was characterized by two important changes of material in this period; the use of bricks and slate.[1] The same was true of other regions, Coventry, for instance. Bricks involved the greater use of coal, as did pottery and glass. All forms of investment implied an enormous demand for wheelwrights, carpenters, the makers of harness, both in leather and metal. In a quiet and unobtrusive way, the workers of England were being weaned away from their traditional agricultural activities and more and more engaged on industrial work.

[1] W. G. Hoskins, *The Midland peasant* (London, 1959), pp. 304–5.

V

Perhaps the unique importance of the years 1680–1750 lies in the emergence, for the first time, of a situation in which the terms of trade between manufactures and primary products turned in favour of the former for reasons other than a fall in population. Until then the major variable had been the size of population, and relative changes in these two categories of production followed as a consequence. The reasons for the change are to be found partly in the appearance of major innovations in agriculture, and partly in the increasing share of raw materials in British imports. In this way, the first half of the eighteenth century has a marked family likeness to subsequent periods when there was a sharp fall in the price of primary products. In some respects, these years – and especially the reigns of the first two Hanoverians – are not unlike the inter-war years of the present century. In both, terms of trade favoured manufactures: although in the eighteenth century the relationship existing within the country was of greater importance than that between England and her overseas markets. In the same way, too, there occurred a re-deployment of resources caused to some extent by a re-disposition of incomes, and the same cushioning of change by cheap food. There was, to carry the comparison still further, a depression in branches of the staple industries where change proved difficult in the face of new conditions. And in both periods refugee craftsmen made their contribution to a new pattern of industrial activity.

The re-deployment of resources, which arose from these conditions, was of the greatest importance. Arable cultivation spread over increasing areas of the lighter soils and, in a measure, was balanced by the conversion of heavier soils to grassland. In southern England, stagnation in the west country woollen industry was paralleled by the growth of output in East Anglia and Devon. More remarkable still was the expansion of manufacturing activity in areas peripheral to the older industrial centres. The regions which give the impression of most active growth are Yorkshire, Lancashire, the north and west Midlands and a thin elongation of this arc through south

Wales to Cornwall. There were doubtless a number of factors to account for this. The influence of inertia was probably strong in the older industrial areas, and there was the need to develop new sources of raw materials and more satisfactory supplies of water power. Most important of all, however, was the fact that labour – the largest element in industrial costs – was cheaper in these northern and western areas. The growth of the Leicester–Nottingham worsted stocking industry with labour partly, at least, displaced by enclosure and the conversion of arable to grass is the outstanding example of this; but the same principle held elsewhere. It might be said that the home market, no less than the foreign one, conformed to the persuasive demand for cheaper products.

The effects of linking new markets with expanding industrial areas were far-reaching. In the first place, it took the country, by 1750, a good way from being a mere collection of regional economies to achieving some form of economic unity. The improvements in transport, distribution and financial facilities were all expressions of this. In 1680, the premium on an inland bill of exchange from Newcastle-upon-Tyne to London, before the sailing of the coal fleet, was 5 per cent; and Oxford college rents seem to have been remitted from London only with the greatest difficulty. Premiums on bills from various parts of the country continued into the nineteenth century, but they were of a very different order of magnitude even by 1760. In this process of financial unification the work of the outriders in organizing means of payment was an essential step towards country banking; as, indeed, was the growing need for money implied by the greater volume of provincial transactions. The growth of provincial trade also meant a decline in the importance of London in the economy in a way which is not fully revealed in the proportion of imports and exports which entered and left the Thames.[1] In the second place, the expansion of industry in new areas helped to diversify society by increasing the number of craftsmen of all kinds. When the first cotton-spinning factory was erected at Cromford, it was not merely women and children to tend the new machines that were required, but also wood turners 'accustomed to wheel-making, Spole-turning, etc.', smiths, and 'clock-makers or others that

[1] I am grateful to Professor Fisher for pointing this out to me.

understand Tooth and Pinion'.[1] The growth of these new groups in society, in turn, enhanced the potential wealth of entrepreneurial ability, and enlarged the number prepared to invest their savings in other than land. This was important when the technical unit was small and personal contacts bulked large in investment decisions. It was in adding to the number of these men that the period before the industrial revolution was so important.

It can be argued that the difficulties of the home market, as much as any other cause, contributed in the 1760s to the adoption of those textile innovations which were to prove so significant. The growth of the industry during the preceding fifty years, accelerated by an expansion of foreign trade after 1750, must have tended to push up the average costs of cotton manufacture as spinning and weaving – especially spinning – were spread over widening areas. Cotton wool, which had cost 8d.–10d. a lb during the 1730s, and the supply of which had been protected during the 1740s by our naval superiority during the war rose to 24d. in 1752 and was 18d. in 1754 largely as the result of French and Dutch demands.[2] During the early 1760s the price was 14d., but apparently rose towards the end of the decade,[3] possibly because of the greater profitability of sugar-growing in the West Indies. This rise was sharper than that of wool prices, although both they and the price of linen yarn went up pretty steeply. In addition dyes were more expensive and credit was dear until 1766. With these increases in costs went the fact that the long decline in food prices came to an end in 1762. Almost every year of the 1760s was a bad one from the point of view of food supplies. As a consequence domestic demand fell and was matched by a fall in exports. Ground between these two forces, manufacturers made every effort to reduce that element of cost most firmly in their grasp. They extended truck; they refused to employ dyers who would not buy their raw materials from them; and they turned to machinery which would reduce labour costs more directly. It is therefore not surprising that the spinning jenny, the flying shuttle

[1] R. S. Fitton and A. P. Wadsworth, *The Strutts and the Arkwrights* (Manchester, 1958), p. 65.

[2] BM Add. MSS. 38342, ff. 232–6 and Wadsworth and Mann, *Cotton trade*, p. 155.

[3] Wadsworth and Mann, *Cotton trade*, p. 159.

and finally, Arkwright's power spinning, were widely adopted in this decade: and once adopted their subsequent development was continuous.

VI

The first half of the eighteenth century – especially the decades 1720 to 1740 – has been regarded as a period of economic stagnation. But to interpret it in this way is to misrepresent its character. The importance of foreign trade seems to have been greater than is suggested by official statistics, especially in the development of the ancillary activities of commerce until 1750. In addition, exports of English manufactures and produce rose with great rapidity from the late 1740s until 1761, under the influence of a variety of forces. But side by side with this went the effect of important internal factors. Contemporaries wrote a great deal about the 'luxury' of English craftsmen and artisans, and in a comparative sense their remarks had a substantive meaning. In the century after the Restoration there was a rise of internal demand which permanently affected the level of expectation of most classes in English society. When population growth re-asserted itself, this was to have a powerful effect on the economy. One might say that the appetite for mass-consumption had been roused. Finally, it has recently been said that 'not least among [the] reasons' why the industrial revolution occurred in England was 'the size of Britain's home and colonial markets which gave her a good start in the race for expansion in the trading area as a whole. By the mid-eighteenth century the United Kingdom was the largest free-trade area in the world.'[1] If this was so, a large measure of the credit for an effective free-trade area must go to agricultural improvement which coincided with a long period of slowly growing population.

[1] K. Berrill, 'International trade and the rate of economic growth', *Economic History Review* 2nd series, XII (1960), 358.

Bibliographical Essay

N.B. *Unless otherwise stated the place of publication is London.*

Several guides to statistics are available, notably G. N. Clark, *Guide to English commercial statistics, 1696–1782* (Royal Historical Society, 1938) and R. C. Jarvis, 'Official trade and revenue statistics', *Economic History Review*, 2nd series, XVII (1964), 43–62. Bibliographies dealing with particular topics are contained in two further articles by R. C. Jarvis: 'Sources for the history of ports', *Journal of Transport History*, III (1957–8), 76–93 and 'Sources for the history of ships and shipping', *Journal of Transport History*, III (1957–8), 212–34. The volume by Clark mentioned above contains some guidance for those who wish to use the port books but see also Sven-Erik Åström, *From cloth to iron, The Anglo-Baltic trade in the late seventeenth century, Part II, The customs accounts as sources for the study of trade* (Helsingfors: Societas Scientiarum Fennica, Commentationes Humanarum Litterarum XXXVIII, 3, 1965) and his 'The reliability of the English port books', *Scandinavian Economic History Review*, XVI (1968), 125–36, J. H. Andrews, 'Two problems in the interpretation of the port books', *Economic History Review*, 2nd series, IX (1956), 119–22 and R. C. Jarvis, 'The appointment of ports', *Economic History Review*, 2nd series, XI (1959), 455–66.

Though posing some problems of interpretation, as critics have pointed out,[1] the best collection of trade statistics for the period from the end of the seventeenth century is provided by Elizabeth Boody Schumpeter, *English overseas trade statistics, 1697–1808* (Oxford: Clarendon Press, 1960) based on two series of national statistics. In his introduction T. S. Ashton discusses

[1] See the reviews by W. A. Cole in *Economic History Review*, 2nd series, XIV 1962), 564–6; Phyllis Deane in *Economic Journal*, LXXI (1961), 801–3; and W. E. Minchinton in *William and Mary Quarterly*, 3rd series, XVIII (1961), 585–7. For comments on the figures for woollen exports see Phyllis Deane and W. A. Cole, *British economic growth, 1688–1959* (Cambridge University Press, 1962), p. 322. Phyllis Deane also notes (*The first industrial revolution* (Cambridge University Press, 1965), p. 60) that the series for exports of grain is omitted and Ralph Davis warns (*A commercial revolution: English overseas trade in the seventeenth and eighteenth centuries* (Historical Association, 1967), p. 24) that aggregates derived from these statistics are misleading as they are only a selection.

the general conclusions that can be drawn from this material. Other series of figures are to be found in B. R. Mitchell and Phyllis Deane, *Abstract of British economic statistics* (Cambridge University Press, 1962) and Werner Schlote, *British overseas trade from 1700 to the 1930s* (Oxford: Blackwell, 1952) which is mainly concerned with the period after 1800. As with Schumpeter the reservations of critics should be noted. An eighteenth-century compilation by Sir Charles Whitworth, *State of the trade of Great Britain in its imports and exports progressively from the year 1697* (1776) also deserves mention. Scattered trade figures can be found in various eighteenth- and early nineteenth-century publications, including George Chalmers, *An estimate of the comparative strength of Great Britain* (1794) and David Macpherson, *Annals of Commerce, Manufactures, Fisheries and Navigation* (1805). A useful guide to these sources is provided by J. R. McCulloch, *The literature of political economy: a classified catalogue* (1845: reprinted London School of Economics, 1938).

For smuggling, apart from Professor Cole's article, see Hoh-Cheung and Lorna H. Mui, 'Smuggling and the British tea trade before 1784', *American Historical Review*, LXXIII (1968), 44–73 and G. D. Ramsay, 'The smugglers' trade: a neglected aspect of English commercial development', *Transactions of the Royal Historical Society*, 5th series, II (1952), 131–58, reprinted in his *English overseas trade during the centuries of emergence* (Macmillan, 1957). R. C. Jarvis discusses the 'Illicit trade with the Isle of Man 1671–1765', *Transactions of the Lancashire and Cheshire Antiquarian Society*, LVIII (1945–6), 245–67; Alfred Rive provides 'A short history of tobacco smuggling', *Economic History*, I (1929), 554–69; T. C. Barker investigates 'Smuggling in the eighteenth century: the evidence of the Scottish tobacco trade', *Virginia Magazine of History and Biography*, LXII (1954), 387–99, and F. G. James examines the question of 'Irish smuggling in the eighteenth century', *Irish Historical Studies*, XII (1961), 299–317. Some reference is also made to smuggling in E. E. Hoon, *The organisation of the English customs system, 1696–1786* (New York: Appleton-Century, 1938: 2nd ed. with an introduction by R. C. Jarvis, Newton Abbot: David & Charles, 1968), in L. A. Harper, *The English navigation laws, a study in social engineering in the seventeenth century* (New York: Columbia University Press, 1939) and in H. Atton and H. H. Holland, *The king's customs* (1908). A popular account of smuggling over a much longer period is N. J. Williams, *Contraband cargoes* (Longmans, 1959). For some documents, see A. L. Cross, *Eighteenth-century documents relating to the royal forests, the sheriffs and smuggling* (New York: Macmillan, 1928).

English overseas trade in the seventeenth and eighteenth centuries is put in perspective by J. H. Parry, *The age of reconnaissance* (Weidenfeld & Nicolson, 1963) in J. Holland Rose, A. P. Newton and E. A. Benians, (eds). *The Cambridge history of the British Empire, Vol. I, The old empire from the beginnings to 1783*. (Cambridge University Press, 1929) and the chapter by Charles Wilson on 'Trade, society and the state' in E. E. Rich and C. H. Wilson (eds.), *The Cambridge economic history of Europe, Vol. IV, The economy of expanding Europe in the sixteenth and seventeenth centuries* (Cambridge University Press, 1967). The most detailed recent discussion of English foreign trade between 1600 and 1770 is provided by the articles here printed but G. D. Ramsay, *English overseas trade during the centuries of emergence: studies in some modern origins of the English-speaking world* (Macmillan, 1957) contains seven studies which deal with particular aspects of the subject. It also has a detailed bibliography. For a short account see R. Davis, *A commercial revolution: English overseas trade in the seventeenth and eighteenth centuries* (Historical Association, 1967).

There is room for discussion not only of the long-term trends but also of the year-to-year fluctuations. Overall for the period between 1600 and 1720, W. R. Scott, *The constitution and finance of English, Scottish and Irish joint-stock companies to 1720* (Cambridge University Press, 1912) is still useful but there have been a number of more modern studies dealing with shorter periods. See, in particular, B. E. Supple, *Commercial crisis and change in England, 1600–1642* (Cambridge University Press, 1959) which supersedes Scott's work for the early seventeenth century: Astrid Friis, *Alderman Cockayne's project: the commercial policy of England in its main aspects, 1603–25* (Copenhagen: Levin & Munksgaard, 1927): Maurice Ashley, *Financial and commercial policy under the Cromwellian Protectorate* (Oxford University Press, 1934: Cass, 1962) and Charles Wilson, *Profit and power: a study of England and the Dutch wars* (Longmans, 1957). For the eighteenth century, the best account is contained in T. S. Ashton, *Economic fluctuations in England, 1700–1800*

(Oxford: Clarendon Press, 1959) but see also R. Davis, 'Seamen's sixpences: an index of commercial activity, 1697–1828', *Economica*, XXIII (1956), 328–43.

Closer study of English overseas trade inevitably means paying attention to individual branches of trade. England's nearest neighbours were Ireland and Scotland. For trade with Ireland see L. M. Cullen, *Anglo-Irish trade, 1660–1800* (Manchester University Press, 1968) which contains an up-to-date bibliography of this branch of commerce. For trade with Scotland, see Theodora Keith, *Commercial relations of England and Scotland, 1603–1707* (Cambridge University Press, 1910) and T. C. Smout, *Scottish trade on the eve of Union, 1660–1707* (Edinburgh: Oliver & Boyd, 1963). No extended discussion of English trade with Scandinavia and the Baltic exists but some information can be found in A. E. Christensen, *Dutch trade to the Baltic about 1600* (Copenhagen: Munksgaard, 1941), in Sven-Erik Åström, *From Stockholm to St Petersburg: commercial factors in the political relations between England and Sweden, 1675–1700* (Helsinki: Finnish Historical Society, Studia Historica II, 1962) and his *From cloth to iron, the Anglo-Baltic trade in the late seventeenth century* (Helsingfors: Societas Scientarum Fennica, 2 vols., 1961 and 1965) and in E. F. Hecksher, *An economic history of Sweden* (Cambridge, Mass.: Harvard University Press, 1954). Statistics of shipping through the Sound are collected in N. Bang, *Tabeller over Skibsfart og Varetransport gennem Øresund 1497–1660* (Copenhagen, 3 vols., 1906–22) and N. Bang and K. Korst, *Tabeller over Skibsfart og Varetransport gennem Øresund 1661–1783 og gennem Storebaelt 1701–1748* (Copenhagen, 3 vols. 1930–45). Little attention has been paid to trade with Hamburg and Bremen apart from A. Friis's book already mentioned nor to Dutch trade in the seventeenth century but Charles Wilson discusses *Anglo-Dutch commerce and finance in the eighteenth century* (Cambridge University Press, 1941, reprinted 1966). Trade with France also awaits its historian. In addition to Dr Fisher's article, for trade with Portugal see V. M. Shillington and A. B. Chapman, *The commercial relations of England and Portugal* (Routledge, 1907) and for trade with Spain, J. O. McLachlan, *Trade and peace with old Spain, 1667–1750* (Cambridge University Press, 1940). For the trade via Spain and Portugal with Latin America see below. An article by R. Davis in F. J. Fisher (ed.), *Esssays in the economic and social history of Tudor and Stuart England* (Cambridge University Press, 1961) discusses 'England and the Mediterranean, 1570–1670', while H. Koenigsberger has written on 'English merchants in Naples and Sicily in the seventeenth century', *English Historical Review*, LXII (1947), 302–66 and G. Ambrose on 'English traders at Aleppo, 1658–1756', *Economic History Review*, III (1931–2), 246–67. Some light on trade with Madeira is cast by A. Simon (ed.), *The Bolton letters* (T. Werner Laurie, 1928).

Much has been written about the slave trade between West Africa, the West Indies and North America, but see in particular, Elizabeth Donnan, *Documents illustrative of the history of the slave trade to America* (Washington, DC: Carnegie Institute, 1930–35: reprinted New York: Octagon Press, 1965), T. S. Ashton (ed.), *Letters of a West African trader, Edward Grace, 1767–80* (Business Archives Council, 1950), Eric Williams, *Capitalism and slavery* (Chapel Hill, NC: University of North Carolina Press, 1944: Deutsch, 1964) and J. P. Mannix and M. Cowley, *Black cargoes* (Longmans, 1963). Among articles the following should be noted: W. E. Minchinton, 'The voyage of the snow *Africa*', *Mariner's Mirror*, XXXVII (1951), 187–96; Francis E. Hyde, Bradbury B. Parkinson and Sheila Marriner, 'The nature and profitability of the Liverpool slave trade', *Economic History Review*, 2nd series, V (1953), 368–77; and R. Sheridan, 'The commercial and financial organisation of the British slave trade, 1750–1807', *Economic History Review*, 2nd series, XI (1958), 249–63.

Most of the recent writing on trade with the West Indies has come from the pen of the late Richard Pares, notably *War and trade in the West Indies, 1739–1763* (Oxford University Press, 1936: Cass, 1963), *A West-India fortune* (Longmans, 1950), 'A London West-India merchant house, 1740–69' in R. Pares and A. J. P. Taylor (eds.), *Essays presented to Sir Lewis Namier* (Macmillan, 1956) and *Merchants and planters, Economic History Review*, Supplement 4 (1960). In addition see K. G. Davies, 'The origins of the commission system in the West India trade', *Transactions of the Royal Historical Society*, 5th series, II (1952), 89–108.

The fullest account of trade with the American mainland colonies is still provided by Emory Johnson, T. W. Van

Metre *et al.* *History of domestic and foreign commerce of the United States* (Washington, DC: Carnegie Institute, 1915) but see also B. Bailyn, 'Communications and trade: the Atlantic in the 17th century', *Journal of Economic History*, XIII (1953), 378–87 and J. H. Andrews, 'Anglo-American trade in the early eighteenth century', *Geographical Review*, XLV (1955), 99–110. The activities of merchants are documented in a number of volumes: Stuart Bruchey (ed.), *The colonial merchant* (New York: Harcourt, Brace & World Inc. 1966); Anne R. Cunningham (ed.), *Letters and diary of John Rowe, Boston merchant, 1759–1962, 1764–1779* (Boston, Mass.: W. B. Clarke, 1903); *The commerce of Rhode Island, 1726–1800* (Boston, Mass.: Massachusetts Historical Society Collections, 7th series, ix–x, 1914–15); Dorothy Barck (ed.), *Letter book of John Watts of New York, 1762–1776* (New York: New-York Historical Society Collections, 1928); *Philip White* (ed.), *The Beekman mercantile papers, 1746–1799* (New York: New-York Historical Society Collections, 3 vols. 1956); Frances Norton Mason, *John Norton & Sons: merchants of London and Virginia* (Richmond, Va.: Dietz Press, 1937, reprinted with a new introduction by Samuel Rosenblatt, Newton Abbot: David & Charles, 1968); Philip M. Hamer *et al.* (ed.), *The papers of Henry Laurens, I: Sept. 11, 1746–Oct. 31, 1755* (Columbia, SC: University of South Carolina Press, 1968; Lilla Mills Hawes (ed.), *The letter book of Thomas Rasberry, 1758–1761* (Savannah: Georgia Historical Society Collections, XIII, 1959).

Among the more important discussions of commercial activity in the American mainland colonies are: Bernard Bailyn, *The New England merchants in the seventeenth century* (Cambridge Mass.: Harvard University Press, 1955: 2nd ed. New York: Harper & Row, 1964); Byron Fairchild, *Messrs William Pepperrell* (Ithaca, NY: Cornell University Press, 1954); William T. Baxter, *The House of Hancock: business in Boston, 1724–1775* (Cambridge, Mass.: Harvard University Press, 1945); James B. Hedges, *The Browns of Providence Plantations* (Cambridge, Mass.: Harvard University Press, 1952); Margaret E. Martin, *Merchants and trade of the Connecticut River valley, 1750–1820* (Northampton, Mass.: Smith College Studies in History, XXIV, 1939); Glenn Weaver, *Jonathan Trumbell, Connecticut's merchant magistrate, 1710–1785* (Hartford, Conn.: Connecticut

Historical Society, 1956); Virginia Harrington, *The New York merchant on the eve of the Revolution* (New York: Columbia University Press, 1935); Philip White, *The Beekmans of New York in politics and commerce, 1647–1877* (New York: New-York Historical Society Collections, 1956); Frederick Tolles, *Meeting house and counting house: the Quaker merchants of colonial Philadelphia* (Chapel Hill, NC: University of North Carolina Press, 1948); Arthur Pierce Middleton, *Tobacco Coast: a maritime history of Chesapeake Bay in the colonial era* (Newport News, Va.: Mariners' Museum, 1953); Charles C. Crittenden, *The commerce of North Carolina, 1763–1789* (Yale Historical Publications Miscellany, XXIX, New Haven: Yale University Press, 1936); Leila Sellers, *Charleston business on the eve of the Revolution* (Chapel Hill, NC: University of North Carolina Press, 1934).

For some aspects of commerce with Latin America see C. R. Boxer, 'English shipping in the Brazil trade, 1640–65', *Mariner's Mirror*, XXXVII (1951), 197–230; C. P. Nettels, 'England and the Spanish-American trade, 1680–1715', *Journal of Modern History*, III (1931), 1–32 and Allan Christelow, 'Great Britain and the trades from Cadiz and Lisbon to Spanish America and Brazil, 1759–1783', *Hispanic American Historical Review*, XXVIII (1947), 1–29. An overall view of English participation in this whole trading area is provided by D. A. Farnie, 'The commercial empire of the Atlantic, 1607–1783', *Economic History Review*, 2nd series, XV (1962), 205–18.

Trade with the Far East has been discussed by William Foster, *England's quest of eastern trade* (A. & C. Black, 1933) and D. K. Bassett, 'The trade of the East India Company in the Far East, 1623–1684', *Journal of the Royal Asiatic Society*, 1960, 32–47, 145–57; but for trade with India see also S. A. Khan, *The East India trade in the seventeenth century* (Oxford University Press, 1923), Bal Krishna, *Commercial relations between India and England, 1601–1757* (Routledge, 1924) and the publications of K. N. Chaudhuri noted below in the section on trading companies.

Accounts of trade with particular areas obviously include a discussion of the major commodities in which business was done but there are a handful of books and articles which deal with specific products. For sugar, see Noel Deerr, *A history of sugar* (Chapman & Hall, 1949) and Richard Pares, 'The London sugar market, 1740–69', *Economic History Review*, 2nd series, IX (1956), 254–70: for tobacco, A. P. Middleton, *Tobacco Coast: a maritime history of Chesapeake Bay in the colonial era* (Newport News, Virginia: Mariners' Museum, 1953), Jacob M. Price, *The tobacco adventure to Russia: enterprise, politics and diplomacy in the quest for a northern market for English colonial tobacco, 1676–1722* (Philadelphia: American Philosophical Society, 1961), his 'The economic growth of the Chesapeake and the European market, 1697–1775', *Journal of Economic History*, XXIV (1964), 496–511, and Neville Williams, 'England's tobacco trade in the reign of Charles I', *Virginia Magazine of History and Biography*, LXV (1957), 403–49. For timber, see H. S. K. Kent, 'The Anglo-Norwegian timber trade in the eighteenth century', *Economic History Review*, 2nd series, VII (1955), 62–74, R. Albion, *Forests and sea power: the timber problem of the Royal Navy* (Cambridge, Mass: Harvard University Press, 1926) and J. J. Malone, *Pine trees and politics* (Longmans, 1964). For tar, see K. Hautala, *European and American tar in the English market during the eighteenth and early nineteenth centuries* (Helsinki: Suomalainen Tiedeakatemia, 1963) and for the Newfoundland fisheries, H. A. Innis, *The cod fisheries: the history of an international economy* (Toronto University Press, 1940, revised ed. 1954) and R. G. Lounsbury, *The British fishery at Newfoundland, 1634–1763* (Cambridge, Mass.: Harvard University Press, 1934).

Of the English ports, little is available for the most important, London, apart from the writings of Professor Fisher though an increasing number of historians are in Mrs Millard's debt for her so-far unpublished tables of London's exports, 1600–1640. Nor is there much available for the south coast ports apart from Exeter. For this port, see W. B. Stephens, *Seventeenth century Exeter, a study of industrial and commercial development, 1620–88* (Exeter: University of Exeter, 1958), E. A. G. Clark, *The ports of the Exe estuary, 1660–1860, a study in historical geography* (Exeter: University of Exeter, 1960) and W. G. Hoskins, *Industry, trade and people of Exeter, 1688–1800* (Manchester University Press, 1935: University of Exeter, 1968) and for Cornwall see J. C. A. Whetter, 'Cornish trade in the seventeenth century: an analysis of the port books', *Journal of the Royal Institution of Cornwall*, new series, IV (1964), 388–413. The history of the overseas trade of the smaller ports of the Bristol Channel has been sparsely discussed apart from D. Trevor Williams, 'The port books of Swansea and Neath, 1709–19', *Archaeologia Cambrensis*, xcv (1940), 192–209 and 'The maritime trade of the Swansea Bay ports with the Channel Islands from the records of the Port Books of 1709–1719', *Société Guernésiaise*, xv (1953), 270–85. So far no more than an outline of Bristol's trade is available in C. M. MacInnes, *A gateway of empire* (Bristol: Arrowsmith, 1939: Newton Abbot: David & Charles, 1968) but in a series of volumes published by the Bristol Record Society the trade of Bristol has been lavishly documented: see P. V. McGrath, *Records relating to the Society of Merchant Venturers of Bristol in the seventeenth century*, xviii (1951) and *Merchants and merchandise in seventeenth century Bristol*, xix (1955) and W. E. Minchinton, *The trade of Bristol in the eighteenth century*, xx (1957), and *Politics and the port of Bristol in the eighteenth century*, xxiii (1961). See also W. E. Minchinton, 'Bristol – metropolis of the west in the eighteenth century', *Transactions of the Royal Historical Society*, 5th series, iv (1954), 69–89 and *The port of Bristol in the eighteenth century* (Bristol branch of the Historical Association, 1962). Much less has so far been published about Liverpool: an outline account is provided by C. N. Parkinson, *The rise of the port of Liverpool* (Liverpool University Press, 1952) but see also T. Baines, *History of the commerce and town of Liverpool* (Liverpool, 1852), T. C. Barker, 'Lancashire coal, Cheshire salt and the rise of Liverpool,' *Transactions of the Historic Society of Lancashire and Cheshire*, cii (1951), 83–101, and R. C. Jarvis (ed.), *The Customs letterbooks of the port of Liverpool, 1711–1813* (Chetham Society, 1954). Of the smaller west coast ports, for Chester see Robert Craig, 'Some aspects of the trade and shipping of the river Dee in the eighteenth century', *Transactions of the Historic Society of Lancashire and Cheshire*, cxiv (1962), 99–128 and 'Shipping and ship-building in the port of Chester in the eighteenth and early nineteenth centuries', *Transactions of the Historic Society of Lancashire and Cheshire*, cxvi (1964), 39–68: for Lancaster, see M. Schofield, *Outlines of an economic history of Lancaster from 1680–1860, part I, Lancaster from 1680–1800* (Lancaster Historical Association, 1946) and Robert Craig and M. Schofield, 'The trade of Lancaster, in the early eighteenth century' in J. D. Marshall (ed.), *Autobiography of William Stout of Lancaster, 1665–1752* (Manchester University Press, 1967); and for Cumberland,

see P. Ford, 'Tobacco and coal: a note on the economic history
of Whitehaven', *Economica*, IX (1929), 192–6, R. C. Jarvis,
'Cumberland shipping in the eighteenth century', *Transactions
of the Cumberland and Westmorland Antiquarian and Archaeological
Society*, LIV (1954), 212–35, J. E. Williams, 'Whitehaven in the
eighteenth century', *Economic History Review*, 2nd series, VII
(1956), 393–404 and Edward Hughes, *North country life in the
eighteenth century: volume II, Cumberland and Westmorland, 1700–
1830* (Oxford University Press, 1965).

There has been much less discussion of the history of the east
coast ports but for Newcastle see *Extracts from the records of the
Merchant Adventurers of Newcastle-on-Tyne* (Surtees Society,
volume 93 (1895) and volume 101 (1899)) and Edward Hughes,
*North country life in the eighteenth century: volume I, the north-
east, 1700–1750* (Oxford University Press, 1952); for Hull see
Ralph Davis, *The trade and shipping of Hull, 1500–1700* (York:
East Yorkshire Local History Society, 1964); for Ipswich see
V. B. Redstone, 'Ipswich port books', *Transactions of the Suffolk
Institute of Archaeology*, XIV (1912), 238–42; for Boston see
R. W. K. Hinton, *The port books of Boston, 1601–1640* (Lincoln
Record Society, 1956) and for Norwich see M. F. Lloyd
Pritchard, 'The decline of Norwich', *Economic History Review*,
2nd series, III (1951), 371–7.

Because of the availability of their records, the trading companies have been well served by historians. Overall as an introduction, W. R. Scott, *The constitution and finance of English,
Scottish and Irish joint stock companies to 1720* (Cambridge University Press, 3 vols. 1910–12) is useful. See also K. G. Davies,
'Joint stock investment in the late seventeenth century', *Economic History Review*, 2nd series, IV (1952), 283–301. Then there
are the histories of individual companies: K. G. Davies, *The
Royal Africa Company* (Longmans, 1957), A. C. Wood, *A history
of the Levant Company* (Oxford University Press, 1935: Cass,
1964) and R. W. K. Hinton, *The Eastland trade and the common
weal in the seventeenth century* (Cambridge University Press, 1959)
which is primarily concerned with the activities of the Eastland
Company. There is no single-volume account of the most important trading company, the East India Company, over the
whole period but see K. N. Chaudhuri, *The English East India
Company: the study of an early joint stock company, 1600–1640* (Cass,

1965), his article, 'Treasure and trade balances, the East India Company's export trade', *Economic History Review*, 2nd series, XXI (1968), 480–502 and H. Furber, *John Company at work* (Cambridge, Mass.: Harvard University Press, 1951). Some of its papers have been published in George Birdwood and William Foster (ed.), *The register of letters &c of the Governor and Company of merchants of London trading into the East Indies, 1600–1619* (Bernard Quaritch, 1893, new ed. 1965) and H. B. Morse (ed.), *The chronicles of the East India Company trading to China, 1635–1834* (Oxford University Press, 1926). See also H. B. Morse, 'The supercargo in the China trade about the year 1700', *English Historical Review*, XXXVI (1921), 199–209. For the only other joint-stock trading company of consequence in this period, see E. E. Rich, *The history of the Hudson's Bay Company, I, 1670–1783* (Hudson's Bay Record Society, 1958) as well as a massive shelf of volumes of the Hudson's Bay Record Society too numerous to list here.

Because of the relative scarcity of the records of merchant houses the activities of individual merchants have not received the attention they deserve. Of the few contributions worthy of notice, see in particular, Lucy Sutherland, *A London merchant, 1695–1774* (Oxford University Press, 1933: Cass, 1962) which is a study of William Braund who engaged principally in the Anglo-Portuguese trade; Richard Pares, *A West-India fortune* (Longmans, 1950) which records the interests of the Pinneys of Bristol; R. H. Tawney, *Business and politics in the reign of James I, Lionel Cranfield as merchant and statesman* (Cambridge University Press, 1958), the first half of which deals with his mercantile activities, some of whose correspondence is printed in *Calendar of the manuscripts of the right honourable Lord Sackville of Knole, Sevenoaks, Kent: volume II, Letters relating to Lionel Cranfield's business overseas, 1597–1612*, edited by F. J. Fisher (Historical Manuscripts Commission, 80: HMSO, 1966); Conrad Gill, *Merchants and mariners of the 18th century* (Arnold, 1961) which centres on the activities of a London merchant, Thomas Hall, mainly in the East India trade and Ralph Davis, *Aleppo and Devonshire Square: English traders in the Levant in the eighteenth century* (Macmillan, 1967) based on the Radcliffe papers. See also a clutch of articles: W. E. Minchinton, 'The merchants in England in the eighteenth century', *Explorations in Entrepre-*

neurial History, x (1957), 62–71, reprinted in Hugh Aitkin (ed.), *Explorations in enterprise* (Cambridge, Mass.: Harvard University Press, 1965); L. B. Namier, 'Anthony Bacon, MP, an eighteenth century merchant', *Journal of Economic and Business History*, II (1929–30), 20–70, reprinted in W. E. Minchinton (ed.), *Industrial south Wales* (Cass, 1969) and A. H. John, 'Miles Nightingale – drysalter: a study in eighteenth century trade', *Economic History Review*, 2nd series, XVIII (1965), 152–63.

English overseas trade would have been impossible without ships. The most important study is Ralph Davis, *The rise of the English shipping industry in the seventeenth and eighteenth centuries* (Macmillan, 1962) but see also V. Barbour, 'Dutch and English merchant shipping in the seventeenth century', *Economic History Review*, II (1930), 261–90 while in a series of articles including 'Sources of productivity change in American colonial shipping, 1675–1775', *Economic History Review*, 2nd series, XX (1967), 67–78, 'A measure of productivity change in American colonial shipping', *Economic History Review*, 2nd series, XXI (1968), 268–82 and 'New evidence on colonial commerce', *Journal of Economic History*, XXVII (1968), 363–89, Gary M. Walton has given closer attention to the utilization of shipping in one main area of English overseas trade.

The relationship between trade and economic growth figures in many of the discussions of economic growth such as W. W. Rostow, *The stages of economic growth* (Cambridge University Press, 1960), W. W. Rostow (ed.), *The economics of take-off into sustained growth* (Macmillan, 1963) and in Phyllis Deane and W. A. Cole, *British economic growth, 1698–1959* (Cambridge University Press, 1962). See also K. Berrill, 'International trade and the rate of economic growth', *Economic History Review*, 2nd series, XII (1960), 351–9. Professor A. H. John has touched on this question in some of his other articles: see, in particular, 'Agricultural productivity and economic growth in England, 1700–1750', *Journal of Economic History*, XXV (1965), 19–34, reprinted in E. L. Jones (ed.), *Agriculture and economic growth in England* (Methuen, 1967). For the case for domestic demand see also D. E. C. Eversley, 'The home market and economic growth in England, 1750–80' in E. L. Jones and G. E. Mingay (eds.), *Land, labour and population in the Industrial Revolution: essays presented to J. D. Chambers* (Arnold, 1967). Recent discussions of the beginnings of industrialization in England also touch on the connection between overseas trade and English industrialization: see Charles Wilson, *England's apprenticeship, 1603–1763* (Longmans, 1965), Phyllis Deane, *The first industrial revolution* (Cambridge University Press, 1965) and Michael Flinn, *Origins of the industrial revolution* (Longmans, 1966).